"As parents, we all want our kids to be healthy, happy, and success-ful—as *Christian* parents, however, we want much more. We want to raise children with a genuine, vibrant, and world-changing faith in Jesus Christ. In *Talking with Your Kids about Jesus*, Natasha Crain reminds us how important it is to integrate conversations about faith into our everyday lives with our sons and daughters. This compelling resource will equip you as a mom or dad to point your child to the truth of Jesus's life, death, and eternal reign."

John Fuller, vice president of Focus on the Family and cohost
of the *Focus on the Family* radio broadcast

"When it comes to learning how to communicate with kids about God, I turn to Natasha Crain. She's funny, relatable, and most im-portant, deeply rooted in the Bible. *Talking with Your Kids about Jesus* is part of a series of books (you need to get them all) that is soaked in Scripture and awash with powerful evidence, fantastic examples, and thought-provoking discussion questions. It's so sneaky the way Natasha gets me thinking more deeply about my own faith as I learn how to help my kids deepen theirs."

Jeff Myers, PhD, president of Summit Ministries and author
of *Unquestioned Answers: Rethinking Ten Christian Clichés
to Rediscover Biblical Truths*

"Wow! Natasha Crain has compiled a power-packed guide that *every* parent should read! Mom and Dad, this one is a *priority*! In a world where there is so much confusion about Christ, you will gain clarity and confidence and your kids will gain *courage* from this clearly written and biblically solid manual. *Talking with Your Kids about Jesus* is a wealth of vital information written in an easy-to-understand way. Some great conversations await you and your family!"

Pam Farrel, author of nearly fifty books, including the
bestselling *Men Are Like Waffles, Women Are Like Spaghetti*
and *The 10 Best Decisions Every Parent Can Make*

"Natasha Crain should be a household name for every Christian parent longing to furnish their kids with a biblical worldview. Once again, this mother of three lays down tried and true principles about the most important conversations a parent can have with their kids about Christianity. What can be more important than that? Buckle up, parents, for an eye-opening read as this wordsmith skillfully navigates you through the terrain of thirty must-have conversations about Jesus."

Bobby Conway, host of The One Minute Apologist and author of *Doubting Toward Faith*

"This book is an answer to my prayers! Natasha Crain has provided thoughtful, practical, kid-friendly talking points I can use with my boys to equip them to face a world that often opposes their faith in Jesus. *Talking with Your Kids about Jesus* is a must-read for every parent!"

Amber Lia, bestselling coauthor of *Triggers* and *Parenting Scripts*

"For many years, we've recognized the need for a resource that parents could use to become the best Christian 'case makers' their kids will ever know. Natasha Crain has delivered that resource. *Talking with Your Kids about Jesus* will help you engage your kids in conversations that will make a difference for eternity. Get this book *today*, and use it to answer your kids' questions, respond to the claims of skeptics, and guide your young believers to the truth."

J. Warner and Susie Wallace, creators of CaseMakersAcademy.com and authors of *Cold-Case Christianity*, *God's Crime Scene*, and *Forensic Faith for Kids*

"These are uncertain times, and yet these are the very times that the Bible has anticipated. Jesus Christ told us there would be days like this, and you and I, as well as our children, have a front-row seat to it all! In light of this reality, our children need to be equipped with God's Word in such a way as will help them navigate the challenges ahead. Parents no longer can assume that the local church or a favorite ministry will rightly and intentionally teach their children the answer to life's most important question: 'Who is Jesus Christ?' That's why I am happy to endorse *Talking with Your Kids about Jesus*. Natasha Crain brings a timely clarion call to parents of faith to reengage the debate and to consider afresh just who Jesus Christ is according to the Bible as well as how to effectively teach their children not only the truth but also how to argue in defense of the truth. This excellent read is worthy to be in your hands right now and in the hearts and minds of your children for the rest of their lives!"

Jack Hibbs, senior pastor of Calvary Chapel Chino Hills and host of *Real Life with Jack Hibbs*

"Jesus of Nazareth was undeniably the most influential human being of all time. But he was (and is) much more than that. He literally holds the key to eternity for all of us. How well do you know him? How about your kids? If you get *Talking with Your Kids about Jesus*, you'll not only be able to gracefully equip your entire family with essential truths about Jesus, but you'll also be able to inoculate them against all the misinformation about Christianity posted on the web and social media. As in all of her books, Natasha Crain brilliantly communicates what you and your children need to know to be bright lights in a world that continues to slide into darkness. Prevent your kids from succumbing to the darkness by reading this with them now!"

Frank Turek, PhD, president of CrossExamined.org and author of *I Don't Have Enough Faith to Be an Atheist*

"Christian parents, this might be the most important book you ever buy to help you disciple your kids. In a culture that often presents Jesus as nothing more than a good moral teacher or all-inclusive postmodern guru, it's never been more important to clearly teach them who the object of their faith truly is. Natasha Crain has done a masterful job presenting the authentic Jesus from Scripture and illuminating what Jesus actually taught about things like judgment and love and what it means to put our faith in him."

Alisa Childers, speaker, author, and host
of *The Alisa Childers Podcast*

"Today, it's easy enough to raise kids who call themselves Christians and yet wind up claiming beliefs about Jesus that are completely contrary to the historic Christian faith. I've seen this tragic situation play out among my kids' peers, as a church elder, and in my media career as a Christian voice in the broader culture. In *Talking with Your Kids about Jesus*, Natasha Crain gives parents tools to fortify their kids' faith (and their own!) against the ruinous effects of the antiauthority, antitruth culture they will inevitably encounter both outside and inside the church. The way she distills the latest objections and the up-to-date scholarship answering those objections so that an ordinary layperson can understand it (and lead kids into a discussion about it) is breathtaking. We've had Natasha on our show several times. She is always clear, current, and solidly rooted in sound doctrine. That's what you'll find in these pages!"

Bill Martin, cohost of *The Morning Cruise* on The JOY FM
and director of spiritual formation at Cornerstone Church
of Lakewood Ranch

"This book is a practical guide to having your most important discussions with the most precious people in your life. Use it, and your kids will grow in knowledge and faith—and you'll grow with them!"

Mark Mittelberg, bestselling author of *Confident Faith* and executive director of the Strobel Center
at Colorado Christian University

"Natasha Crain has done it again! This collection of the most important conversations parents should have with their kids about Jesus is truly a must-have. Natasha writes excellent summaries without sacrificing important details and will equip you to confidently engage with your kids on these vital subjects."

Hillary Morgan Ferrer, founder of Mama Bear Apologetics and coauthor and general editor of *Mama Bear Apologetics: Empowering Your Kids to Challenge Cultural Lies*

"In this book, Natasha provides parents the cheat sheet to the most vital conversations to help their kids answer the most challenging questions that confront their faith. Every parent needs not only intentionality but also the tools to prepare kids to defend their beliefs. I am always recommending Natasha's books in this series because they create the most compelling conversations with your kids."

Ron Hunter Jr., PhD, founder of D6, director of D6 Conference, and author of *Toy Box Leadership* and *The DNA of D6*

"Today's child is being soaked in social media and video games, steeped in popular culture but not in spiritual life. Even as parents, we can be distracted and busy, never getting around to those important conversations that go deeper about Jesus. Or we may feel ill-equipped to answer questions that go beyond kids' church and inviting Jesus into their hearts. Enter Natasha Crain. She's a mom who has done the research and who communicates in a way you'll understand. Read a chapter a day. Your faith and knowledge will grow and, as a result, so will your child's."

Arlene Pellicane, speaker and author of *Parents Rising*

TALKING
with YOUR KIDS
about JESUS

TALKING
with YOUR KIDS
about
Jesus

30 Conversations
Every Christian Parent
MUST HAVE

NATASHA CRAIN

BakerBooks
a division of Baker Publishing Group
Grand Rapids, Michigan

Published by Baker Books
a division of Baker Publishing Group
PO Box 6287, Grand Rapids, MI 49516-6287
www.bakerbooks.com

Printed in the United States of America

Library of Congress Cataloging-in-Publication Data
Names: Crain, Natasha, 1976– author.
Title: Talking with your kids about Jesus : 30 conversations every Christian parent must have / Natasha Crain.
Description: Grand Rapids, Michigan : Baker Books, a division of Baker Publishing Group, 2020. | Includes bibliographical references.
Identifiers: LCCN 2019040129 | ISBN 9780801075537 (paperback)
Subjects: LCSH: Jesus Christ—Person and offices—Study and teaching. | Christian education of children.
Classification: LCC BT203 .C744 2020 | DDC 248.8/45—dc23
LC record available at https://lccn.loc.gov/2019040129

HANDS concept is from *Putting Jesus in His Place* by Robert M. Bowman Jr. and J. Ed Komoszewski. Published by Kregel Publications, Grand Rapids, MI, 2007. Used by permission.

20 21 22 23 24 25 26   7 6 5 4 3 2 1

To all of my family—
my husband, kids, parents, and in-laws—
I'm so blessed to love and be loved by you.

Contents

Part 5: The Difference Jesus Makes

Foreword

My descent into skepticism started early. When I was a youngster, I began asking questions about God, but nobody was willing to answer them. My conclusion was that Christians didn't want to discuss spiritual doubts because they didn't have any good responses.

Then, as a freshman biology student in high school, I was taught that Darwin's theory of evolution explained the origin and diversity of life. As a result, I concluded that science had put God out of a job.

Finally, when I was a freshman in college, I took a course on the historical Jesus from a cynic who convinced me that the Jesus of the four Gospels was not really the Son of God. My journey was complete: *I became an adamant atheist.*

Years later, prompted by my wife's conversion to Christianity, I dug deeper into these issues and discovered that the scientific evidence actually points toward a Creator and that history shows that Jesus did demonstrate his divinity by returning from the dead. Based on the facts, I put my trust in Christ—and instantly I became concerned about other young people who were embarking on the same path toward atheism that I had traveled.

We live in a world of increasing skepticism—and even hostility—toward Christianity. Youngsters who lack a solid foundation for their faith are at risk as they are challenged by doubters who pick up their often-inaccurate information from friends, the internet, or even their parents. In fact, a Christian friend told me recently that his daughter—*a kindergartner*—was taunted on the playground by a classmate who mocked her by saying, "Why do you believe in fairy tales?"

Finally, Natasha Crain comes to the rescue.

A wife of twenty years and the mother of three children, Natasha knows what parents face as they seek to spiritually nurture the next generation. She has an uncanny combination of a warm and winsome writing style, keen insights born out of personal experience, and a wealth of knowledge about Christian apologetics, or evidence for the faith.

In short, she is a trusted source for parents who want to provide their children with a vibrant and well-informed belief in Jesus. They have come to trust Natasha for her practical and highly accessible teaching, which she unfolds in this book through thirty conversations about Jesus that every Christian parent should have with their kids.

My own kids are grown and—thank God!—faithfully serving the Lord. But now I'm the grandparent of four young ones—and you bet I'm putting this book, as well as Natasha's other resources, into action in our extended family!

Here is another benefit of using Natasha's materials: your own faith will be bolstered as you are reminded once again that Christianity is not built on legend, mythology, make-believe, or wishful thinking but is firmly anchored to a bedrock of scientific and historical evidence and in the eternal truth of Scripture.

Fairy tales? No, our faith is much more than creative fiction. Let Natasha partner with you to help your children not only defend what they believe but also share it in a positive way with their spiritually curious friends.

So turn the page and dive in. Keep a highlighter handy—you're going to need it!

Lee Strobel, author of *The Case for Christ*
and *The Case for Faith*

Introduction

I was scrolling through Facebook recently when I saw an article that stopped me in my tracks: "5 Things People with Tidy Homes Don't Do."

Oh boy. This is one I need to read. Immediately.

I am constantly fighting a messy house. Whenever I take my kids to a friend's home, I'm amazed at how relatively clean it is. How do they not have a pencil on every seat cushion? How do they not have returned homework papers carelessly scattered across the floor? How do they not have sticky spots on their counters and stacks of mail stuck to the sticky spots? What do these parents know that I don't?

The article I clicked on that day provided a tantalizing clue to the answer. The author wrote:

> Tidy People don't act like a slob all day, and then get their house tidy in one fell swoop. . . . The number one thing I've learned from Tidy People is how valuable it is to develop some simple, non-drastic, tiny habits that when added together will change the level of tidiness in your home. Tidy People are in a constant state of low-grade tidying.[1]

Low-grade tidying. The point hit me like a ton of bricks (which, if they were in my house, would be all over the floor, and we'd continue to step over them for weeks before someone moved them outside). You see, my running assumption had been that I must have particularly messy kids. But I've since come to realize that—gasp!— the vast majority of kids are quite messy. Those clean houses I visit aren't the product of naturally clean kids. They're the product of parents with good habits—parents who are constantly in a state of low-grade tidying.

Low-Grade Tidying Is the Key to Faith Conversations

As parents, we're often as overwhelmed by the task of having deep faith conversations with our kids as I am by the task of keeping a clean house. We have a rough idea of how our *spiritual* house should look, but we feel we've let things get messier than they should be. We know we should have more faith conversations than we do, the ones we do have don't go as we'd like, and discouragement sets in when we don't feel equipped to answer the questions our kids raise. These subtle disappointments are like pencils on seat cushions— nagging reminders that things aren't where we'd like them to be.

Now you're holding a book telling you there are *thirty* conversations you must have with your child about Jesus. It's like I just dumped a laundry pile in your living room.

But that's not all. I've written two *other* books with "must have" conversations. My first one, *Keeping Your Kids on God's Side*, walks parents through forty important faith conversations in the subject areas of God, truth and worldviews, Jesus, the Bible, and science.[2] My second one, *Talking with Your Kids about God*, takes parents deeper into thirty conversations specifically about God (for example, the evidence for God's existence).[3] *Talking with Your Kids about Jesus* now goes deeper into thirty conversations about—you guessed it—Jesus.

All together, that's *one hundred* faith conversations I'm saying every Christian parent needs to have with their kids! (And there are many other important topics I haven't covered.)

Lest anyone read my books with the guilt or pressure I feel when stepping into clean houses, I want to suggest a healthier mind-set: *know that impactful faith conversations happen through consistent low-grade tidying—not massive house clean-outs.*

A massive house clean-out requires you to set aside blocks of hours upon hours, as you attempt to order and beautify everything in one fell swoop. That's overwhelming. I want you instead to look at this book (and my others) as your guide to long-term, low-grade spiritual tidying through ongoing conversation. This book will help you do that in three key ways.

First, it will help you focus on what most needs tidying in your child's understanding of Jesus, given the challenging world in which they're growing up. No one can clean absolutely everything, so having focus is key. Interestingly, many of the subjects in this book are ones your child won't hear discussed in church (at least in much depth). Sunday school programs tend to teach only the basics of Christianity, and those basics are leaving kids unequipped to encounter today's secular world. Research consistently shows that at least 60 percent of kids who grow up in a Christian home walk away from Christianity by their early twenties, largely in response to intellectual challenges to their faith.[4] Our kids need specific training for what they'll encounter today, and they need that training from *you*. That can sound intimidating, but this book will help you get focused on the kind of training they need most. We'll look at challenges from atheists, challenges from those who adhere to non-Christian religions, and even challenges from Christians who promote ideas that vary from what the Bible teaches. All are vital subjects that should continually be revisited as your child grows to both refresh and deepen their understanding over time.

Second, this book will help you learn the most essential points your child should understand about each subject. Much more could be said in any given chapter, but this book isn't about doing the deepest possible "cleaning" on the areas covered. Rather, the goal is to help you develop clarity on the essential points to emphasize in your conversations over time.

Third, this book will give you a vision for how *to do your tidying.* The chapter content itself is written for you, the parent. But at the end of each chapter, you'll find a step-by-step guide with questions designed to help you facilitate conversation with your child about the chapter's subject. The first question ("Open the Conversation") is an easy one to get your child talking. The subsequent questions ("Advance the Conversation") then open the door to discussion about more detailed content from the chapter. In "Apply the Conversation," you'll find a quote from a person who in some way challenges what was learned. These quotes are intended to give older kids practice applying their understanding. While each guide can be used in a single sitting, it's also intended to be a flexible tool you can use to revisit these subjects as your child grows. For example, with young kids, you might use the first question as a conversation starter, then casually discuss a few basic points from the chapter without using the remaining questions. With older elementary-age kids, you might use all the discussion questions but explain only a couple of key points in response to each one. With tweens and teens, I encourage you to walk through the full discussion guide, covering as much detail as you can from each chapter.

What this book won't do is create the actual *habit* of tidying. That's up to you. You'll have the tools for doing your work, but you'll need to make the time. If you need some ideas for when and how to weave these conversations into daily life, I've created a page on my website with tips to help; see this endnote.[5]

Homes where deep and meaningful faith conversations happen regularly aren't the product of lucky parents. They're the product of intentional parents who believe nothing is more important than raising kids to know and love Jesus. All those sports events, music practices, play rehearsals, and other activities that fill our weeks can be great, but Jesus must come first. Getting our spiritual house in order starts with that simple commitment. Once that's in place, we're ready for cleaning—one tidying step at a time.

PART 1
The Identity of Jesus

Overview

When I graduated from college, I realized that I hadn't taken my faith very seriously for a while. I decided I needed to spend time studying Christianity more deeply, so I headed to my local bookstore's "Christian" section one morning.

After haphazardly thumbing through a few titles, I eventually settled on a book called *Jesus: A Revolutionary Biography* by New Testament scholar John Dominic Crossan. I liked the idea of learning more about Jesus's historical context, and this book seemed to contain a lot of material in that area that I had never heard about while growing up in church. I returned home eager to reinvigorate my fledgling faith.

The cover of the book described it as a "startling account of what we can know about the life of Jesus." And it delivered on that claim—I was completely *startled* by what I read. As it turned out, Jesus wasn't who I thought he was at all! He was a peasant who didn't perform the many miracles in the Gospels, didn't die for the sins of humankind, and didn't physically rise from the dead. The only thing that made him extraordinary was how he lived.

I was confused. Here was someone who identified himself as a Christian but in his scholarly work described a Jesus who was nothing like the Jesus I had always known. And as far as I could tell from the book, most scholars agreed with Crossan's assessment. I distinctly remember wondering, *Was everything I learned in church all those years wrong, or did I profoundly misunderstand what I was taught?*

What I didn't know at the time was that Crossan's thinking was no different from that of many other liberal New Testament scholars. Crossan is the cofounder of the now famous Jesus Seminar, which was organized in 1985 to determine who the historical Jesus "really" was. Fellows of the Seminar met regularly to debate the authenticity of various words and deeds attributed to Jesus and to cast votes to obtain consensus. They eventually concluded that only about 18 percent of Jesus's sayings and 16 percent of his deeds (as recorded in the Gospels) are authentic.[1] The Jesus who remained—like the Jesus in Crossan's book—was unrecognizable compared to the Jesus I grew up worshiping in church.

The Jesus Seminar isn't the only group with an understanding of Jesus's identity that differs from what the Bible says, of course. There are many diverse ideas today of who Jesus is:

- Some believe he never existed (we'll address this in chapter 1).
- Some believe he was a failed Messiah (we'll address this in chapter 2).
- Some believe he was simply a good moral teacher or someone who had unique spiritual insights but never claimed to be God (we'll address this in chapter 3).
- Some believe he was a special part of God's plan in the world (even a "savior" in some cases) but not God himself (we'll address this in chapters 3–6 and part 4).

With so many competing ideas of who Jesus is, how can we know which one is correct? That's the fundamental question we need to help our kids answer, and it's the question I wasn't prepared to address when I picked up Crossan's book . . . despite having spent hundreds of hours in church.

As parents, we often focus more on the *teachings* of Jesus than on his *identity* because we're preoccupied with the task of shaping our kids' behavior. When we're faced with the daily parenting drama of kids fighting, lying, gossiping, hitting, cheating, back talking, yelling, and so on (all before 9 a.m., of course!), we have a multitude of natural opportunities to share how Jesus taught us to live. It's not so natural, however, to inject conversations into the mix about who Jesus is and how we can know who he is. But that doesn't make doing so any less important. Let's be clear: if Jesus was only a human, his teachings are no more authoritative for our kids' most recent behavioral issue than those of our next-door neighbor. Jesus's identity is foundational to *everything* we believe as Christians.

In part 1, we'll look at key questions kids should understand about who Jesus is. I'm going to warn you: these chapters contain a lot of detail, even though they're short. Don't just skim through them! Be patient and take the time to really understand the content, because these chapters will serve as an essential foundation for appreciating the importance of what Jesus taught, which we'll study in part 2.

Three Keys to Impactful Conversations about the Identity of Jesus

1. *Establish the importance of Jesus's identity before beginning these conversations.* For kids who have grown up in a Christian home or who have spent a lot of time in a Christian church, the identity of Jesus as God is often a foregone conclusion—so much so that they may never have considered the implications of that fact. Share examples from this overview about other Jesus beliefs and discuss how those beliefs result in people having very different worldviews.

2. *Make it clear that Jesus's identity isn't a matter of blind belief.* When you introduce competing ideas of who Jesus is, your child might assume that everyone just has to choose the belief that makes the most sense to them. It's important for them to understand, however, that we should form our beliefs about Jesus's identity based on the evidence we have. Knowing who Jesus is doesn't mean we blindly pick a belief but rather that we search for what is *true* of him.

3. *Emphasize how Jesus's identity is what makes him relevant to our lives today.* Skeptics like to say they don't care about a book written two thousand years ago or about a man who lived then. If Jesus were just another human, perhaps what he taught two thousand years ago *would* be irrelevant today. But if Jesus is God incarnate—perfectly knowing the past, present, and future—then what he taught couldn't be more important, no matter *how* long ago it was.

1. Is Jesus a Myth?

Four words make the hairs of annoyance stand up on my arms more than any others: "Mommy, I can't find . . ." Of course, it's not the words alone that annoy me. It's the frenzied tone and timing—always the last possible moment before we need to go somewhere. Shoes are the most frustrating example. There's not a single school morning that kids don't need shoes, so they should automatically know they'll need them and plan accordingly. Yet they regularly look at me when we're trying to leave as if to say, "I have *no* idea where these crazy things called shoes are that you unexpectedly want me to find, so you have to help me search."

The reason it's so maddening when kids say they can't find something is that we know they haven't *really* looked. "I can't find" means they quickly glanced around whatever room they happened to be in at the moment, then gave up. But as adults, we know that if we're going to find something, we have to look in the right place, and we have to look thoroughly. Otherwise, we'll draw the wrong conclusions.

In the same way, an increasing number of people today say they can't find the historical Jesus . . . at all. Jesus "mythicists" claim there's no reliable evidence he existed. In other words, they say they're looking in the right places and are searching thoroughly, but Jesus just isn't there.

The idea that Jesus is a myth has been around for hundreds of years, but it's become more popular recently. For example, the *Washington Post* featured an article just in time for Christmas titled "Did Historical Jesus Really Exist? The Evidence Just Doesn't Add Up."[1] This isn't an isolated example of something otherwise unheard of. Research shows that 8 percent of Americans don't believe Jesus was a real person, with the number significantly higher for millennials (13 percent).[2] In England, *40 percent* of people don't believe Jesus existed![3]

When you think of having conversations with your child about Jesus, you're probably not thinking about explaining how we know he was a real person in history, but that's where we need to start given the popular claims today.

What Evidence Should We *Expect* to Find?

When we're looking for a pair of shoes, we know exactly what we're looking for, and when we find them, we know it. When we're looking for someone in history, however, things aren't so obvious. We can't travel back in time, so there's no way to *prove* anything historical. Nonetheless, we can confidently reconstruct much of history by piecing together the evidence that remains today.

In order to establish that a person existed, historians like to have physical evidence such as photographs of or writings by the individual. But because such evidence is often not available, historians also look for written references to the person. Ideally, they want a number of sources that are (1) independent (not relying on one another for information), (2) dated close to the time of the person they're describing, (3) written by disinterested authors (to minimize bias), and (4) detailed in information.

Mythicists claim we don't have enough evidence matching these criteria to confidently determine that Jesus existed. To understand and evaluate their case, we'll look at the three most important

32

types of historical evidence under scrutiny: (1) early references to Jesus by non-Christians, (2) references to Jesus by the apostle Paul, and (3) references to Jesus by the Gospel writers.

Early References to Jesus by Non-Christians

The biggest objection mythicists have to a historical Jesus is that there's a lack of reliable non-Christian sources from the first century that reference him (Jesus lived until about AD 30). They say that if Jesus was such an important figure, there would have been more writings about him. This is a poor argument, however, because we don't even have many first-century writings about the *rulers* of Roman Palestine (the area where Jesus lived). For example, Pontius Pilate was governor of Judea from AD 26 to AD 36 and was one of the most important figures there during the years he reigned. However, we have no first-century Roman records today that document his rule. *Even so, no one doubts his existence.*

From Roman Palestine, writings survive from only *one* author from the first century—the Jewish historian Josephus. And Josephus mentions Jesus on two occasions in his work *The Antiquities of the Jews*. In one passage, he describes how Ananus, the high priest in Jerusalem, unlawfully put to death a man named James, "the brother of Jesus, who was called Christ." In a second, more descriptive passage, Josephus writes about Jesus being a wise teacher who reportedly did "startling" deeds, was condemned and crucified under Pilate, and had followers who believed he rose from the dead.[4] As a Jew, Josephus did not believe Jesus was the Messiah, but the details he provides clearly point to Jesus's *existence*.

Josephus is the only non-Christian reference to Jesus's existence from the first century, but if we expand our search even thirty years (still within a reasonable one hundred years of Jesus's death), we find three mentions of Jesus by Roman writers.[5] The most valuable one comes from Cornelius Tacitus (AD 56–c. 117), a Roman historian who wrote a history of the Roman Empire covering the years AD 14 to AD 68. In *The Annals of Imperial Rome*, Tacitus describes a devastating fire that raged through Rome during the reign of Emperor Nero. Many people believed Nero was responsible for setting it. Tacitus wrote:

> Therefore, to squelch the rumor, Nero created scapegoats and subjected to the most refined tortures those whom the common people called "Christians," hated for their abominable crimes. Their name comes from Christ, who, during the reign of Tiberius, had been executed by the procurator Pontius Pilate.[6]

Tacitus's statement places Jesus in history by confirming that the time of his execution was during the reign of Tiberius (AD 14–37) and during the governorship of Pilate (AD 26–36). While some have questioned the source of Tacitus's information, claiming it could have been "hearsay," he's generally considered to be a very reliable historian, and there's little reason to claim this particular passage is inaccurate.

As we can see, several early and credible non-Christian sources reference the existence of Jesus. We'll now look at how Christian sources provide further evidence, starting with the letters of Paul.

References to Jesus by the Apostle Paul

The apostle Paul wrote at least seven books of the New Testament, and his writings are considered by New Testament scholars to be the earliest surviving Christian texts (Paul's first letter, 1 Thessalonians, is typically dated to AD 50 or before—within twenty years of Jesus's crucifixion). Their proximity to Jesus's life makes them of special interest to those studying the historical evidence for his existence.

Some mythicists claim that Paul never believed in a historical Jesus and that these early writings instead reflect a belief in a "celestial Jesus"—a purely divine being.[7] The reason this claim has gained traction is that Paul's writings lack biographical details of Jesus's life. Whereas the Gospels tell us much about what Jesus said and did, Paul mentions very little. Mythicists claim that Paul would have talked much more about important details of Jesus's life (such as his miracles and teachings) *if he had known about them.* They say the details we have in the Gospels today were invented years after Paul wrote, in order to historicize what was originally a myth.

It's important to understand, however, that Paul's writings are letters, not biographies. He wrote to address specific needs that churches had, not to recount the details of Jesus's life. Even so, several passages in Paul's letters demonstrate that he knew Jesus was a real human and not simply a spiritual being:

- Jesus was born of a woman and was descended from David "according to the flesh" (Gal. 4:4; Rom. 1:3).
- Jesus had human brothers, and Paul personally met with his brother James (Gal. 1:19; 1 Cor. 9:5).
- Jesus died (1 Cor. 15:3; 2 Cor. 4:10; Gal. 1:1; Col. 1:22).
- Jesus was buried (1 Cor. 15:4).
- Jesus rose after he died (Rom. 1:4; 1 Cor. 15:14; Phil. 3:10).

While mythicists often say these details were later added by Christians to "historicize" Jesus's life, this is pure speculation. There's no textual evidence that these passages were not originally in Paul's writings, and they appear in every manuscript copy of his writings that we have.[8]

References to Jesus by the Gospel Writers

Most of what we know about Jesus's life comes from the Gospels. Mythicists, however, believe these writings are unreliable as historical sources. This is not the place to lay out a defense of the reliability of the Gospels—many extensive books have been written on the subject[9]—but given our current purpose, it's also not necessary. As we've already seen, we have strong historical evidence for Jesus's existence without even considering the Gospels. In addition, a skeptic doesn't need to accept the truth of everything recorded in the Gospels to acknowledge that they must have been written in response to the life of someone who actually existed. As New Testament scholar, agnostic, and ex-Christian Bart Ehrman explains:

> We are not dealing with just one Gospel that reports what Jesus said and did from sometime near the end of the first century. We have a number of surviving Gospels . . . that are either completely independent of one another or independent in a large number of their traditions. These all attest to the existence of Jesus. . . . The vast network of these traditions, numerically significant, widely dispersed, and largely independent of one another, makes it almost certain that whatever one wants to say about Jesus, at the very least one must say he existed.[10]

Articles such as the one in the *Washington Post* may grab people's attention, but they're misleading and sensational. Virtually all historians and New Testament scholars agree that Jesus existed, given the multiple independent sources we have from within just a few decades of his death.

KEY POINTS

- Three important types of historical evidence for Jesus's existence are (1) early references to Jesus by non-Christians, (2) references to Jesus by the apostle Paul, and (3) references to Jesus by the Gospel writers.

- We don't have many non-Christian sources from the first hundred years after Jesus lived that reference him, but we wouldn't expect to. However, the few we do have—especially from Tacitus and Josephus—are strong evidence for Jesus's existence.
- Mythicists often claim that Paul believed in a "celestial" rather than a historical Jesus due to the few life details he recounts. However, Paul's writings are letters, not biographies. Even so, several passages in Paul's letters show that he knew Jesus was a real person.
- A skeptic doesn't need to accept the truth of everything recorded in the Gospels to acknowledge that they must have been written in response to the life of someone who actually existed.

CONVERSATION GUIDE

Open the Conversation

- If you were a historian who wanted to confirm that George Washington existed, what kinds of evidence would you look for? *(Think about what kinds of evidence would be useful to historians—paintings, personal writings, biographies, etc.)*

Advance the Conversation

- Now think about the kinds of evidence you would look for if you wanted to confirm that Jesus existed. What would you hope to find? *(Explore the four criteria historians use for written sources. Introduce the categories of references to Jesus by early non-Christians, Paul, and the Gospel writers.)*
- Some people think there's not enough evidence to believe that Jesus existed because we don't have many early writings from non-Christians that mention him. Would you expect there to

be a lot of early non-Christian writings about Jesus? Why or why not? *(Writings would have to survive for two thousand years, and few survive that mention even the rulers of the time. Discuss the writings we have from Tacitus and Josephus.)*

- There are also people who think the apostle Paul believed that Jesus was only a spiritual being and never existed as a human on earth. Look up what Paul says in 1 Corinthians 15:3–4; and Galatians 1:19 and 4:4. What does this sample of verses tell us Paul believed about Jesus's existence? *(Help make connections to the points that imply Jesus was a real person.)*

- Do you think someone who doesn't believe all that the Gospels tell us about Jesus should also think Jesus didn't exist? Why or why not? *(Read the Bart Ehrman quote and explain that the Gospels represent multiple, independent pieces of evidence for the historical life of Jesus.)*

Apply the Conversation

- In an online article titled "5 Reasons to Suspect That Jesus Never Existed," the author's first two points are (1) "No first-century secular evidence whatsoever exists to support the actuality of [Jesus]," and (2) "The earliest New Testament writers [Paul] seem ignorant of the details of Jesus' life."[11] How would you respond based on what you learned in this chapter?

2. Is Jesus the Jewish Messiah?

When my twins were in first grade, I told them it was time for them to start getting into the habit of reading the Bible on their own—and not just a children's Bible. I suggested they start with Mark (the shortest Gospel) and explained that they wouldn't understand it all, but we would discuss what they read.

That night my heart melted as I went to tuck them in and found them each in bed with the Bible in their hands. I walked into my daughter's room, smiling proudly from ear to ear. Then I saw what she was reading.

Isaiah.

"Um . . . honey, I think that's a *really* tough book to start with. Why not read Mark, as I suggested?"

She shrugged. "Because I wanted to pick my own book."

My son then walked in from his room and said, "I picked Ezekiel! Is that a good one?"

Now, don't get me wrong. These are both very important books in the Bible. But they are also two of the most difficult books my kids could have chosen to read on their own. That night we had a good talk about why the Old Testament can be hard to understand with no background. One of the things I explained was that the Old Testament contains many prophecies (predictions of what would happen in the future). Of particular importance are *messianic* prophecies—the many Old Testament predictions of a coming Savior known as the Messiah. Christians believe these prophecies were uniquely fulfilled in Jesus (the Greek word for Messiah is *christos*, which is where we get the word *Christ*).

As we talked, I realized how rarely most kids hear about the subject of Jesus's messiahship. And I understand why. Messianic prophecy and its fulfillment isn't exactly the easiest subject to explain to kids, and many parents haven't studied it themselves. However, there are some key points kids can and should understand that are powerful evidence for the supernatural nature of the Bible and for Jesus as the anticipated Savior of the world.

Did Jesus *Claim* to Be the Messiah?

A major reason for the complexity of this topic is that the Old Testament doesn't explicitly label *which* verses are talking about the coming Messiah, and a number of verses *could* be, depending on one's interpretation of the context. Because of this, the messianic expectations held by Jewish people before, during, and after the time of Jesus were highly diverse. Their understanding of the messianic mission as well as the means through which the Messiah would accomplish that mission (including the degree of divine assistance) varied widely.[1] Some people thought the Messiah would be a priestly figure, others a royal deliverer. Evidence suggests that at least one Jewish group thought there would be two Messiahs. Although these diverse messianic expectations existed, the theme of a warrior Messiah who would be a political rescuer—an earthly king—dominated Jewish thought because the Jews longed for deliverance from the tyranny of Rome.

With as much expectation as there was for a coming Messiah, one might think Jesus would have claimed the title for himself early and often in his ministry if he was, indeed, that person. But he didn't. For most of his ministry, Jesus told people to keep signs of his identity a secret (a pattern especially seen in Mark). So what's going on? Much could be said, but we'll look at three particularly important events that reveal how Jesus saw his identity.[2]

1. Peter's Confession

The following dialogue between Jesus and Peter is an important starting point for this discussion.

> Jesus and his disciples went on to the villages around Caesarea Philippi. On the way he asked them, "Who do people say I am?"
>
> They replied, "Some say John the Baptist; others say Elijah; and still others, one of the prophets."
>
> "But what about you?" he asked. "Who do you say I am?"
>
> Peter answered, "You are the Messiah."
>
> Jesus warned them not to tell anyone about him.
>
> He then began to teach them that the Son of Man must suffer many things and be rejected by the elders, the chief priests and the teachers of the law, and that he must be killed and after three days rise again. (Mark 8:27–31)

The disciples had accompanied Jesus, heard his teachings, and witnessed his miracles. Now Jesus pressed them to consider what his ministry implied about his identity. When Peter responded that Jesus was the Messiah, Jesus didn't throw him a party for successfully connecting the dots. Instead, he (1) warned the disciples to keep his identity a secret, then (2) immediately prepared them for his upcoming rejection, suffering, and death. The key to understanding Jesus's response is in what we just learned about Jewish expectations of the Messiah. Because the Jews predominantly expected a warrior king, Jesus knew that a public claim of messiahship amounted to a *political claim of kingship* in the minds of many—a misunderstanding that could have led to his premature execution by Roman rulers who didn't want that challenge to their authority. This also explains why Jesus immediately started talking about his upcoming suffering. He knew that wasn't what the disciples were expecting for a Messiah, so he had to prepare them for something very different—the events of his final week on earth.

2. The Triumphal Entry

Jesus entered Jerusalem the Sunday before his crucifixion riding on a donkey never before ridden (an event known as the triumphal entry; Mark 11:1–10). The disciples spread their cloaks on the donkey, and other followers spread their cloaks and palm branches on the road before it. Importantly, this procession resembled the way high-ranking officials entered ancient cities. New Testament scholar Darrell Bock explains, "In mimicking such entries, Jesus was making a social and political statement that was a direct public political challenge to authorities, much more than most of his ministry had been. It left Jesus open to the charge of claiming to be king (John 12:13)."[3] Because Jesus knew his earthly life was ending in a few days, he was now willing to make bolder claims about his identity. This particular action alluded to a claim of royalty, and not just any royalty. Jesus appears to have intentionally evoked an image associated with a messianic prophecy from Zechariah 9:9—that Israel's future king would come riding on a donkey. This was specifically a claim to *messianic* royalty.

3. Examination by Jewish Leadership

Within days of Jesus's triumphal entry, he was betrayed by Judas, arrested, and brought to the Jewish leadership for examination, culminating in the high priest directly asking Jesus if he was the Messiah (Matt. 26:57–68; Mark 14:53–65; Luke 22:66–71). Jesus responded, "I am. . . . And you will see the Son of Man sitting at the right hand of the Mighty One and coming on the clouds of heaven" (Mark 14:62). This affirmation is not as explicit in Matthew and Luke, but all three of these Gospels include Jesus's response that the Son of Man will be seated at the right hand of God ("Son of Man" was how Jesus often referred to himself). Once again, Jesus was applying messianic prophecy in a personal way—the Messiah was to sit at the right hand of God (Ps. 110:1).

Jesus's words about coming on the clouds of heaven (included in Matthew's and Mark's accounts) also referred to messianic prophecy. Daniel 7:13–14 says a son of man figure would come with "the clouds of heaven" and be given all authority, glory, and sovereign power for a kingdom that would never pass away. Jesus, therefore, claimed messiahship in each of these Gospel accounts, either through an explicit "I am" response (in Mark) or through applying messianic prophecies to himself (in Matthew, Mark, and Luke).

These events are important examples of how Jesus claimed to be the Messiah (see also Matt. 5:17; 21:42; Luke 24:27, 44; John 5:46–47). To see why there's good reason to *accept* his claims, we now need to look at the prophecies he fulfilled—a collective profile he couldn't have arranged.

What Prophecies Did Jesus Fulfill?

Given what we've learned, it shouldn't be surprising that the answer to the question "What prophecies did Jesus fulfill?" will differ depending on whom you ask and which Old Testament passages they consider to be prophetic; the number can range from dozens to hundreds. The following list is a select group of those that are most understandable for kids.

- *Lineage.* A descendant of Abraham, through the line of Isaac, Jacob, Judah, Jesse, and King David (Gen. 12:3; 17:19; 49:10; Num. 24:17; Isa. 11:1; Jer. 23:5); *fulfillment: Matthew 1:1–17.*

- *Birth*. Born of a virgin in Bethlehem (Isa. 7:14; Mic. 5:2); *fulfillment: Matthew 1:23; 2:1–2; Luke 2:4.*

- *Miracle worker*. Healer of the blind, deaf, lame, and mute (Isa. 35:5–6; 42:7; 53:4); *fulfillment: Matthew 8:16–17; 11:4– 6; Luke 7:20–23.* (Chapter 4 will discuss miracle claims.)

- *Ministry*. Rejected by his people and with great suffering (Isa. 53); *fulfillment: Luke 23:13–21; John 12:37–41.*

- *Death*. Betrayed by a friend for thirty pieces of silver (Zech. 11:12; 13:6); *fulfillment: Matthew 26:14–15.* Deserted by disciples (Zech. 13:7); *fulfillment: Matthew 26:56.* Mocked (Ps. 22:7); *fulfillment: Matthew 27:27–31.* His hands and feet pierced (Ps. 22:16); *fulfillment: Matthew 27:32–35.* Lots cast for his garments (Ps. 22:18); *fulfillment: Matthew 27:35.* Bones not broken (Ps. 34:20); *fulfillment: John 19:31–36.*

- *Resurrection*. Resurrected to God's right hand (Ps. 110:1; Isa. 25:7–8; part 4 will discuss the fulfillment of this prophecy.)

Any *one* fulfilled prophecy may not be compelling evidence that Jesus was the Messiah, but the prophecies, when taken together, make the probability of fulfillment by one person astonishingly small.[4] *Only Jesus matches the profile.* The implication is that he was the promised Savior of the world and that the Bible accurately told of his arrival hundreds of years before he was born.

KEY POINTS

- The messianic expectations held by Jewish people before, during, and after the time of Jesus were highly diverse because of varied views on which Old Testament verses were prophecies and how best to interpret them.

- Three key events demonstrate that Jesus *claimed* to be the Messiah: (1) Peter's confession, (2) the triumphal entry, and (3) the examination by Jewish leadership.
- Any *one* fulfilled prophecy may not be compelling evidence that Jesus was the Messiah, but the prophecies, when taken together, make the probability of fulfillment by one person astonishingly small. Only Jesus matches the profile.

CONVERSATION GUIDE

Open the Conversation

- When you think of the Old Testament, what events or people come to mind first? *(Ask if your child has heard that the Old Testament made predictions of a coming Savior known as the Messiah. Explain that Christians believe Jesus fulfilled these predictions and why, if he did, that's powerful evidence the Bible is God's Word.)*

Advance the Conversation

- Read Mark 8:27–31. Why do you think Jesus warned Peter to keep his identity a secret if he was the Messiah? *(Explain that Jews at the time of Jesus had varying expectations of the Messiah, depending on their interpretation of the Old Testament. Discuss how the popular view of the Messiah as a political warrior affected the claims Jesus could publicly make.)*
- Read Zechariah 9:9—a messianic prophecy from the Old Testament. Now read Mark 11:1–10. What do Jesus's actions in Mark say about who he claimed to be? *(He intentionally entered Jerusalem in a way consistent with prophecy, so this was a claim to messiahship. With older kids, discuss Jesus's claims in the examination by Jewish leadership as well.)*

- We know that Jesus claimed to be the Messiah from the verses we just read and others. But other people have claimed to be the Messiah too! To know whose claim we should believe, we have to look at who fulfilled prophecies they couldn't have *chosen* to fulfill. *(Walk through the prophecies listed in this chapter in age-appropriate depth. Look up both the prophecy and the fulfillment verses for at least one. Emphasize how small the chance is that all the prophecies could be fulfilled in one person and that Jesus uniquely matches the profile.)*

Apply the Conversation

- In an online forum, a person asked, "Why do Christians believe that Jesus was Christ [Messiah]?" Someone responded, "There is every reason for Christians *not* to believe that Jesus was 'the Christ.' It was [the apostle] Paul, who never knew Jesus . . . who 'made' him into 'the Christ' well after his failure to merit the title."[5] How would you respond to this person's claim that Paul created the idea that Jesus was the Messiah years after Jesus's death?

3. Is Jesus God?

My son loves science kits, and they're a staple on his yearly Christmas list. But as the parent of any science-loving kid knows, the kits are all pretty similar, just packaged in a thousand different ways. No matter what that exciting box looks like, you're probably going to dump out a couple of tubes, a plastic cup, a few basic chemicals, and a small instruction booklet that explains how to make a "volcano."

This year we decided to get him a different kind of science kit, filled with optical illusions to show how our eyes can play tricks on us. One picture, for example, showed hundreds of coffee beans with a man's face hidden in them. It sounds like a face would be easy to spot, but because the shading on it was like that of the beans, it was hard to find at first. However, once you saw it, you couldn't *not* see it. Every time you looked at the picture from that point forward, your eyes gravitated straight to the face. It became obvious.

The question of whether or not the Bible claims that Jesus is God is similar. When you first look at the text, you might assume it doesn't claim that Jesus is divine because Jesus doesn't explicitly say the words "I am God"—and skeptics (as well as adherents to some other religions) are quick to point that out. But once you understand the diverse nature of the ways in which the Bible presents Jesus as God (and the ways in which Jesus presents himself as God), you'll never look at the text the same way again. Those ways, like the face in the beans, become obvious once you've seen them. (We'll look at the question of *how* Jesus can be both God and human in chapter 6.)

Robert M. Bowman Jr. and J. Ed Komoszewski have written an excellent book on this subject called *Putting Jesus in His Place*.[1] They explore the range of evidence for Jesus's deity using the acronym HANDS:

- Honors: Jesus shares the *honors* due to God.
- Attributes: Jesus shares the *attributes* of God.
- Names: Jesus shares the *names* of God.
- Deeds: Jesus shares in the *deeds* that God does.
- Seat: Jesus shares the *seat* of God's throne.

It's important to understand why the fact that Jesus shares these five things with God is so significant. First-century Jews were strict monotheists (believing in only one God). Yet Jewish Christians spoke of Jesus sharing in the *unique identity of God* while continuing to believe only one God exists.[2] To claim that Jesus shared in God's unique identity was to claim that Jesus *is* God.

Because acronyms can be especially useful in helping kids memorize facts, we'll use this organization of content to answer this chapter's question. Given space limitations, we'll cover only a few select points for each letter. I highly recommend *Putting Jesus in His Place* for deeper study.

Jesus Shares the *Honors* Due to God

To give someone honor is to acknowledge their rightful status and position. Jesus was given the honors due to God when people worshiped and prayed to him.

Honor of Worship

There are times in the Bible when people bowed to Jesus, but the context doesn't necessarily imply it was an act of divine worship—bowing was also a custom of showing humility (see Matt. 8:2; 9:18; 20:20). However, at other times, the context demonstrates that a person's response to Jesus was more than mere respect.

In one case, the disciples were in a boat on the Sea of Galilee when they saw Jesus walking toward them on the water. Peter then tried to walk on the water himself, but he began to sink after becoming fearful. Jesus rescued him, and they both got into the boat. The winds stopped, and Matthew 14:33 says that the disciples "worshiped him, saying, 'Truly you are the Son of God.'" Given the context—the disciples had just seen a supernatural display of Jesus's power—it's clear that they were worshiping Jesus as deity, not just as an impressive human.

Another revealing moment is when the disciples met Jesus after his resurrection. Matthew 28:17 says, "When they saw him, they worshiped him." Jesus replied, "All authority in heaven and on earth has been given to me" (v. 18). Jesus didn't refuse their worship. Instead, he *confirmed* that it was an appropriate response to his resurrection.

Honor of Prayer

Throughout the Old Testament, the only proper object of prayer is God. But just days after Jesus's ascension to heaven, a major shift took place: the disciples prayed to *Jesus* for help in choosing a new apostle to replace Judas (Acts 1:24–25). They prayed, "Lord, you know everyone's heart. Show us which of these two you have chosen to take over this apostolic ministry, which Judas left to go where he belongs." "Lord" means Jesus here, because Peter had just referred specifically to "the Lord Jesus" before this prayer (v. 21). The fact that monotheistic Jews prayed to Jesus speaks volumes about their understanding of his identity (see also Acts 7:59–60; 2 Cor. 12:8–9).

Jesus Shares the *Attributes* of God

The New Testament regularly ascribes attributes to Jesus that only God has. One of the most significant ones is preexistence. Bowman and Komoszewski explain the importance of this:

> If Christ existed as a divine person before his human life, then he is the definitive revelation of the nature of God because his nature *is*, in fact, the nature of God. On the other hand, if Christ did not exist before his human life, then he is a revelation of the nature of God only in the sense that in his words and actions we see how God wants us to live. . . . Was Jesus a man through whom God was revealing himself, or was he God revealing himself as a man?[3]

This is a crucial question. And the New Testament repeatedly answers that Jesus existed before his human life:

- Jesus prayed, "And now, Father, glorify me in your presence with the glory I had with you before the world began" (John 17:5).
- "For in him all things were created: things in heaven and on earth, visible and invisible, whether thrones or powers or rulers or authorities; all things have been created through him and for him" (Col. 1:16).
- "In these last days he has spoken to us by his Son, whom he appointed heir of all things, and through whom also he made the universe" (Heb. 1:2).

It should be noted that preexistent doesn't *necessarily* mean eternal, but other passages make it clear that Jesus preexisted in an eternal, divine way, equal with God himself. For example, in

John 8:58, Jesus says, "Very truly I tell you . . . before Abraham was born, I am!" The wording "I am" echoes the name God revealed for himself in Exodus 3:14. Jesus's critics understood he was claiming to be the same God—they picked up stones to kill him for blasphemy.

In addition to preexistence, some other key divine attributes ascribed to Jesus include omnipotence (all-powerful—Eph. 1:21), omnipresence (all-present—Mark 7:24–30; Luke 7:1–10), and omniscience (all-knowing—Matt. 9:4; 11:21–24; 12:25; Mark 2:6–8; Luke 6:8).

Jesus Shares the *Names* of God

When the New Testament uses titles for Jesus, it often does so by quoting from or alluding to Old Testament passages about God. For example, the Old Testament speaks of God as the bridegroom and husband of Israel (Isa. 54:5; 62:5). In the New Testament, Jesus claims to be the bridegroom as well. When people asked why Jesus's disciples weren't fasting, he answered, "How can the guests of the bridegroom fast while he is with them? They cannot, so long as they have him with them" (Mark 2:19; see also Matt. 22:2; 25:1–13; John 3:29; 2 Cor. 11:2; Eph. 5:23–27).

As another example, the Old Testament almost always uses the title Savior to refer to God—the only exception being a few references to the judges of Israel (Judg. 3:9, 15; Neh. 9:27; translated as "deliverer"). When Savior is applied to Jesus in the New Testament, however, the context shows that something much greater than a human savior is in mind. Jesus is specifically referred to as the Savior of the world (John 4:42; 1 John 4:14), a Savior from heaven (Phil. 3:20), and a Savior who brings deliverance from sin and death (Acts 5:31; Titus 2:13–14).

Other Old Testament names and/or titles Jesus shares with God include King of kings and Lord of lords (Rev. 17:14), name above every name (Phil. 2:9–11), I am (see the prior section), and the first and the last (Rev. 2:8).

Jesus Shares in the *Deeds* That God Does

Jesus Created All and Sustains All

The Jewish people believed that the God of Israel was the *sole* Creator and Ruler of all things, yet the New Testament clearly teaches that creation owes its existence to *Jesus*. In addition to the verses pointing to Jesus's preexistence, the apostle Paul says in 1 Corinthians 8:6, "For us there is but one God, the Father, from whom all things came and for whom we live; and there is but one Lord, Jesus Christ, through whom all things came and through whom we live." Similarly, Paul says that God "himself gives everyone life and breath and everything else. . . . 'For in him we live and move and have our being'" (Acts 17:25, 28). The implication is clear: Jesus shares in the work of creating and sustaining because he shares in the identity of God.

Jesus Acts with God's Authority and Power

A core part of Jesus's ministry was his miracle working—signs used to confirm that he acted directly with God's authority and power. This is such an important subject to understand that we'll devote the following chapter to it.

Jesus Will Judge All

The Old Testament teaches that God is the sole Judge of humankind (Gen. 18:25; Pss. 7:11; 50:6; 75:7). But Jesus teaches that *he* is that judge: "The Father judges no one, but has entrusted all judgment to the Son" (John 5:22; see also Matt. 16:27; Acts 17:31). Paul says that Jesus will carry out that judgment from "the judgment seat of Christ" (2 Cor. 5:10). This brings us to the final letter of the HANDS acronym—the significance of the judgment seat.

Jesus Shares the *Seat* of God's Throne

In various ways, the New Testament says that Jesus's judgment seat is God's throne. Bowman and Komoszewski explain, "Someone sitting on God's throne and exercising God's ultimate prerogatives is, in at least a very practical sense, God. He occupies God's position and in doing so has the rightful expectation that we respond to him as to God himself."[4] The Bible expresses this in several ways:

- Jesus is pictured as sitting on God's throne (Rev. 22:1, 3).
- Jesus is said to exercise universal rule over all things—language characteristically used in Judaism to communicate God's unique sovereignty from his throne (John 3:35; 13:3; 16:15; Acts 10:36; 1 Cor. 15:27–28).
- Jesus is said to be exalted above all of God's heavenly "court," such as angels and other supernatural powers (Eph. 1:21; Phil. 2:10; 1 Pet. 3:22).

Phew! I know we covered a lot in this chapter. Don't worry if you don't remember the details. Focus on learning the acronym and helping your child understand the *type* of evidence represented by each letter. You can always come back later for specifics.

KEY POINTS

- The case for the deity of Jesus can be remembered using the HANDS acronym. Jesus shares the:
  - Honors due to God (worship and prayer)

- Attributes of God (preexistence, omnipotence, omnipresence, and omniscience)
- Names of God (bridegroom, Savior, King of kings and Lord of lords, name above every name, I am, and the first and the last)
- Deeds that God does (created all and sustains all, acts with God's authority and power, and will judge all)
- Seat of God's throne (exercises rule over all and is exalted over all)

CONVERSATION GUIDE

Open the Conversation

- Christians believe that Jesus is God, but the Bible never tells us that Jesus specifically said, "I am God." Based on what you know of Jesus's life, why do you think his followers believed he was God?

Advance the Conversation

- Even though Jesus doesn't say the exact words "I am God" in the Bible, there are a lot of *other* ways the Bible tells us he's God. *(Explain the HANDS acronym as a way of remembering these ways. Pick at least one example for each letter, taking the time to read the corresponding verses.)*

Apply the Conversation

- In an online forum, a person asked, "Is there a [Christian] denomination I fit into or do I [have] to find another religion? I agree with everything except for the whole Jesus is God [thing]."[5] What are some points you could share on how the Bible affirms that Jesus is God?

4. Did Jesus Really Perform Miracles?

Since starting my blog, *Christian Mom Thoughts*, in 2011, I've received several thousands of comments—many of which have been from skeptics. Sometimes skeptics' comments are relevant to a given blog post, but other times people just want to tell me how ridiculous they think Christianity is. Here's one I received this week of a more general nature:

> Why do you believe outlandish claims about a god [sic] speaking things into existence, or about a man being swallowed by a fish for a few days and surviving, a worldwide flood (and ark) that fit all of the animals in it and eight people, or a story about a virgin getting pregnant? None of that makes sense, you don't have any proof that it happened, but you still think it's true. Why do you prefer to believe outlandish claims because they're religious?

Now, "outlandish" means that something is bizarre or unfamiliar. From that perspective, this skeptic is right—miracles *are* bizarre! If they weren't, they wouldn't be miracles; they would be ordinary events. So logically speaking, we can't determine whether a miracle happened based on how crazy it sounds to us; miracles are, by definition, extraordinary.

At the same time, if we're honest, we should empathize with this commenter's skepticism. Even young kids, who are accustomed to reading fantastical stories, often ask if biblical accounts really happened. As rational humans, we should want good reason to believe that reports of events so foreign to our knowledge of how the world *normally* works are true. More specifically, as Christians, we should especially want good reason to believe the miracle reports surrounding Jesus because they're important for establishing his identity. It's one thing for the New Testament writers to *claim* he was God (as we saw in the previous chapter), but it's another thing to have good reason for *believing* that claim. That's why this chapter's subject is so important. *If Jesus performed the many miracles attributed to him, this validates the Bible's claim of his deity, and that in turn has numerous implications for our lives.* But if the miracle reports are just baseless legends that developed over time, our faith is useless (1 Cor. 15:14).

So how can we know the answer to such an important question—one that revolves around events that allegedly happened two thousand years ago? That's what we'll consider in this chapter. But before we look at New Testament miracles specifically, we need to look at the broader philosophical question of whether miracles are *ever* possible.

Are Miracles *Ever* Possible?

A miracle is "an extraordinary event manifesting divine intervention in human affairs."[1] They aren't simply surprising or unusual events, though we often call those kinds of things "miracles" in casual conversation. When we ask if miracles are possible, we are specifically asking if it's possible there are exceptional events in our universe with a *supernatural* cause—a cause from outside of nature.

When we define the question this way, we can see that the answer depends on whether anything outside of nature exists. If the natural world is all there is, it follows that miracles aren't possible; nothing can have a supernatural cause if nothing supernatural exists. But if a being does exist beyond nature—such as God—it's at least logically possible that he chooses to intervene in the natural world.

The question of whether miracles are possible, therefore, is really a question of whether God exists. This is one of the many reasons why it's so important for kids to understand the evidence for the existence of God—the plausibility of biblical miracles (including the resurrection!) depends on it. Because I devoted several chapters in *Talking with Your Kids about God* to explaining this evidence, I won't recap it here. For this chapter's question, we'll assume that miracles are at least *possible*, given the evidence for God's existence. Now we'll turn to the evidence that Jesus actually performed them.

Did Jesus Perform Miracles?

There are seven key pieces of evidence that support the historicity of Jesus's miracle reports.

1. Jesus's Miracles Appear in the Earliest Sources about Him

The books of the New Testament were written over several decades in the first century. Scholars are often especially interested in what the Gospel of Mark says, because it's considered to be the earliest Gospel we have (critical scholars assume that the later the writing, the more time for legend to be added). And there's no doubt that Mark presents a miracle-performing Jesus: almost one-third of the verses in Mark, or about 40 percent of his narrative, involve miracles in some way. New Testament scholar

Craig S. Keener says, "Very few critics would deny the presence of any miracles in the earliest material about Jesus."[2]

2. Jesus's Miracles Appear in Multiple, Independent Sources

If we read of Jesus's miracles in only one or two of the four Gospels, we might question why the others don't mention such amazing events. But all the Gospels report multiple miracles, and miracles are referenced throughout the rest of the New Testament as well. There's no trace of a Jesus who didn't perform miracles in any existing sources.

3. Miracle Working Was an Integral Part of Jesus's Ministry

People often believe they can separate Jesus's teachings from the miracle claims of the New Testament and regard him simply as a good moral teacher. However, as Keener says, "So central are miracle reports to the Gospels that one could remove them only if one regarded the Gospels as preserving barely any genuine information about Jesus."[3] In other words, throwing out miracle claims as an add-on to the stuff that "really" matters is not a legitimate option. Miracle claims are so central to the Gospels that without them most of the remaining text doesn't make sense.

4. Jesus Attracted Large Crowds Because of His Works

There's no controversy among scholars that Jesus drew large crowds in response to his works.[4] This isn't to say that scholars necessarily accept that what Jesus did was *miraculous* in nature but rather that he did things that were considered amazing enough by observers to draw crowds. This is evidenced by many reports in the Gospels (Matt. 4:25; 8:1, 18; 14:13; 19:2) as well as in non-Christian sources (recall from chapter 1 that even the Jewish historian Josephus reported that Jesus did "startling deeds").

5. Jesus's Opponents Didn't Deny the Amazing Nature of His Works

If Jesus never actually did incredible deeds, we would expect his enemies to state as much. But *none* of the ancient sources that mention Jesus deny the surprising nature of what he did or that people believed he did amazing things. For example:

- Matthew 12:9–13 says that Jesus healed a man with a shriveled hand on the Sabbath. The Pharisees didn't challenge Jesus by denying he performed a miracle. They went out and plotted how they might kill him for it (v. 14).
- Paul wrote in 1 Corinthians 15:7–8 that he encountered the risen Jesus while he was an enemy of the church. Paul became a Christian after experiencing what he believed to be a miraculous event.
- Ancient Jewish writings called the Talmud comment negatively about Jesus but say he performed miracles. Rather than deny the claims, they attributed them to sorcery.

6. There Is Strong Historical Evidence for the Resurrection

Although historical evidence doesn't exist for most of Jesus's specific miracles (such as healing a blind man), there is strong historical evidence for the most important miracle of all: the resurrection. And if there's good reason to believe the resurrection happened, we have good reason to believe the rest of Jesus's miracles happened as well. (We'll devote six chapters to looking at the evidence for the resurrection in part 4.)

7. Jesus's Reported Miracles Have a Reasonable Purpose

The following point is admittedly more subjective than the first six, but it's well worth considering. Contrary to popular thinking, the Bible doesn't read like one long fairy tale with miracles on every page. *Biblical miracles reportedly served a specific purpose in God's plan.* In particular, miracles were most often recorded when God needed to authenticate his messengers. It's easy to see why miracles would be both necessary and effective for this purpose. Any human could claim to speak for God. But if a person truly *was* speaking for God, how would we know? Only a sign that was clearly of supernatural origin—a *miracle*—would validate their message. And this is indeed the context for the vast majority of biblical miracle accounts, including those surrounding Jesus. For example, when John the Baptist's disciples asked Jesus if he really was the Christ, Jesus pointed to his miracles as evidence (Matt. 11:2–6; Luke 7:18–23). In Luke 11:20, Jesus said that his casting out of demons demonstrated that the kingdom of God had arrived. The Gospel of John specifically calls the miracles of Jesus "signs," implying that they were for the purpose of confirming his claims. We see this consistently throughout the Gospels.

So what do we have? Early, multiple, independent sources that claim Jesus worked miracles as an integral part of his ministry, drawing large crowds in response and encountering opponents who never denied the incredible nature of his deeds. In addition, we have strong historical evidence of the resurrection specifically, the credibility of which supports the likelihood that the other miracle claims are true. Finally, these reported miracles occurred in a context that is consistent with what we might expect from a God who wanted to authenticate his messengers.

From the evidence for God's existence, we have good reason to believe that miracles are possible, and from the evidence of historical texts, we have good reason to believe that Jesus's miracles actually happened. Importantly, those miracles testify to the Bible's claim that *Jesus is God.*

KEY POINTS

- The question of whether miracles are *ever* possible is really a question of whether God exists. If God exists, miracles are possible; if God doesn't exist, miracles are not possible.
- Seven pieces of evidence make a persuasive case that Jesus performed miracles.
  1. Jesus's miracles appear in the earliest sources about him.
  2. Jesus's miracles appear in multiple, independent sources.
  3. Miracle working was an integral part of Jesus's ministry.
  4. Jesus attracted large crowds because of his works.
  5. Jesus's opponents didn't deny the amazing nature of his works.
  6. There is strong historical evidence for the resurrection.
  7. Jesus's reported miracles are presented as having a reasonable purpose.

CONVERSATION GUIDE

Open the Conversation

- When you think of Jesus's miracles in the Bible, which are the first that come to mind?
- Do you find it easy or hard to believe that Jesus's miracles happened? Why?

Advance the Conversation

- Some people think miracles never happen. Why do you think they say that? What do you think they're assuming? *(Define what a miracle is from this chapter's discussion, and explain how this is really a question of God's existence. If God exists, miracles are possible.)*

- If you were a historian who wanted to investigate whether Jesus actually performed miracles, what kinds of evidence would you look for? *(Walk your child through the seven points in this chapter.)*
- What do you think is the best explanation for the seven pieces of evidence we just discussed? Why? *(Discuss how Jesus truly performing miracles makes the best sense of the historical evidence.)*

Apply the Conversation

- Read the quote from the commenter at the beginning of this chapter. How would you respond to their question regarding Jesus's miracles: "Why do you prefer to believe outlandish claims because they're religious?"

5. Did Ancient People Believe in Miracles Because They Were More Gullible?

My son was overjoyed to receive a book gift from a friend this year titled *The Fantastic Flatulent Fart Brothers' Second Big Book of Farty Facts.* What could possibly sound more awesome to a ten-year-old boy? For a couple of weeks, he entertained us with an ongoing stream of smelly facts. But I'll never forget the joy on his face when he ran to tell me about one in particular: there is a people group with a *fart god.* Yes, I confirmed it's true.

Matshishkapeu (literally "Fart Man") is the most powerful spirit for the Innu people of northeastern Canada. According to the Innu, he communicates with people each time gas is passed. That's right—every fart is a message from their god. (Go ahead and take a minute to consider how often Matshishkapeu might be communicating with you in a given day.) The Innu apparently vary in their ability to translate the messages, but elders in the tribe are revered for their gaseous insight. In case you're wondering (as I was) whether the Innu themselves find all of this funny, researchers say yes.[1] *Not* because it's hard to believe but because they think Matshishkapeu is humorous to reveal himself in this way.

There's a reason the fart god is included in a book of humorous farty facts. Unless you're an Innu, the existence of such a god sounds pretty silly. We can't imagine how anyone today could believe there is a god who communicates with varying degrees of frequency based on what we eat.

Many skeptics similarly think we should discount the kinds of evidence we looked at in the previous chapter because beliefs about gods, divine interaction with humans, miracles, and the like were plentiful in the ancient world. In other words, they think there's no reason to take the miracle claims of Jesus's followers any more seriously than the claims of those who believe in a god communicating through gas—both are rooted in the *gullibility* of ancient people.

Are People Who Believe in the Supernatural Gullible?

In his essay "Kooks and Quacks of the Roman Empire: A Look into the World of the Gospels," historian and atheist activist Richard Carrier says:

> There is abundant evidence that these were times replete with kooks and quacks of all varieties, from sincere lunatics to ingenious frauds, even innocent men mistaken for divine, and there was no end to the fools and loons who would follow and praise them. Placed in this context, the Gospels no longer seem to be so remarkable, and this leads us to an important fact: when the Gospels were written, skeptics and informed or critical minds were a small minority. Although the gullible, the credulous, and those ready to believe or exaggerate stories of the supernatural are still abundant today, they were much more common in antiquity, and taken far more seriously.[2]

Carrier goes on to give specific examples of all these "kooks and quacks" to argue that (1) we should immediately discount the credibility of the Gospels because they were written in a time when people believed some bizarre things, and (2) the content of the Gospels is similar in nature to that of other writings from the time period. There are three key points to understand about such claims.

First, given that Carrier says people *today* continue to gullibly believe in the supernatural, it's clear he isn't dismissing only ancient claims—he's dismissing any worldview that involves the supernatural. Because he *assumes beforehand* that nothing supernatural exists, he labels people gullible (ancient or modern) for believing otherwise. That's not an argument, however; it's simply an assumption and a corresponding label based on his own worldview.

Second, setting aside the assumption that nothing supernatural exists, we can see how the logic of his case fails on its own merits. It's like saying, "Throughout history, there have been all kinds of medical 'cures' that we no longer believe work. Some of them were pretty crazy, and yet there were times in history when many people believed in them! Therefore, we should immediately discount *all* claimed medical cures in history (and today)." Carrier wouldn't say that, of course, because he surely believes that some medical cures are legitimate and wouldn't dismiss *all* of them just because *some* of them are false. Medical cures vary widely in their nature and evidential support, so we have to consider their credibility on a case-by-case basis—unless we're assuming beforehand that *no* medical cures are possible. In the same way, supernatural claims vary widely, so we can't carelessly lump them together for evaluation.

Third, though Carrier says there's nothing remarkably different about the claims of the Gospels compared with others from the ancient world, a careful evaluation shows otherwise. Many scholars recognize that the nature of the biblical worldview is vastly different from that of other supernatural worldviews throughout history. In *The Bible among the Myths*, Old Testament scholar

John N. Oswalt details the differences between ancient worldviews and concludes:

> That one's deity could act in history was no new idea. But that this was the *only* place he acted that had significance for human beings, that those actions were according to a consistent, long-term purpose, that he was using the details of human-historical behavior to reveal that purpose, and that he was just as capable of using enemies as he was friends to accomplish his good purposes—that, I maintain, is not found anywhere else in the world, ancient or modern, outside of the Bible and its direct derivatives.[3]

Not only is the *nature* of the biblical worldview different, but so is the *quality of the evidence* for the miracle claims surrounding Jesus. That brings us to our second question.

Are People Who Believe in Miracles Gullible?

For the same reason that it's unreasonable to lump all supernatural claims together for evaluation, it's unreasonable to lump all miracle claims together for evaluation. They, too, must be considered on a case-by-case basis. To declare that *anyone* who believes *any* miracle claim is gullible is to assume the supernatural doesn't exist. As we already saw, that's an assumption, not an argument. So let's now look more specifically at whether there's good reason to believe that those who claimed Jesus performed miracles were gullible.

It's true that in the ancient world there were many kinds of reported miracles.[4] However, we know from historical writings that ancient people didn't indiscriminately believe everything they heard, as skeptics often suggest. In his book *Miracles: The Credibility of the New Testament Accounts*, New Testament scholar Craig S. Keener says, "The majority of ancient historians were critical of some reports while accepting the possibility of others; that is, they did not a priori decide all claims of paranormal events to be either authentic or inauthentic."[5] Based on his extensive historical analysis, Keener shows that ancient people were like us—some readily accepted miracle claims, while others were more skeptical.

Ancient people did widely believe that deities could heal.[6] Those who merely *heard* of Jesus's healings would not necessarily have been as skeptical of the idea as many are today. But recall from the last chapter that there's strong historical evidence that Jesus drew large crowds in response to his acts. This is very telling. These were people who witnessed what he did *firsthand* and followed him because of what they *saw*. To claim that people believed in Jesus's healings and other miracles out of gullibility, therefore, is to claim that crowds were deceived by something they actually witnessed—not just something they heard secondhand. This is possible, but it's a much harder case to make. It raises several more questions about how so many eyewitnesses were fooled in multiple contexts and locations and whether Jesus was the kind of person who would have intentionally fooled people.

Even more telling, however, is what ancient people believed about the kind of resurrection miracle the apostles claimed for Jesus (a new embodied life for an individual after death). *No one believed that kind of miracle could happen.* New Testament scholar N. T. Wright, in his classic work *The Resurrection of the Son of God*, explains the thought world of Jesus's time:

> Death was all-powerful. One could neither escape it in the first place nor break its power once it had come. The ancient world was thus divided into those who said that resurrection couldn't happen, though they might have wanted it to, and those who said they didn't want it to happen, knowing that it couldn't anyway. . . . When the early Christians spoke of Jesus being raised from the dead, the natural meaning of that statement, throughout the ancient world, was the claim that something had happened to Jesus which had happened to nobody else. A great many things supposedly happened to the dead, but resurrection did not.[7]

We see this skepticism of resurrection in the Gospels themselves. Matthew 28:17 says that when the disciples met the risen Jesus in Galilee, they worshiped him, but "some doubted." In Luke 24:36–43, Jesus had to eat a piece of fish in front of the disciples to convince them he wasn't a ghost. In John 20:24–29, Thomas didn't accept the resurrection reports from the other disciples and said he would have to *personally* see the marks on Jesus's hands and side to believe Jesus had been raised.

In no way do the Gospels read as if the resurrection was a miracle everyone casually accepted. People in the ancient world didn't believe in this kind of resurrection miracle, and neither did the disciples—until they became convinced it had happened. They were then willing to risk their lives to proclaim what they had witnessed (Luke 1:1–4; John 21:24–25; 2 Pet. 1:16). This is powerful historical evidence that belief in the resurrection— Jesus's most important miracle—wasn't simply a product of a gullible culture. The disciples believed Jesus had been raised from the dead *despite* their culture's belief that such a thing couldn't happen.

Could the disciples have lied or been mistaken for reasons other than gullibility? We'll see why those theories don't hold up in part 4. For now, it's enough to see that the supposed gullibility of ancient people is not a valid reason to immediately dismiss the miracle claims found in the Gospels. There's strong evidence to support these claims, *regardless* of how many bizarre things people have believed throughout history.

KEY POINTS

- Claiming that people (ancient *or* modern) are gullible simply because they believe something exists beyond nature is not an argument. It's an assumption that the natural world is all there is.

- Supernatural claims, and miracle claims more specifically, vary widely in their nature and evidential support, so we have to evaluate them on a case-by-case basis.

- There's strong evidence to support the miracle claims of the Gospels, *regardless* of how many bizarre things people have believed throughout history.

- People in the ancient world didn't believe the kind of resurrection miracle that was claimed for Jesus could happen. The disciples believed Jesus had been raised from the dead *despite* their culture's opposing belief.

CONVERSATION GUIDE

Open the Conversation

- The Innu people of Canada believe in a fart god who communicates with people each time they pass gas. What would it take to convince you that gas is actually a message from a god? *(Get your child to think about what makes something believable.)*

Advance the Conversation

- People sometimes think there's no reason to take claims of Jesus's miracles any more seriously than claims about a god communicating through gas. They think people who lived a long time ago were just really gullible—easily fooled into believing things. Do you think we can determine whether Jesus performed miracles based on the fact that people have believed some bizarre things in history? Why or why not? *(If your child has trouble answering, read them the example about medical cures and ask what the problem is with the logic. Focus on the point that claims have to be evaluated on a case-by-case basis. Explain that ruling out anything supernatural before considering the evidence is just a worldview assumption and not an argument.)*

- Read Matthew 28:16–17; Luke 24:36–43; and John 20:24–29. Do these verses suggest that the disciples easily believed Jesus had been raised from the dead? Why or why not? *(These passages do not paint a picture of people who easily accepted a resurrection. Explain how no one at the time thought this kind of resurrection was possible. The disciples believed it happened to Jesus despite their culture's opposing assumption.)*

Apply the Conversation

- How would you respond to Richard Carrier's quote from the beginning of this chapter?

6. How Can Jesus Be Both God and Human?

My kids and I have a great time making up characters that we spontaneously act out. "Christina," for example, is a mom we created who has no understanding of acceptable personal space. When Christina asks her kids simple questions like "How was school today?" she gets close enough to them that her nose touches their faces. They politely back away, but Christina presses in again to remind them of how much she loves being close. Other favorite characters we have are "Mo" (a mom who constantly seeks validation from her kids and giggles like an overjoyed schoolgirl when they tell her she's a good mom) and "Abraham" (a precocious four-year-old who speaks with an East Coast accent and wants to marry my youngest daughter someday).

It's usually my quirky sense of humor that results in us creating these characters, but I was thrilled one day when my daughter created one on her own: "Indonesio." When I asked her who Indonesio is, she excitedly offered a description: "She hates ice cream, loves fighting, asks many questions, and is a spirit made of matter!" I laughed and explained, "A spirit can't be made of matter—spirits are immaterial." My daughter replied, "I know, but Indonesio is . . . she's like Jesus!"

And just like that, God graciously provided the perfect introduction to this chapter.

The Son of God becoming man (called the incarnation) is a foundational truth of Christianity, but it can be difficult to grasp. If we aren't intentional about giving our kids an accurate understanding of the incarnation, they can end up developing their own Indonesio-like idea that isn't exactly biblical. While part 1 has focused on establishing that Jesus is the Jewish Messiah and God himself, this final chapter in the section will help you articulate the *theology* of what it means for Jesus to be both God and human.

Jesus Is Fully Human

At the time 1 John was written, an erroneous belief was circulating in the church that Jesus was not fully human—a heresy that came to be known as Docetism. In response to docetic beliefs, John wrote about the importance of believing that Jesus truly took on human flesh: "Every spirit that acknowledges that Jesus Christ has come in the flesh is from God, but every spirit that does not acknowledge Jesus is not from God" (1 John 4:2–3; see also 2 John 1:7). In today's world, people are far more likely to challenge Jesus's deity than his humanity. But as Christians, we often focus so much on how Jesus is God that we forget he is fully human as well: Jesus was born (Luke 1:35; 2:6–7), had a human mind (Mark 13:32; Luke 2:52), needed food (Luke 4:2), became thirsty (John 19:28), became tired (John 4:6), needed sleep (Luke 8:23), experienced human emotions (Matt. 26:38; John 11:35), and died (John 19:33).

Acknowledging Jesus's full humanity is important for two major reasons.

First, because Jesus is fully human, we can find comfort in knowing that he can relate to our human sufferings. We don't have a God who is content to simply watch from afar while we experience the many trials of this world. Instead, he willingly subjected himself to the same difficulties, sufferings, and temptations we face. As Hebrews 4:15 says, "We do not have a high priest who is unable to empathize with our weaknesses, but we have one who has been tempted in every way, just as we are—yet he did not sin" (see also Heb. 2:18; 1 Pet. 2:21).

Second, Jesus had to be human to die in our place as payment for our sins. The penalty for human sin is death (Rom. 6:23), and that penalty must be paid by a human (more will be said on this in part 3). But a person who is a sinner cannot pay for the sins of others—he's in debt to God himself! That means Jesus not only had to be human but also had to live the sinless life *we* couldn't live in order to pay for our sins. His perfect obedience to God the Father qualified him to bear the sins of all. Hebrews 2:17 says, "For this reason he had to be made like them, fully human in every way, in order that he might become a merciful and faithful high priest in service to God, and that he might make atonement for the sins of the people" (see also Rom. 5:19; Heb. 2:10; 5:9; 7:27–28).

Jesus Is Fully God

We already learned in chapter 3 how the Bible presents Jesus as fully God (recall the HANDS acronym). We won't repeat that discussion here, but some brief additional notes about the nature of the Trinity are relevant for our current topic.

The doctrine of the Trinity affirms that (1) there is one God, (2) God is three distinct persons, and (3) each person is fully God. We see this in Scripture as follows:

- The Bible repeatedly affirms that there is only one God (Deut. 6:4; Isa. 43:10; Mark 12:29–30; Gal. 3:20).

- While the Bible never uses the word *Trinity*, it speaks of the Father, the Son, and the Holy Spirit as three distinct persons (Matt. 3:16–17; John 14:26; Acts 10:37–38).
- The Bible equates each member of the Trinity with God himself. The Father is God (John 6:27; Rom. 1:7; 1 Cor. 8:6), the Son Jesus is God (John 1:1, 14; Rom. 9:5; Col. 1:16), and the Holy Spirit is God (Matt. 10:20; Rom. 8:9; 1 Cor. 3:16).

An appropriate understanding of the Trinity is important for understanding what it means that Jesus is fully God, because only God *the Son* became incarnate, not God the Father or God the Holy Spirit. This explains why, for example, Jesus prayed to God even though he *is* God—he was praying to God the Father. We often take such concepts for granted as adult Christians, but we have to remember how confusing these things can be for kids! It's important to take the time to teach them these theological foundations. (For more on how to talk with your child about the Trinity—and bad analogies you shouldn't use!—see chapter 17 in *Talking with Your Kids about God*.)

How Do Jesus's Humanity and Deity Relate to Each Other?

We've seen so far that the Bible presents Jesus as both fully human and fully God. But how do these natures relate to each other? Throughout history, people have tried to resolve this mystery in ways that don't fit with the biblical picture we've established. For example, Apollinaris was a bishop who lived in the late fourth century and taught that Jesus had a human body filled *only* with a divine nature (a divine mind and spirit). However, this view takes away from Jesus's full humanity. Another early bishop, Eutyches, taught that Jesus's human and divine natures mixed together into a third kind of nature. If this were the case, however, Jesus would no longer be both God and human but rather a completely different kind of being. A third view, Nestorianism, taught that there were two separate *persons* in Jesus—one human and one divine. The Bible, however, always speaks of Jesus as being *one* person.

In order to address these disagreements, a council was called in the city of Chalcedon (near modern Istanbul) in AD 451. The Council of Chalcedon developed a statement on the relationship between Jesus's natures called the Chalcedonian Definition. To this day, it's considered by both Protestants and Catholics to be the orthodox definition of the person of Jesus. This statement affirms that Jesus has "two natures, inconfusedly, unchangeably, indivisibly, inseparably; the distinction of natures being by no means taken away by the union, but rather the property of each nature being preserved, and concurring in one Person and one Subsistence, not parted or divided into two persons."[1] In other words, Jesus has two distinct natures—divine *and* human—that are united in a single person. This is known as the hypostatic union.

But How Does That Actually Work?

The Council of Chalcedon formalized a statement of orthodoxy that's faithful to the biblical witness, but that doesn't mean it's easy to understand how Jesus's two natures work together in practice. To some degree, the incarnation is a mystery we can never fully comprehend, because it's unlike anything we've ever experienced. However, an understanding of Jesus's two natures does help us make sense of some difficult verses. For example, as we saw in Hebrews 4:15, Jesus was tempted. However, James 1:13 says that God cannot be tempted by evil. If Jesus is God, that sounds like a contradiction. But this is an example of one verse speaking of something that's true about Jesus's human nature (he was tempted), while another verse is speaking of something that's true about his divine nature (he cannot be tempted).

Another example is found in Matthew 24:36, where Jesus speaks about the timing of his second coming: "About that day or hour no one knows, not even the angels in heaven, nor the Son, but only the Father." This sometimes seems shocking to Christians—how can he not know something if he's God? And other verses specifically affirm his omniscience (John 2:25; 16:30; 21:17). We can make sense of this again by understanding that Jesus has two natures. In his divinity, he knows all things. In his humanity, his knowledge is limited. It was from his humanity that Jesus spoke in Matthew 24:36.

In the same way, understanding Jesus's two natures can help us understand his preexistence and omnipresence (from chapter 3). In his divine nature, he has always existed and is everywhere at once. But in his humanity, he has a body that came into existence at a particular moment in his mother's womb, and that body was in one place at a time during his years on earth.

Unlike my daughter's "Indonesio" character, Jesus is not a spirit made of matter (though it's not hard to see why Jesus's nature is difficult for kids to grasp!). He is fully human and fully God—one person with two distinct natures.

KEY POINTS

- The Bible affirms that Jesus is both fully human and fully God.
- Jesus's full humanity is important for two major reasons: (1) we can find comfort in knowing that he can relate to our human sufferings, and (2) Jesus had to be (a sinless) human to die in our place as payment for our sins.
- An appropriate understanding of the Trinity is important for understanding what it means that Jesus is fully God. Only

God the Son became incarnate, not God the Father or God the Holy Spirit.

- The Council of Chalcedon provided the statement of orthodoxy on the relationship between Jesus's humanity and his divinity. He has two distinct natures—divine and human—that are united in one person.

CONVERSATION GUIDE

Open the Conversation

- The Bible teaches that Jesus is fully human *and* fully God, but sometimes we think of him as more one than the other. Do you tend to think more about how he is human or how he is God? *(Emphasize that Jesus is completely human and completely God—not some of each.)*

Advance the Conversation

- Let's think about Jesus being fully human for a moment. What are some ways he was like us while on earth? *(Discuss examples from this chapter.)*
- Why do you think Jesus needed to become a human? Why couldn't he have just stayed in heaven? *(There are many possible answers, but be sure to discuss the two given in this chapter.)*
- Now let's think about Jesus being fully God. What are some ways he showed *that* part of who he is? *(Review the points learned in chapters 3 and 4.)*
- The Bible says several times that Jesus prayed to God. How do you think that's possible if he's God himself? *(Review the basics of the Trinity—one God in three persons. Only God the Son became incarnate.)*

- *(For older kids)* Hundreds of years ago, a church leader taught that Jesus's human and divine natures mixed together into a third nature. Why is this not an accurate understanding of what the Bible teaches? *(Jesus retains his two natures separately. Discuss the Council of Chalcedon.)*

Apply the Conversation

- A Muslim wrote online, "The Gospel of Mark, Chapter 13, verse 32 states this . . . 'No one knows about that day or hour [of Jesus's second coming], not even the angels in heaven, nor the Son, but only the Father.' This verse clearly shows that Jesus is not [all knowing] and therefore cannot be God."[2] How would you respond to the claim that this verse shows Jesus isn't God?

PART 2
The Teachings
of Jesus

Overview

I'm a disaster when it comes to finding my car keys. In theory, this shouldn't be difficult. If I just always put them in the same place—preferably by the door—I'd always know where to find them. Many things sound great in theory that don't pan out in real life, though. In *theory*, my kids should have no trouble putting their dirty clothes in their laundry baskets at the end of the day, but in reality, those clothes go straight onto the floor (and usually inches away from the basket).

My keys end up in the kitchen junk drawer, by the bathroom sink, on my desk, on my nightstand, between couch cushions, next to the stove, or in my purse. I've even left them hanging from the door lock outside overnight (welcome, prospective intruders)! Apparently, I'm not much more organized than my kids. But I discovered a solution last year that changed everything: a little device called Tile. Here's how the magic works. You put the Tile app on your cell phone and then attach a small Tile device to anything you have trouble finding—your keys or wallet, for example. When you need to find something connected to a Tile device, you just open the app and click on a button. The device will ring from wherever it is. Assuming your lost item is within earshot, you follow the sound and easily locate what you're looking for.

I've become completely dependent on Tile. I don't even *try* to put my keys in a memorable place or look for them when I'm ready to go. When I need them, I just call them from my cell phone. I've officially relinquished all mental responsibility for my keys to technology.

In the same way, kids often develop a dependence on other people for their understanding of Christianity. Rather than putting effort into personally studying the Bible, they "Tile it out" to their parents, youth leaders, pastors, friends, media, celebrities, and others. Sometimes there's obvious tension in what they hear. They know, for example, that "God exists" and "God doesn't exist" can't be true at the same time. But in many cases, they absorb things that *sound* right yet aren't actually biblical. Oftentimes these misunderstandings even come from Christians. And when they do, they're often about the teachings of Jesus.

As one example, *New York Times* bestselling author Rachel Hollis (a professing Christian) says in her popular book *Girl, Wash Your Face*:

> Just because you believe it doesn't mean it's true for everyone. . . .
> Faith is one of the most abused instances of this. We decide that our
> religion is right; therefore, every other religion must be wrong. . . .
> I don't know the central tenet of your faith, but the central tenet
> of mine is "love thy neighbor."[1]

To be sure, Jesus did tell us that loving God and loving our neighbor are the two greatest commandments (Matt. 22:37–40). Does it follow from that, however, that multiple religions can be true or that it's arrogant to believe any one religion is right? As we'll see in chapter 7, this is a common belief today—even among professing Christians—but it's not biblical.

In part 2, we'll sort out truth from cultural fiction on this and five other important subjects on which Jesus taught. To be clear, the goal here is not to summarize *all* of what Jesus taught. Rather, we'll be looking at selected topics that (1) often come up at a popular level and (2) are frequently misunderstood by both Christians and nonbelievers. Because the popular-level understanding of these subjects typically contains at least partial truths (as in the quote we just looked at), these conversations are necessarily nuanced. They require a willingness to go beyond our sometimes culturally conditioned views and really dig into what the Bible says. Let's leave the Tile devices behind and help our kids learn to lean on God's Word for their understanding of what Jesus taught—not on the world around them.

Three Keys to Impactful Conversations about the Teachings of Jesus

1. *Emphasize that the importance of Jesus's teachings follows from his identity.* Kids need to explicitly hear *why* Jesus's teachings should be so important to them—it's because he's God. As we learned in part 1, Jesus wasn't just a good moral teacher who lived two thousand years ago and had some interesting insights about how to best live our lives. Remind them before you begin these conversations that Jesus has the knowledge and the authority to teach us all that he does because he's our Creator and Sustainer.

2. *Explain that when someone states "The Bible says . . ." or "Jesus says . . . ," it doesn't necessarily mean that what they say is accurate.* Anyone can claim to pass on a biblical teaching, but sometimes people intentionally mischaracterize what the Bible says, and other times there can be a genuine misunderstanding. Talk to your child about the importance of studying the Bible personally and not just relying on what they hear from secondary sources (including this book!). Take

the time to look up the many Bible verses in these chapters so your child can see firsthand how to seek answers.

3. *Distinguish between reading an isolated Bible verse and understanding context.* Oftentimes misunderstandings about what the Bible says arise because verses are taken out of context. For example, people often like to quote Jesus's words "Do not judge, or you too will be judged" (Matt. 7:1) but fail to understand the wider context of that passage, which makes it clear that Jesus is *not* saying to withhold all judgment (see chapter 11). As you research the passages in part 2, point out the importance of going beyond isolated verses to understand the wider context of what Jesus taught.

7. Did Jesus Teach That He's the Only Way to God?

Michael A. Walrond Jr. is the pastor of a ten-thousand-plus-member Baptist church in Harlem, New York. In 2018, a video clip from one of his sermons went viral after he told his congregation that believing Jesus is the only way to God is "insanity." Walrond preached:

> There was a time when you would see people in the pulpit say, "Well, if you don't believe in Jesus [you're] going to hell." That's insanity in many ways because that is not what Jesus even believes. And so the key is you believe in God. And whatever your path is to God I celebrate that.[1]

Walrond is not alone as a pastor (or a layperson) questioning the historic Christian view that Jesus is the exclusive path to God. Prominent Presbyterian pastor Shannon Johnson Kershner similarly made the news when she told the *Chicago Sun-Times*, "For me, the Christian tradition is the way to understand God and my relationship with the world and other humans . . . but I'm not about to say what God can and cannot do in other ways and with other spiritual experiences."[2]

Non-Christians have long claimed that believing there's only one way to God is narrow-minded and arrogant. But that claim is now increasingly being made *within* the church, as these examples show. Our kids need a clear understanding of what the Bible actually teaches to know how to respond to such claims and not be swayed by statements that simply sound good.

What Does It *Mean* for Jesus to Be "the Only Way"?

In 2008, the Pew Forum on Religion & Public Life conducted an in-depth national survey that found that 65 percent of all Christians believe many religions can lead to eternal life.[3] The *New York Times* featured the findings in an article they titled "Survey Shows U.S. Religious Tolerance."[4] If that headline didn't strike you as problematic, read it again. The *New York Times* conflated a belief in the exclusivity of Jesus as the path to eternal life with intolerance. *This subject has nothing to do with tolerance.* Tolerance doesn't mean that a person should accept multiple views as equally true—that would require accepting beliefs that often *cannot* logically be true at the same time. Tolerance only means a willingness to bear with ideas other than your own. The person who asserts that Jesus is *not* the only way to God is making an exclusive truth claim as much as the person who asserts that Jesus *is* the only way to God. The surveyed Christians who believe that many religions can lead to eternal life aren't any more tolerant than those who believe that Jesus is the only way. But they do hold beliefs that aren't supported by the Bible, as we will soon see.

Setting aside the irrelevant issue of tolerance, we can now evaluate three views that *are* relevant to whether Jesus is the only way to God:

1. Jesus isn't a necessary path to God; people can find eternal life in many ways.

2. Jesus's death was necessary to provide a path to God, and all people will now have eternal life through him.

3. Jesus's death was necessary to provide a path to God, but people must *accept* Jesus to have eternal life.

Separating the first view from the other two views is the question of the necessity of Jesus's atonement (his sacrifice on the cross to make payment for sin and allow for the reconciliation of humankind to God). Let's consider that question first.

Is Jesus's Atonement Necessary for People to Have Eternal Life?

The key to understanding the answer to this question is in what the Bible says about the nature of sin and the nature of God.

Sin is a transgression of God's moral law (1 John 3:4). The Bible says that all people have this law written on their hearts (Rom. 2:14–15) and are guilty of breaking it (Isa. 64:6; Rom. 3:10, 23). When we sin, we rebel against God, and our sins relationally separate us from him (Isa. 59:2). This separation from our Creator and Sustainer is the fundamental problem of human existence (see chapters 14 and 28 for more on this).

Two attributes of God's nature frame what we need to understand about how God deals with this sin: his lovingness and his justness. First John 4:8 says, "God is love," and the Bible is filled with references to his loving nature (Pss. 86:15; 136:1; John 3:16; Rom. 8:37–39). The Bible also tells us repeatedly that God is just—he can, should, and will judge perfectly between right and wrong and dispense justice accordingly (Deut. 32:4; Pss. 9:7–8; 33:5; Isa. 61:8). Because God is just, he must act in judgment against sin—and he has set the penalty as death (Rom. 6:23). Overlooking sin would make God unjust and imperfect because he would be letting people do whatever they want, even if it's wrong, without paying any consequences.

God could have chosen to leave us in our universal state of sinfulness and judge humankind accordingly. In this sense, the atonement wasn't something God *had* to do. But once God, in his love, decided to offer a way for humans to be justly forgiven of sin, *some kind of atonement was necessary*. He made payment for our sins himself through Jesus's sacrifice on the cross (John 3:16).

Could God have chosen another kind of atonement? This is something theologians debate. The important point here, however, is that Jesus's sacrifice on the cross was, in fact, the way God offered atonement to humankind—and the *only* way: "Salvation is found in no one else, for there is no other name under heaven given to mankind by which we must be saved" (Acts 4:12; see also Rom. 3:25; 1 Cor. 15:3; 2 Cor. 5:21; 1 Tim. 2:5).

In John 14, Jesus tells his disciples that he is going to prepare a place for them. The disciple Thomas responds, "Lord, we don't know where you are going, so how can we know the way?" Jesus replies, "I am the way and the truth and the life. No one comes to the Father except through me" (vv. 5–6). While the meaning of Jesus's words in isolation *might* be debatable, verses such as Acts 4:12 leave no doubt as to what he taught: only through him can anyone have eternal life.

Will *Everyone* Have Eternal Life through Jesus's Atonement?

As we just saw, Jesus's atonement was the only way God provided for the forgiveness of sin. But now we have to discern between the second and third views outlined earlier: Will Jesus's atonement eventually reconcile all people to God, or must people accept Jesus's sacrifice to have eternal life?

The belief that all people will eventually be saved is called universalism. *Unitarian* universalism teaches that everyone of all faiths will be saved and that Jesus's death on the cross didn't provide any special access to God. As we already learned, this view is biblically untenable. The view we're considering now, however, is called *Christian* universalism. This view teaches that Jesus's atonement *was* necessary and that *all* will be reconciled to God because of his sacrifice. Christian universalists typically believe that hell exists but that it's only a temporary punishment and ultimately all will be saved.

In the next chapter, we'll look at what the Bible teaches about hell specifically, but to answer our current question, we need only address whether the Bible says there are people who will *not* have eternal life with God. The verse that perhaps most directly answers this is the most famous verse in the Bible: "For God so loved the world that he gave his one and only Son, that whoever believes in him shall not perish but have eternal life" (John 3:16). Here Jesus explicitly states that there is an alternative to eternal life and that eternal life is given specifically to *those who believe in him*. Jesus also warned repeatedly that not everyone will be saved in passages such as Matthew 7:21: "Not everyone who says to me, 'Lord, Lord,' will enter the kingdom of heaven, but only the one who does the will of my Father who is in heaven" (see also Matt. 7:13–14; 25:34, 41, 46).

If the Bible is clear on this, how do Christian universalists—who typically say they accept the Bible as God's Word—come to the conclusion that all people will eventually be reconciled to God? Though space doesn't allow for an in-depth examination of the case they make, we can briefly note three verses commonly used to support their belief:

1. "For as in Adam all die, so in Christ all will be made alive" (1 Cor. 15:22).

    As with any verse in the Bible, context is key here. The very next verse says, "But each in turn: Christ, the firstfruits; then, when he comes, those who belong to him" (v. 23). In other words, the "all" who will be made alive are the "all" who belong to Jesus—not all humankind.

2. "At the name of Jesus every knee should bow, in heaven and on earth and under the earth" (Phil. 2:10).

   This verse speaks of the time when Jesus will return to reclaim creation, and no one will be able to deny his sovereignty. With his reign, judgment will come to those who rejected him previously (see Phil. 1:28; 3:18–19 for context).

3. "For God was pleased to have all his fullness dwell in him, and through him to reconcile to himself all things, whether things on earth or things in heaven, by making peace through his blood, shed on the cross" (Col. 1:19–20).

   While these verses alone seem to suggest universal reconciliation, once again the context demonstrates otherwise. Just two verses later, the apostle Paul writes, "He has reconciled you by Christ's physical body through death to present you holy in his sight, without blemish and free from accusation—*if you continue in your faith*, established and firm, and do not move from the hope held out in the gospel" (vv. 22–23, emphasis mine). Paul was not implying in verses 19–20 that reconciliation is unconditional; he says it depends on the continuation of faith.

In short, the Bible affirms that Jesus is the only way to God in two senses: (1) his atonement alone makes reconciliation possible, and (2) only those who believe in him will inherit the eternal life his atonement offers.

KEY POINTS

- Given the nature of sin (the cause of separation from God) and the nature of God (both loving and just), some kind of atonement was necessary if God wanted to reconcile humankind to himself.

- The Bible repeatedly tells us that Jesus's sacrifice on the cross was the one and only way God offered atonement to humankind. This makes Unitarian universalism—the idea that there are multiple equally valid paths to God—untenable for Christians.

- Christian universalists believe that Jesus's atonement was necessary and that all will be reconciled to God because of his sacrifice. However, Jesus warned many times that not everyone will find eternal life.

- Jesus is the only way to God because his atonement alone makes reconciliation possible, and only those who believe in him will inherit the eternal life his atonement offers.

CONVERSATION GUIDE

Open the Conversation

- Do you think people of all religions will have eternal life with God? Why or why not? *(Listen to your child's reasoning and ask questions to dig deeper into why they believe what they do. If they already have an understanding that the Bible says Jesus is the only way to God, challenge them to tell you what, specifically, it says.)*

Advance the Conversation

- Would God be the most loving if he gave everyone eternal life, regardless of what they believed or did? Why or why not? *(Take time to define the word* sin *and look up the related verses discussed in this chapter: Isaiah 59:2; Romans 2:14–15; 3:23; 1 John 3:4. Explain how a God who is both loving and just can't overlook sin—some kind of atonement was necessary to reconcile God and humankind. Jesus's sacrifice on the cross was the atonement God chose.)*

- Read John 14:6. What do you think Jesus is teaching here about the various paths people try to take to God? *(Discuss the clear meaning of his words—he is the only path to God—then read related verses as well: Acts 4:12; Romans 3:25; 1 Corinthians 15:3; 2 Corinthians 5:21; 1 Timothy 2:5.)*

- Some people called Christian universalists believe that Jesus is the only path to God but that all people will receive eternal life because he made that path. Read Matthew 7:13, 14, and 21; and 25:34, 41, and 46. What does Jesus teach about this view? *(For older kids, go deeper into discussion with a conversation about the verses Christian universalists use to support their views.)*

Apply the Conversation

- Reread the quote from Pastor Walrond at the beginning of this chapter. How would you respond to his claim that it's "insanity" to believe Jesus is the only way to God?

8. What Did Jesus Teach about Hell?

While I dream of our school evenings being filled with the kids peacefully frolicking around the house, the reality is far more stressful. And I have to admit, I'm the one who usually sucks the playfulness out of our nights—by necessity. Someone has to constantly direct the "to dos" or nothing happens (a burden felt by parents around the world, I know). The collective commentary to my three kids typically sounds something like this:

> Please pick up the pile of stuff on the stairs. Did you do your homework? Remember to set out your baseball stuff for the game. I haven't heard you practice piano yet. Did you water the plants and unload the dishwasher? Why is there a dirty sock everywhere I turn? Your science project is due tomorrow—why haven't I seen you working on it? No, I don't know where your soccer cleats are, but you need to be ready for practice in three minutes. Stop picking your nose.

One night my daughter suddenly huffed off in the middle of a conversation about what she needed to do. When I asked where she was going, she replied, "I just don't want to hear anything more if it's not something *fun*!"

Wouldn't it be great if we all had the luxury of deciding we're not going to deal with anything that isn't fun in life (and without repercussions)? As a starting point, I'd never go to the dentist again. But adults know we can't realistically expect everything to be fun. We do often try to avoid uncomfortable subjects, however, and hell probably tops the "uncomfortable list" in Christianity. In fact, you may be thinking right now that you'll skip this chapter with your child because you'd rather focus on God's love. Or maybe you feel like a mom I know who wanted to wait until her child was a teenager before having conversations about hell so he wouldn't be scared. While I certainly understand why parents sometimes come to these conclusions, it's a mistake to avoid talking about hell or treating it like a PG-13 subject. It's part of the truth God has revealed about eternity. When we discuss it matter-of-factly and put it in its appropriate theological context, there's nothing for us *or* our kids to fear.[1]

Hell Is Real

Skeptics often say that Christianity is a dangerously harmful religion for parents to teach their kids because the idea of hell is too frightening. This common claim, however, makes a big assumption—that hell isn't real. If hell *is* real, and it's a devastating destination, parents would obviously be harming their children by *not* warning them about it. We have no problem warning our kids about the dangers of doing drugs because we believe that drugs are a real thing to fear. We should similarly have no problem warning our kids about hell if it, too, is a real thing to fear. Let's begin, then, by looking at what Jesus says about hell's existence.

As some background for Jesus's teachings, the Old Testament says little about the afterlife in general, though there are hints of it in a few books (for example, Job 19:25–27; Pss. 49:15; 73:24; Isa.

26:19). Perhaps the most direct reference is found in Daniel 12:2: "Multitudes who sleep in the dust of the earth will awake: some to everlasting life, others to shame and everlasting contempt." In the intertestamental period (the roughly four hundred years between the time covered by the Old and New Testaments), Jewish writings about the afterlife increased in number and detail. They typically portrayed hell with images of fire, darkness, and great lament. By the first century, the dominant Jewish view was that hell is a terrible place of punishment after death for those who don't follow God.

When Jesus began his ministry, he sometimes challenged and corrected prevailing Jewish ideas (for example, in Mark 3:1–6). When it came to hell, however, *his words mirrored and expanded on the Jewish views of the day.* Far from denying the existence of the hell in which first-century Jews believed, Jesus spoke of it as a stark reality to be avoided at all costs. And he didn't do so in a passing mention. Jesus said more about hell than anyone else in the Bible.

Hell Is a Punishment after Final Judgment

Jesus didn't merely affirm that hell exists. He also affirmed the common Jewish belief about what it is: a place of punishment after death. Nonetheless, it has become popular for people—even Christians—to speculate that hell is something very different. For example, Roger Wolsey, an ordained United Methodist pastor, says, "I—along with many other Christians—am agnostic about the afterlife. I don't know if there's a heaven or a hell. I rather suspect that the only hells that exist are the ones that we create and allow at this time."[2] Though Rev. Wolsey says that he suspects hell is about what happens on earth, Jesus's own words leave no doubt that this is not what he taught. For example, consider the most detailed account of judgment day in the Gospels (judgment day is the day of God's final judgment on humankind):

> When the Son of Man comes in his glory, and all the angels with him, he will sit on his glorious throne. All the nations will be gathered before him, and he will separate the people one from another as a shepherd separates the sheep from the goats. . . .
>
> Then the King will say to those on his right, "Come, you who are blessed by my Father; take your inheritance, the kingdom prepared for you since the creation of the world. . . ."
>
> Then he will say to those on his left, "Depart from me, you who are cursed, into the eternal fire prepared for the devil and his angels. . . ."
>
> Then they will go away to eternal punishment, but the righteous to eternal life. (Matt. 25:31–32, 34, 41, 46)

We can note three important things about hell from this passage alone. First, Jesus explicitly states that the alternative to eternal life with God is eternal *punishment*.[3] He doesn't say that this alternative is corrective or that it's an opportunity for people to reconsider their decisions; nothing in the Bible suggests there is a second chance for salvation after death. Second, Jesus spoke about hell in the context of judgment at the end of time, not as some kind of condemnation in the here and now as Rev. Wolsey speculates (see also John 5:28–29; 12:48; Acts 17:31; Heb. 9:27; Rev. 20:11–15). Third, Jesus (the "Son of Man") is the one who will judge between those who go on to eternal life and those who face eternal punishment. How will he make that decision? John 3:16 gives us the answer: "For God so loved the world that he gave his one and only Son, that *whoever believes in him* shall not perish but have eternal life" (emphasis mine). Of course, true belief in Jesus results in a transformed life (as Matt. 25:31–46 makes clear)—John 3:16 isn't talking about some kind of vague intellectual affirmation of who Jesus is. We'll talk more about what it means to be a Christian and what it means to be saved in chapters 25 and 28.

Jesus will grant eternal life to those who put their trust in him for the forgiveness of sin. Hell is real and is a punishment after final judgment, but no one has to go there. (Out of scope for this chapter is the debate over whether the punishment of hell will be forever, or if those in hell will eventually cease to exist. See the endnote for a further reading recommendation.)[4]

Hell Is Not Something to Take Lightly

Finally, let's look at how Jesus described hell itself:

- "If your hand causes you to stumble, cut it off. It is better for you to enter life maimed than with two hands to go into hell, where the fire never goes out. And if your foot causes you to stumble, cut it off. It is better for you to enter life crippled than to have two feet and be thrown into hell. And if your eye causes you to stumble, pluck it out. It is better for you to enter the kingdom of God with one eye than to have two eyes and be thrown into hell, where 'the worms that eat them do not die, and the fire is not quenched'" (Mark 9:43–48; see also Matt. 18:8–9).

- "As the weeds are pulled up and burned in the fire, so it will be at the end of the age. The Son of Man will send out his angels, and they will weed out of his kingdom everything that causes sin and all who do evil. They will throw them into the blazing furnace, where there will be weeping and gnashing of teeth" (Matt. 13:40–42).

- "His winnowing fork is in his hand, and he will clear his threshing floor, gathering his wheat into the barn and burning up the chaff with unquenchable fire" (Matt. 3:12; see also Luke 3:17).

These are unquestionably images meant to get our attention and tell us that hell is not a place we want to go. That said, most theologians agree that they're not meant to be taken as a literal depiction of what hell is—after all, a literal fire emits light and hell is also pictured as utter darkness (Matt. 22:13). Whatever the precise nature of hell may be, however, the message of Jesus's words is clear: hell is a stark reality.

Does this mean that Christianity is a "fear-based religion," as skeptics so often claim? It depends on what you mean by "fear-based." If you mean it's a religion that includes claims about reality that people should fear if true, then yes. The reality of hell *should* be feared by those not in right relationship with God. But if you mean it's a religion people adhere to *because* of fear, then no. While that might be the case for any given individual (people hold beliefs for many different reasons), that's not why the Bible itself claims people should follow Jesus. Christians follow Jesus out of *love* for him. We believe that God so *loved* the world that he provided a way for us to be forgiven of our sins and reconciled to him. Sin against a holy God is a serious matter with serious consequences, as Jesus indeed warned, but Christianity is ultimately a story of love. Jesus captured the essence of this when he summarized all the "Law and Prophets" with two commands: to love God and to love others (Matt. 22:36–40). Christians need not fear hell because there is "no condemnation for those who are in Christ Jesus" (Rom. 8:1).

KEY POINTS

- Jesus affirmed the existence of hell and warned about its severity.
- While the idea that hell is something we experience on earth is increasingly popular today, it contradicts the clear teaching

of Jesus: hell is a punishment after final judgment for those who have not put their trust in him for the forgiveness of sin.

- Christians need not fear hell because there is "no condemnation for those who are in Christ Jesus" (Rom. 8:1).

CONVERSATION GUIDE

Note: These questions assume your child already has some idea of what hell is. If that's not the case, explain hell using the key points of this chapter rather than working through this guide.

Open the Conversation

- Research shows that more people believe in heaven than hell.[5] Why do you think that is? *(People sometimes choose to believe what they like rather than what Jesus taught. Emphasize the importance of basing our beliefs on what the Bible says and that the Bible teaches that hell is as real as heaven.)*

Advance the Conversation

- If a friend asked you what hell is and who goes there, what would you say? *(Listen for now; correct any misunderstandings as you continue the conversation.)*
- Read Matthew 25:31–46. This is Jesus's description of what will happen on judgment day—the day of God's final judgment on humankind. What can we learn about hell from this passage? *(Explain the three key points discussed in this chapter regarding these verses.)*
- Do you think hell is something Christians should fear? Why or why not? *(Read John 3:16; Romans 8:1; 1 John 4:18. Christians never need to fear hell because there is no condemnation for those*

in Christ. Hell is something to fear only for those not in right relationship with God.)

Apply the Conversation

- Read Rev. Wolsey's quote in this chapter. How would you respond based on what you've learned?

9. What Did Jesus Teach about Religion?

In 2012, twenty-two-year-old Jefferson Bethke became an overnight sensation after he posted a four-minute spoken word video on YouTube titled "Why I Hate Religion, But Love Jesus."[1] Bethke began by asking, "What if I told you Jesus came to abolish religion?" He then lyrically described how Jesus and religion are at irreconcilable odds. The video was viewed seven million times in its first forty-eight hours, and views have now climbed to over thirty-four million. Bethke went on to write a *New York Times* bestselling book based on his message.[2] Clearly, the video hit a nerve. Millions of people resonated with the idea that it's okay to love Jesus but hate so-called religion.

The thought that Christians can and should disentangle themselves from the trappings of organized religion and "just" follow Jesus is everywhere today, and it's a favorite topic of many writers. One blogger, for example, wrote, "Jesus minus organized religion equals biblical Christianity. . . . Even the church of the New Testament was corrupted within its first generation, as the apostles make clear. . . . What then shall we do? Forsake organized religion and love Jesus Christ."[3]

If Jesus truly hates religion, the popularity of the idea that Jesus and religion are at odds wouldn't be an issue. The problem is that Jesus doesn't hate religion. He hates *false* religion. And missing this important distinction can lead young people to have erroneous beliefs about the nature of truth, the authority of the Bible, and/or the importance of the church. We'll talk more about that slippery slope, but first we need to establish some definitions. Much of this conversation hinges on what a person means by the word *religion*.

What Is Religion?

By definition, religion is "an organized system of beliefs, cere-monies, and rules used to worship a god or a group of gods."[4] This includes diverse belief systems such as Christianity, Judaism, Mormonism, Islam, Scientology, Jehovah's Witnesses, Christian Science, and many more. In other words, religion is simply a broad descriptive term for any set of beliefs about a god or gods and carries no inherent evaluation of the truth of those beliefs or of the behavior of those who hold them.

For many people, however, the word *religion* has become syn-onymous with narrow-mindedness, hypocrisy, condemnation, and empty rituals. It often functions as a shorthand reference for all the things people don't like about churches they've attended, re-ligious people they've known, or what the Bible says. In Bethke's video, "religion" starts wars, builds huge churches but fails to feed the poor, preaches grace but practices something else, ridicules God's people, focuses only on behavior modification, puts you in bondage, makes you blind, and more. But religion, by definition, doesn't do any of those things. People who adhere to religions sometimes do—and that may or may not be consistent with what their religion actually teaches. Blanket statements about what "re-ligion" does fail to make this critical distinction. Jesus, however, had plenty to say about it.

What Did Jesus Say about False Religion?

Jesus frequently clashed with members of a Jewish sect called the Pharisees, who were strong opponents of his ministry. The Pharisees strictly kept the law given to Moses centuries earlier and followed an elaborate system of oral tradition to help them do so. One of the Mosaic laws, for example, was to keep the Sabbath holy, which meant that Jews were not to work on Saturdays. But to clarify what constituted "work," many layers of specific restrictions were developed over time, down to the details of how many steps a person could take. The Pharisees had elevated such laws to the level of Scripture and prided themselves on how well they kept them. Meanwhile, they harshly condemned others for not meeting the same standards. When Jesus himself didn't follow these added laws, his actions created conflict between him and the religious leaders.

People today often have this turbulent relationship in mind when they claim that Jesus hates religion. It's important to understand, however, that Jesus wasn't against the Pharisees because they were *religious*. He never said or implied that becoming *irreligious* would solve their problems. Rather, it was their self-righteous legalism, hypocrisy, and rejection of himself that Jesus condemned. In Luke 11, for example, a Pharisee expressed surprise when Jesus didn't wash before a meal. Jesus responded with a lengthy condemnation of their ways (vv. 37–52; see also Matt. 23). He criticized them for things such as tithing according to the law but neglecting justice and the love of God (Luke 11:42), loving the most important seats in the synagogues and respectful greetings in the marketplaces (v. 43), and loading people down with the burdens of a law they could hardly carry (v. 46)—not for being "religious." In Mark 12:38–40, Jesus similarly criticized the teachers of the law for devouring widows' houses while making lengthy prayers just for show. Jesus made it clear that the Pharisees honored God externally, but their hearts were far from him (Matt. 15:8).

Does that mean the Mosaic law—part of the Jewish religion—was bad? Not at all. The apostle Paul tells us that the law was holy and good for the purposes God had (Rom. 7:12). And Jesus explicitly said that his criticisms of how the Pharisees *used* the law didn't imply that he was in any way opposed to the law itself:

> Do not think that I have come to abolish the Law or the Prophets; I have not come to abolish them but to fulfill them. For truly I tell you, until heaven and earth disappear, not the smallest letter, not the least stroke of a pen, will by any means disappear from the Law until everything is accomplished. (Matt. 5:17–18)

Jesus participated in and validated other aspects of the "organized system of beliefs"—*religion*—that the Jewish people had as well. He went to synagogue on the Sabbath (Luke 4:16); taught in the synagogue (Mark 6:2); considered what we now call the Old Testament to be God's Word (Matt. 15:3; Mark 7:13); and observed Jewish religious traditions such as Passover (John 2:13), the Festival of Tabernacles (John 7:2, 10), and the Festival of Dedication (John 10:22). When Jesus was preparing for the end of his earthly ministry, he told Peter that he would be the rock on which he would build his church (Matt. 16:18)—the body of believers who would share faith in him and live out their beliefs accordingly. He even gave some specific instructions for practicing faith in what would come to be known as the Christian religion. At the Last Supper, he broke bread and commanded the disciples to "do this in remembrance of me" (Luke 22:19). He also told them to "make disciples of all nations" and to baptize people "in the name of the Father and of the Son and of the Holy Spirit" (Matt. 28:19).

As we can see, there's no need to separate Jesus from religion that is *true*. Christianity is simply the name for the religion whose beliefs center on who Jesus is and that calls us to know, worship, serve, and obey him. It's a religion centered on relationship (when religion is appropriately defined).

What's the Downside of Believing Religion Is Bad?

You may wonder why we need to split hairs over the meaning of words. If people—including our kids—believe religion is bad based on an unnuanced definition yet have a relationship with Jesus, why should we care?

Assuming religion is a bad thing can lead people to erroneous conclusions that significantly affect the *nature* of their relationship with Jesus. To see the potential problem, let's circle back to the three common areas of slippery slope mentioned earlier: the nature of truth, the authority of the Bible, and the importance of the church.

In an opinion piece for the *Huffington Post*, writer Mick Mooney explains why he chooses to live his faith "outside of organized religion":

> While it seems popular to think Jesus came to build an army of sorts for God, and to then organize his followers to build him an empire on earth, I personally don't subscribe to such a concept. In fact, I think Christ came to do the opposite; I believe he came to end empire thinking and bring each of us back to a personal, individual experience of God. . . . The thoughts and questions that God stirs my heart with—and the answers I find—are never going to be the same as everyone else, because my relationship with God is personal. Contrary to this is organized religion. Religion creates a corporate identity. When we buy into religion we end up speaking, sounding, even looking like everyone else within that corporate branded identity. Same thoughts. Same beliefs. Same well-defined doctrines.[5]

In this one statement, we can see how the idea that religion is bad and Jesus is good has led to confusion over all three issues we identified. First, Mooney uses the contrast between religion and Jesus to seemingly abandon the notion of objective truth—that there can be a well-defined set of doctrines that are true for all people regardless of a person's own experience. He sees such uniform religious belief as a bad thing. However, if Jesus was who he claimed to be (God) and revealed to humankind what he *knows* to be true about the world he created, then uniform assent to those truths isn't a negative—it's the only reasonable response.

Second, Mooney clearly values his personal insights over God's revelation to humankind through the Bible. His personal experience is his authority. But while our personal experience with God is vital, it's not a substitute for the knowledge we have from what God has revealed in Scripture.

Finally, Mooney seems to believe that a "corporate identity" is part of religion's rap sheet. To the contrary, the New Testament repeatedly emphasizes the importance of Christians having a corporate identity in Jesus. We are to be unified in the Holy Spirit (1 Cor. 12:13; Eph. 4:3), in our understanding of the truth (Eph. 4:13; Phil. 2:2), in meeting together with other believers (Heb. 10:25), and in functioning as *one body* with many parts (1 Cor. 12:12–27). A core aspect of a Christian's identity is our connection to the body of Christ.

None of this is to say that all people who believe "Jesus hates religion" will end up thinking in these ways about truth, the Bible, and the church. However, such a belief *is* a justification many people use to abandon what they don't like about what the Bible says and to create their own personalized belief system. It's important for kids to understand that *true* religion (properly defined) glorifies God (James 1:27) and isn't something Christians should denounce in favor of their own customized faith.

KEY POINTS

- Jesus doesn't hate religion—he hates *false* religion, such as what the Pharisees practiced.
- Religion and relationship with Jesus are a false dichotomy. Christianity is a religion *centered* on relationship.
- The assumption that religion is a bad thing can lead people to erroneous conclusions that affect the nature of their relationship with Jesus—including a lowered view of the nature of truth, the authority of the Bible, and the importance of the church.

CONVERSATION GUIDE

Open the Conversation

- How would you define religion—not just Christianity but religion in general? *(Discuss the definition given in this chapter.)*
- What kinds of words do you think come to mind when people think of religion? *(Talk about any positive or negative associations your child mentions and explore why people have such different thoughts about religion.)*

Advance the Conversation

- Sometimes people say they hate religion but love Jesus. What do you think they mean by that? *(If your child is old enough, play the Jefferson Bethke video. Listen to how he describes religion and discuss how that differs from the definition of religion you discussed. For younger kids, simply list some of the things Bethke says religion is and discuss how those are bad things—but those things don't define religion.)*

- How do you think Jesus sees religion? *(Emphasize that he hates false religion, giving examples from his encounters with the Pharisees, but that true religion glorifies God.)*
- If a person says they hate religion but love Jesus, what impact do you think that might have on their faith? *(Use Mick Mooney's quote in this chapter as an example to discuss how this view can lead someone away from Jesus.)*

Apply the Conversation

- How would you respond to Mick Mooney's concern that in organized religion everyone has the same beliefs and well-defined doctrines?

10. What Did Jesus Teach about Loving Others?

For Valentine's Day this year, my husband and I exchanged notes with fifteen affirming words that describe each other. One of the words my husband chose for me included a qualification: "Adventurous (unless there's danger)." When I first saw it, I thought he was joking. How adventurous can a person be if there's no danger? But he defended his questionable choice of a compliment by clarifying that he loves how I embrace the *idea* of adventure, even if I eventually panic when doing something.

One case in point: scuba diving. Before my husband and I had kids, we decided to get scuba certified. To do so, we started by taking classroom lessons. It was in those lessons—before my big toe had even touched the water—that I started having second thoughts. The complexity of diving even caused my normally fearless husband to have some trepidation.

Nonetheless, we continued, and there was one lesson we still laugh about today. The book said something like this: "Before you get to the dive site, discuss the dive objective with your buddy. If you're planning a photography dive but your buddy is planning a trash clean-up dive, the two of you will bring very different tools and want to do very different things."

Trash clean up? Photography? Our only objective as dive buddies was to *not drown*. The idea that the two of us would ever get to a point where I might show up to the boat with a litter grabber only to have my hopes dashed by my husband revealing an exciting new dive camera was ridiculously funny. For years now, whenever we need to make sure we're on the same page about something, we say, "Okay, I was just making sure you weren't planning to pick up trash while I was planning to photograph a lobster."

One of the greatest barriers to civil conversation between people with different worldviews is that they don't stop to determine whether they have the same objectives in mind. Oftentimes they *think* they're on the same page—"Hey! We both want to scuba dive!"—but in reality, one group means they want to pick up trash and the other means they want to do underwater photography. Love is one of the most common subjects where this happens today.

What Does It Mean to Love People?

Nearly everyone in our culture appeals to the necessity of loving one another. Given the importance of love in Christianity, one might think this is an area where the secular world and Christians can align. Unfortunately, however, that's often not the case. The key to understanding why is in Matthew 22:36–40. A Pharisee asked Jesus, "Teacher, which is the greatest commandment in the Law?" Jesus replied:

> "Love the Lord your God with all your heart and with all your soul and with all your mind." This is the first and greatest commandment. And the second is like it: "Love your neighbor as yourself." All the Law and the Prophets hang on these two commandments.

If Jesus says that one commandment is the *greatest*, we need to listen closely; it implies that any other commandments should be obeyed within that context. In this case, he's telling us that *what it means to love others depends on what it means to first love God.* This is why Christians so often clash with culture on what love is—we have different objectives. Christians strive to love others given *God's* standards. The secular world strives to love others given *self-defined* standards. To see why these differing objectives lead to conflicting ideas, let's dig deeper into what Jesus taught.

Loving Others When We First Love God

Since Jesus commanded us specifically to love our *neighbor* as ourselves, we should start by asking, "Who is our neighbor?" Jesus told the famous parable of the good Samaritan to answer that question (Luke 10:25–37). He described a man traveling from Jerusalem to Jericho when he was attacked by robbers and left to die. A priest and a Levite eventually walked by, but neither bothered to help. A Samaritan came along, however, and stopped to save the man's life. Because the Jews and the Samaritans were longtime enemies, Jesus used the story to teach that our neighbor isn't just a person like us—our neighbor is everyone (see also Matt. 5:44, 46).

From this parable, we can see that Christians are undoubtedly to love all people, but what does it mean to love them in the context of loving God first?

Godly Love Means Caring for People's Souls

As we saw in chapters 7 and 8, what people believe about Jesus has eternal significance. For that reason, Jesus told his disciples after his resurrection, "Go and make disciples of all nations, baptizing them in the name of the Father and of the Son and of the Holy Spirit, and teaching them to obey everything I have commanded you" (Matt. 28:19–20). When we love God first, we trust in the truths he has revealed about eternity and salvation, and we obey his commands. Our love for others flows out of that obedience when we share the gospel.

Jesus's command, however, is at odds with the widespread secular view that sharing Christianity as an objective truth is arrogant and/or wrong (an objective truth is something that is true for all people regardless of one's personal opinion). As one atheist wrote, for example, "When the [Christian evangelizes], he or she is proceeding from the assumption that his or her religious beliefs are superior to all others. . . . The arrogance here really is astounding."[1] Unfortunately, many young Christians have been influenced by this view. Research shows that 96 percent of millennials agree that part of their faith "means being a witness about Jesus," but almost half also agree that "it is wrong to share one's personal beliefs with someone of a different faith in hopes that they will one day share the same faith."[2]

Kids must understand that sharing the truth of Jesus with others is one of the greatest ways we can love them. We should confidently share our faith with gentleness and respect (1 Pet. 3:15), because doing so is right in God's eyes—even if not in the eyes of the world.

Godly Love Means Caring for People's Earthly Needs

The fact that we should love others by caring for their souls doesn't mean we can neglect their earthly circumstances. Jesus's heart for the poor runs throughout the Gospels, and he calls those who love him to love the less fortunate in the same way. Perhaps the most well-known example is the story of the rich young ruler. In Luke 18:18, the ruler asks Jesus, "Good teacher, what must I do to inherit eternal life?" Jesus tells him, "Sell everything you have and give to the poor, and you will have treasure in heaven. Then come, follow me" (v. 22). Similarly, in Luke 12:33–34, Jesus tells his disciples to sell their possessions and give to the poor, "for where your treasure is, there your heart will be also." Jesus also says that when we care for people's needs, we serve *him* (Matt. 25:31–46). Our love for God should clearly translate into a tangible care for others' physical needs.

Caring for the poor is something that people of any worldview can agree is important and loving. Even so, there are still sometimes significant differences between the objectives of secular love and those of Christian love in this area. My husband sees this all the time as the chief operating officer of one of the largest gospel rescue missions in the United States. Gospel rescue missions offer faith-based transitional-living programs that help homeless people get off the streets and obtain the job and life skills training they need. They care for the *whole* person—both physically *and* spiritually—because they know that a person's relationship with Jesus is a key factor in breaking the cycle of addiction-related homelessness. Secular organizations that help the homeless, however, typically focus on fixing the symptom of the problem (homelessness) without addressing root issues. Some organizations are now going so far as to *support* drug use and drug user "rights" in the homeless population with the goal of only minimizing risk of disease and overdose.[3] The stated mission of organizations like these is often to "meet people where they are" in a "nonjudgmental" environment.[4] Jesus meets people where they are too . . . but he doesn't want to leave them there. He wants to rescue them, not facilitate continued brokenness. Once again, we see that loving God first can result in a very different understanding of what it means to love others.

Godly Love Means Speaking Truth about Morality in a Fallen World

When Jesus said, "I am the way and the truth and the life" (John 14:6), he made a very pointed claim: he *is* the truth. When we love Jesus, therefore, we love truth, and we must be ready to stand up for it as "salt" and "light" in a fallen world (Matt. 5:13–16).

Despite the negative associations people have with the word *intolerant*, there are many things Christians *should* be intolerant about out of a love for God and others. As Josh McDowell and Sean McDowell say in their book *The Beauty of Intolerance*, "Intolerance can sometimes be beautiful—that is, when you understand it from God's point of view. . . . What is more beautiful than God's intolerance expressed in his moral outrage toward the tragedies of poverty, racism, sexual abuse, slavery, AIDS, bigotry, and other such evils?"[5] We must be lovers, speakers, and doers of truth in order to make an impact on a fallen world.

Oftentimes Christians work side by side with people of other worldviews who find those evils intolerable. Other moral issues, however, lead to great disagreement between the secular world and Christians. When biblical morality conflicts with what is accepted by mainstream society, Christians are often (inappropriately) accused of being intolerant—abortion and sexuality are two of the biggest examples. Loving others, in the secular view, means affirming the individual as the ultimate standard of his or her morality; if something is right *for you*, it's right. In such a view, it's not possible to both love a person and not affirm their choices because love *equals* affirmation. In essence, secular love is wanting for others what they want for themselves. Godly love is wanting for others what God wants for them—even when that's *not* what they want for themselves.

Christians are often quick to say that God is love, and they're certainly right (1 John 4:8). But as we've seen, we can't stop there. Kids need to understand what, exactly, that means and why a love for God *before* a love for others can make all the difference in the world.

KEY POINTS

- Christians often clash with culture over what it means to love others because we have different objectives. Christians strive to love others given *God's* standards. The secular world strives to love others given *self-defined* standards.
- Three key ways Christians express a godly love for others is by caring for people's souls, caring for people's earthly needs, and speaking truth about morality in a fallen world.
- Secular love often means wanting for others what they want for themselves. Godly love is wanting for others what God wants for them—even when that's *not* what they want for themselves.

CONVERSATION GUIDE

Open the Conversation

- When you think of what it means to love others as a Christian, what kinds of things come to mind?

Advance the Conversation

- Read Matthew 22:36–40. Why do you think Jesus says that our love for God must come before our love for others? *(We won't fully understand what it means to love others unless we first understand what it means to love God.)*
- When Jesus said that we should love our *neighbor* as ourselves, who do you think that includes? *(Everyone. Read the parable of the good Samaritan and Matthew 5:44, 46.)*
- Read Matthew 28:19–20. How is obeying Jesus's command in these verses one way of loving others? *(A person's relationship with Jesus has eternal significance. When we share Jesus*

with someone, we are caring for their soul. Discuss how the secular world sometimes views this as a bad thing and why we should not be deterred.)

- Read Matthew 25:31–40; and Luke 12:33–34 and 18:18–22. What is another important way we should love others, according to these passages? *(We must care for their earthly needs. Discuss the example of the rescue mission to show how even in this area Christian love is sometimes different from that of the world.)*

- What are some things in our world that all people—regardless of what they believe about God—agree are morally wrong? What are some things that Christians and nonbelievers may disagree are wrong? *(Use age-appropriate examples, and discuss how Christians love God and others by speaking up for truth in a fallen world.)*

Apply the Conversation

- Singer Lana Del Rey has said, "When someone else's happiness is your happiness, that is love."[6] Is this view consistent with the Christian meaning of love? Why or why not?

11. What Did Jesus Teach about Judging Others?

One of the most popular blog posts I've ever written is titled "10 Signs the Christian Authors You're Following Are (Subtly) Teaching Unbiblical Ideas."[1] While it resonated with many—it's been shared almost twenty thousand times—I also received a stream of emails from people who wanted to let me know the Bible says not to judge. Those emails continue to arrive months after I published the post, with this one coming in just five minutes before this writing:

> If "judge not, lest you be judged" is true, why is judging others a good thing? Not the ultimate sin, but it's a sin. How about the Great Commandment? Love God with all of you, and love your neighbor as yourself. What's not transparent about that? Jesus said it was the commandment to replace ALL OTHERS.

This person's understanding of what the Bible says about judgment is common today: *You just said someone is wrong . . . Jesus said judging others is bad . . . You're the one who's wrong for saying someone else is wrong.* Of course, such thinking puts the person in the ironic position of having made a judgment themselves! Interestingly, both Christians and nonbelievers can share this understanding. Christians sometimes believe it's not their place to judge ("I'm leaving that to God!"), and nonbelievers quote Jesus's words about not judging in order to silence Christians who speak up on moral issues ("Follow the words of your own holy book!").

We saw in the previous chapter why this commenter's understanding of love is misguided. Now it's time to look at the common and related confusion over the nature of judgment. Is judging others really unloving and unbiblical?

What Do You Mean by "Judge"?

My daughter came downstairs one morning with an outfit that was poorly matched. When I told her that the shirt and pants didn't go together, she replied, "Stop judging me!" I did a double take because those aren't words we use in our house. Clearly, she had heard them enough from kids at school that her young mind had already been trained to think that vocalized disagreement = judgment = bad.

The challenge in talking about this subject is that people can mean a number of different things when they use the word *judge*, just as we saw that people can mean a number of different things when they use the words *love* and *religion*. One sense of the word *judge* is "to discern." Discernment is the ability to separate right from wrong and truth from error. Another sense of the word *judge* is "to condemn"—to pass a final sentence (a judge, for example, may condemn a person to death). People also sometimes use the word *judge* as a catch-all for *any* type of perceived disapproval, as my daughter did. But it's the first two senses of the word—to discern and to condemn—that are relevant for our current discussion. The Bible uses the word *judge* in both of these ways, and knowing which sense is intended at a given time is the key to understanding the answer to this chapter's question.

When Judging Is Right . . . and When It's Wrong

The words of Jesus that have so often led to misunderstanding on this subject are from Matthew 7:1: "Do not judge, or you too will be judged." People extract those words from the Bible with razor-like precision, leaving their context in the dust. But read the next four verses:

> For in the same way you judge others, you will be judged, and with the measure you use, it will be measured to you. Why do you look at the speck of sawdust in your brother's eye and pay no attention to the plank in your own eye? How can you say to your brother, "Let me take the speck out of your eye," when all the time there is a plank in your own eye? You hypocrite, first take the plank out of your own eye, and then you will see clearly to remove the speck from your brother's eye. (vv. 2–5)

Despite how Matthew 7:1 sounds in isolation, Jesus isn't saying to never judge! *He tells us how to judge sin rightly.* That requires examining ourselves first. If we're guilty of the same sin we see in others, we need to deal with that "plank" in our eye before trying to remove the speck in theirs. In other words, Jesus's famous statement about not judging is a prelude to his warning against *hypocritical* judgment, not *all* judgment. Similarly, in John 7:24, Jesus tells a crowd, "Stop judging by mere appearances, but instead judge correctly." These cautions imply that we must be slow to judge—examining ourselves first, then seeking to carefully evaluate a situation before attempting to address sin.

The Bible gives several other qualifications on how Christians should and should not judge sin as well.

Judge the Action; Don't Condemn the Person

Jesus's words in Matthew 7 are clearly speaking about discernment (separating right from wrong) and *not* condemnation. Only

119

God has the authority to pass a final sentence on a person's life (Pss. 7:11; 9:8; 50:6; Isa. 33:22). While Jesus did instruct us to carefully call out sin, he never instructed us to condemn another; not one of us is qualified to state what a person's final standing before God will be. This is what James 4:11–12 means when it says, "Brothers and sisters, do not slander one another. . . . There is only one Lawgiver and Judge, the one who is able to save and destroy. But you—who are you to judge your neighbor?" We are to judge *actions* as right or wrong, not condemn *people*.

Much of the time when people say they feel judged, they're assuming (rightly or wrongly) that another person is condemning them—claiming to know how they will ultimately stand before God. It's important that when we speak the truth about sin, we do so in a way that plainly avoids that implication. That said, people sometimes accuse Christians of "playing God" if we say *anything* about sin. We can respond by clarifying that (1) we aren't claiming to be the source of moral law ourselves—it's God's law we're sharing; (2) we aren't claiming to be a moral authority in their lives—God alone holds that position; and (3) we aren't claiming to be better than others—"all have sinned and fall short of the glory of God" (Rom. 3:23).

Judge the Action, Not the Intent

Scripture also cautions us not to judge others' motives. Only God can judge motives because only God can see the heart (1 Sam. 16:7; Ps. 44:21; 1 Cor. 4:5; Heb. 4:12). Instead, we must focus on judging actions, where the sinful intent of the heart is revealed (Matt. 12:33).

Be Motivated by Love

Our own motives are important as well. We should be motivated by love for the other person to help bring repentance, not shame. We can see this in Jesus's carefully sequenced instructions to his followers in Matthew 18:15–17:

If your brother or sister sins, go and point out their fault, just between the two of you. If they listen to you, you have won them over. But if they will not listen, take one or two others along, so that "every matter may be established by the testimony of two or three witnesses." If they still refuse to listen, tell it to the church; and if they refuse to listen even to the church, treat them as you would a pagan or a tax collector.

Paul also addressed the gracious handling of sin, telling the Galatians, "Brothers and sisters, if someone is caught in a sin, you who live by the Spirit should restore that person gently" (Gal. 6:1). Speaking the truth about sin isn't about "winning" or making ourselves look better than others. It's about loving restoration.

What about Judging Doctrine?

So far we've addressed judgment in the context of sin. But there's another area in which we must appropriately judge as well: doctrine. In the emailed comment I quoted at the beginning of this chapter, my great sin was calling out unbiblical ideas taught by popular Christian writers. The underlying assumption of the commenter was that Christians shouldn't judge what other Christians believe and/or teach. But that's a judgment as well—and one the Bible doesn't support.

In Ephesians 4:11–15, Paul tells Christians to speak the truth in love rather than being like infants "tossed back and forth by the waves, and blown here and there by every wind of teaching." The result, he says, is that we will "grow to become in every respect the mature body of him who is the head, that is, Christ." Paul speaks to the importance of sound doctrine in his instructions to Timothy as well:

Preach the word; be prepared in season and out of season; *correct, rebuke and encourage—with great patience and careful instruction.*

For the time will come when people will not put up with sound doctrine. Instead, to suit their own desires, they will gather around them a great number of teachers to say what their itching ears want to hear. They will turn their ears away from the truth and turn aside to myths. (2 Tim. 4:2–4, emphasis mine)

As brothers and sisters in Christ, we must carefully guard the truths God has given us. The Bible in no way suggests that we are to accept all ideas put forth in the name of Christ as equally valid or to remain silent. On the contrary, we are to discern truth from error because falsehood abounds (1 John 4:1–3), and we are to bring error to light because poor doctrine can lead people away from God (1 Tim. 4:16). This should, of course, be done in a loving manner.

We've seen in this chapter that the subject of judgment is one with many nuances. As such, one of the best things we can teach our kids to do when they hear someone say that Christians are judgmental is to ask, "What do you mean by judgmental?" Once assumptions are identified, much more productive conversations can be had.

KEY POINTS

- Jesus's famous words "Do not judge, or you too will be judged" are a prelude to his warning about *hypocritical* judgment, not *all* judgment.
- While Jesus instructed us to carefully call out sin (*discerning* between right and wrong), he never instructed us to *condemn* another. Only God has the authority to pass a final sentence on a person's life.
- When addressing sin, we should be motivated by love for the other person, seeking to help bring repentance.

- Christians must also judge between right and wrong doctrine because falsehoods abound and poor doctrine can lead people away from God.

CONVERSATION GUIDE

Open the Conversation

- Eighty-seven percent of young non-Christians say that Christianity is "judgmental."[2] What do you think they mean by that? *(With younger kids, instead ask if they've heard someone say, "Don't judge me!" and what they think that means.)*

Advance the Conversation

- Read Matthew 7:1–5. What is Jesus saying about when we should and shouldn't judge others? *(Jesus is warning against hypocritical judgment, but people often stop reading after Matthew 7:1 and think we should never judge at all.)*
- Read James 4:11–12. How is the kind of judgment God has the right to make different from the kind of judgment Jesus told *us* to make in Matthew 7:1–5? *(Only God has the authority to pass a final judgment on a person's life. We are not to condemn people in this way.)*
- Imagine that you have a Christian friend who is bullying another kid. Based on the verses we've read, what would be a biblical way of addressing their actions with them, and what would be an unbiblical way? *(Biblical: Make sure you're not guilty of the same sin, confirm your understanding of the situation, pull the friend aside privately, and share that what they're doing is not right for a Christian. Unbiblical: Not say anything at all, say something in front of everyone to shame them, or tell the friend they're going to hell.)*

- If you confronted the friend in a biblical way and they replied, "You're a Christian! You're not supposed to judge me!" what would you say? *(Explain how the Bible calls us to judge rightly.)*
- Now imagine that you have a Christian friend who believes something about Jesus that's untrue according to the Bible. Do you think you should say something? Why or why not? And is saying something being "judgmental"? *(It's judgmental in the sense of discerning between truth and error, and the Bible does call us to that kind of discernment. Read Ephesians 4:11–15; 2 Timothy 4:2–4.)*

Apply the Conversation

- A blogger wrote, "I think in general, we judge everyone way more than we should. Jesus never judged, He's always loved. If we're trying to live like Jesus, [then] loving is the best thing we can do."[3] How would you respond?

12. How Can We Know What Jesus Would Have Taught on Subjects He Didn't Address?

One evening my daughter shared with me about a difficult situation with some friends at school. It was clear that she needed to let her teacher know that another student wasn't being treated well. Rather than just telling her to do that, however, I tried to get her to think through the situation from a biblical perspective. I asked, "What do you think Jesus would say about how to handle this situation?"

She looked at me with a blank stare and furrowed brow, then replied, "I don't know. How *would* I know? He didn't say anything about that."

I had to laugh. She was right. Jesus didn't say anything specifically about what to do when a group of second graders is treating a classmate poorly behind the teacher's back. But, of course, he did say plenty that would inform a decision on how to respond in a godly way.

For an adult Christian, this was a no-brainer application of biblical truth, and kids typically grow into that kind of understanding over time. There are other subjects Jesus is "silent" on, however, that are more complex in nature and consequently require more proactive teaching. Kids need to understand that just because Jesus didn't explicitly address a given subject doesn't mean we can't have a good idea of what he would have said.

The Bible Is More Than Jesus's Recorded Words

In 2007, pastor and popular speaker Tony Campolo founded a group called the Red Letter Christians. The group's name is a reference to the fact that some Bibles print Jesus's words in red. Campolo explains, "We emphasize the 'red letters' because we believe that you can only understand the rest of the Bible when you read it from the perspective provided by Christ."[1] In particular, the group believes that Christians spend too much time talking about subjects Jesus didn't specifically address—Campolo mentions abortion and homosexuality as key examples.

Many people today have never heard of Campolo's group but are effectively Red Letter Christians themselves. If Jesus didn't plainly say something about a given subject—even if it's otherwise addressed in the Bible—they treat it as a secondary concern or reject the applicable biblical teachings completely. There are several reasons why this is a problematic approach.

First, as a purely logical point, just because Jesus is "silent" on an issue doesn't mean we're free to conclude anything we want about it. The Gospels don't record Jesus saying anything about child abuse, infanticide, racism, or domestic violence, yet few would argue these things are unimportant or morally acceptable. Jesus couldn't possibly have addressed everything, so we can't use his silence on a given issue to determine our evaluation of it.

Second, Jesus validated the Old Testament as God's Word, so he didn't need to repeat everything God had already said; it was assumed he was building on it. Recall from chapter 9 that Jesus said he did not come to abolish the Law or the Prophets but to fulfill them (Matt. 5:17–18; see also Matt. 22:29; Luke 16:31; 24:27; John 5:47). Ironically, therefore, Jesus's own words show why he would disagree with the approach of Red Letter Christians: he makes it clear that the Old Testament is equally authoritative and important for his followers. This means that the Old Testament, when appropriately applied, should inform our understanding on subjects Jesus didn't directly address.

Third, the Gospels represent just four out of twenty-seven books in the New Testament that are equally authoritative for Christians. Second Timothy 3:16 says that *all* Scripture is God-breathed, and the process of New Testament Scripture recognition began very early in the life of the church. For example, in 1 Timothy 5:18, the apostle Paul was already quoting from Luke's writings, calling them part of "Scripture." Similarly, 2 Peter references Paul's letters as Scripture (3:15–16). The twenty-three books after the Gospels add much to our understanding of theology and cannot be ignored in the interest of prioritizing Jesus's words alone.

In short, there is no biblical basis for treating Jesus's words differently than the rest of the Bible. With that established, let's now look at three examples of how we can apply the whole witness of Scripture where Jesus is technically silent.

Old Testament Cultural Concessions Jesus Didn't Condemn (Example: Polygamy)

Skeptics often claim that because the Bible doesn't condemn polygamy (one man married to multiple wives) and because some godly men of the Old Testament had multiple wives (for example, Abraham, Jacob, and David), Christians should believe that God endorses the practice. They use the same logic to claim that the Bible endorses slavery.[2]

Polygamy, however, is one of many cultural concessions God apparently made in ancient Israel that we know didn't reflect his *ideal*. We can see God's ideal for marriage in the second chapter of Genesis: "That is why a man leaves his father and mother and is united to his wife, and they become one flesh" (v. 24). When the Pharisees challenged Jesus on the morality of divorce (also a marriage issue), Jesus appealed to the authority of those same words:

> "Haven't you read," he replied, "that at the beginning the Creator 'made them male and female,' and said, 'For this reason a man will leave his father and mother and be united to his wife, and the two will become one flesh'? So they are no longer two, but one flesh. Therefore what God has joined together, let no one separate." (Matt. 19:4–6)

The Pharisees then asked why, if this (ideal) was true, Moses commanded that a man give his wife a certificate of divorce and send her away. Jesus explained that a concession was made: "Moses permitted you to divorce your wives because your hearts were hard. But it was not this way from the beginning. I tell you that anyone who divorces his wife, except for sexual immorality, and marries another woman commits adultery" (vv. 8–9).

God made certain cultural concessions, but we can see when those practices did not reflect his ideal—even when not explicitly condemned. The consistent witness of both the Old and the New Testament is that God's ideal for marriage is one man and one woman (see also Eph. 5:31–32; 1 Tim. 3:2).

Old Testament Prohibitions Jesus Didn't Overturn (Example: Mixed Fabrics)

Two passages in the Old Testament law prohibit wearing clothing woven of two kinds of material (Lev. 19:19; Deut. 22:11). The rest of the Bible never says that this specific law has been overturned, yet Christians have no problem today mixing wool and linen. Skeptics often use this fact to mock Christians who adhere to Old Testament teachings on *morality*; they claim that if we don't follow laws on things such as mixed fabrics and shellfish (Lev. 11:10–12), then we're being inconsistent.

While there is uncertainty as to why the mixed fabrics law was in place, many theologians believe it was to set apart the garments of the high priest, who wore mixed wool and linen himself (Exod. 28:6–8; 39:4–5). Though other interpretations have been offered, the key point to understand doesn't change: this was one of many laws specific to the people of ancient Israel and not a command for all people of all times. The nation of Israel, for example, had civil laws that were intended to deal with disputes between individuals. We don't follow those laws today because we don't live in the ancient nation of Israel; we follow our own country's civil laws. Other laws were ceremonial in nature, instructing the Israelites on proper worship and purity. Christians don't follow ceremonial laws because Jesus fulfilled the sacrificial system once and for all (Matt. 5:17–18; see chapter 14). This is not to suggest, however, that we don't follow *any* of the laws the ancient Israelites did. Some laws reflect the character of God himself and apply to people of all times because God is unchanging. For example, the Israelites were not to murder, and neither are we. Mixing fabrics, however, is not an issue of God's character. This is one of many rules that no longer apply today.

Issues on Which the Whole Bible Is "Silent" (Example: Abortion)

Pro-choice advocates often emphasize that the Bible doesn't explicitly say anything about abortion—and this is true. But they raise the point to suggest that silence implies permissibility. As we've already seen, this in and of itself is poor logic. Abortion is a good example of a subject the Bible is technically "silent" on but about which much can be inferred from what the Bible *does* say. Let's look at two very basic points.

First, we know that every human life has value because we are all made in the image of God (Gen. 1:27). Although the Bible doesn't directly state that the preborn are equally human, it speaks in ways that assume as much. For example, consider God's words to Jeremiah: "Before I formed you in the womb I knew you, before you were born I set you apart; I appointed you as a prophet to the nations" (1:5; see also Job 31:15; Ps. 139:13; Isa. 44:24; Luke 1:41, 44; Gal. 1:15). Second, the Bible consistently condemns the unjust taking of human life (Exod. 23:7; Ps. 106:37–38; Prov. 6:16–19; Matt. 5:21). Putting these points together, we can infer a biblical view that abortion is wrong because it intentionally and unjustly kills a human being—an image bearer of God. This, of course, is a very brief case. For deeper discussion, I highly recommend Scott Klusendorf's book *The Case for Life: Equipping Christians to Engage the Culture*.[3]

Though much more could be said on any of these three examples, discussing the basic points will help your child begin to think through some of the important aspects of reading and applying Scripture today.

KEY POINTS

- Just because Jesus is "silent" on an issue doesn't mean we're free to conclude anything we want about it. Both the Old and the New Testament should inform our understanding.
- The example of polygamy demonstrates that God made certain cultural concessions, but we can see when those practices did not reflect his ideal—even when not explicitly *condemned* elsewhere in the Bible.

- The example of mixed fabrics demonstrates that certain Old Testament laws were intended only for the people of ancient Israel and are no longer applicable today—even when not explicitly *overturned* elsewhere in the Bible.
- The example of abortion demonstrates that even when the whole Bible is technically "silent" on an issue, much can be inferred from what the Bible *does* say.

CONVERSATION GUIDE

Open the Conversation

- Think of the last time you faced a difficult situation. If you could have asked Jesus what to do, what do you think he would have said? *(Explore how your child knows what Jesus would say even if the Bible doesn't speak to their exact problem.)*

Advance the Conversation

- There are many subjects Jesus didn't directly talk about. What are some reasons why he wouldn't have talked about *everything* we want to know? *(He couldn't possibly have addressed everything in his short ministry; some things were already addressed in the Old Testament; and some things weren't relevant to the people of his day.)*
- If Jesus *did* talk about a subject, do you think that means it's more important than things he *didn't* talk about? Why or why not? *(We can't assume anything about something's importance or morality based on silence.)*
- In the Old Testament, some of the godly men we read about, like King David, had multiple wives. The Bible never says that this practice is not allowed, but Christians today believe it's wrong. Why do you think that is? *(Read Genesis 2:24 and*

explain God's ideal for marriage. Discuss how God made conces-
sions in ancient Israel that don't reflect his ideal. Use Jesus's words
on divorce as an example.)

- The Old Testament contains many laws that sound pretty
  strange to us today. For example, one law says that people
  shouldn't wear clothing woven of two kinds of material! Why
  do you think we don't pay attention to that rule today even
  though the Bible doesn't say it's okay not to obey it now?
  (Explain how the Old Testament contains civil and ceremonial laws
  that applied only to the people of Israel. Contrast this with moral laws
  based on God's unchanging nature.)

- *(If you're comfortable discussing abortion with your child, explain*
  that the Bible doesn't directly address the subject. Ask them to think
  about things the Bible does say that would be relevant to the issue.
  Cover the two basic points from this chapter.)

Apply the Conversation

- A young adult commented online, "I've often asked my (de-
  vout Christian) parents why some things [from the Old Testa-
  ment] were okay, and others were not, and they reply with,
  'That's the Old Testament, not the New! We don't have to
  live that way anymore!' Ooooo . . . kay . . . That's not how
  it works . . . you can't pick and choose what you want to be
  for and against; you either follow all or none."[4] How would
  you respond to *both* the parents and this commenter about
  their statements?

PART 3
The Death of Jesus

Overview

I love the concept of family movie night, when everyone gathers together to watch something of mutual enjoyment and eat buttery popcorn. Okay, it's mostly the buttery popcorn I love. Truth be told, I don't really enjoy movies. I like the *idea* of everyone watching something together, but it's impossible to find something we can all agree on.

My husband and son like movies like the Lord of the Rings series. I remember doing my husband a favor by seeing the first one with him years ago, and I stared at the screen in disbelief when it ended. I couldn't believe I had lost precious hours of my life watching mythical creatures fight their way through a forest and never get where they were headed (apparently you have to watch the *next* movie to find out what happens). No thanks. But I digress. My daughters usually want to watch mediocre kids' movies that we've already seen twenty times, and I only want to watch something if it's a documentary or based on a true story. You can see why family movie night is tough in our house.

Compromise on everyone's part has landed us on something we're all at least somewhat interested in: nature shows. We all enjoy the beauty of God's breathtaking creation. But I have to admit that I'm bothered when those shows involve graphic scenes of predators attacking, gruesomely killing, and eating their prey. Yes, I know that's part of God's world too, but I just find it hard to watch.

In jarring contrast to my own feelings, there's often a narrator calmly commenting on the "grandeur" of such events. He points out the majestic strength of the lion, the amazing speed of the cheetah, or the impressive cunning of the bobcat. It's sometimes hard to believe we're watching the same thing—it's ugliness to me, beauty to him.

That same contrast can be seen in how people view the death of Jesus. For Christians, the cross is a glorious display of God's love. It's where Jesus willingly gave his life as payment for our sins so we could be reconciled to God and have eternal life. While the death of Jesus was physically brutal, we see the beauty of its *significance*. At the same time, skeptics see the cross as a bloody event Christians have strangely turned into something worth celebrating. One ex-Christian pastor, for example, wrote a book called *Obsessed with Blood: The Crazy Things Christians Believe*. The book's description says:

> Christians are obsessed with blood! They sing about it, declare they are washed in it and even drink it! In this book you will discover the crazy background to this Christian obsession and the truth about the bloodthirsty God they claim to know and serve. . . . The stories of blood sacrifice in the Bible are just another example of Christianity propagating Bronze Age myths.[1]

It's not just skeptics who have trouble seeing the beauty in Jesus's sacrifice on the cross. Those who identify as "progressive" Christians often find the idea of Jesus shedding blood on our behalf troubling as well.[2] In an article on talking with kids about Easter, children's pastor (and progressive Christian) Anna Skates writes about why she doesn't want to teach kids that "Jesus died for you / your sins." She explains:

While I realize that statement won't psychologically damage every kid, if it damages ONE, it's not worth using. Period. To that end, I can list hundreds of people for whom this sentiment was harmful. We have to find better words and be VERY intentional with our language. And the reality is, Jesus didn't die specifically for your kid. I know that's a bit blunt but technically—Jesus died publicly and grotesquely because he was a political and religious threat to those in power.[3]

In part 3, we'll look at six questions that will help kids more deeply understand the cosmic significance of the cross. Yes, Jesus died a public and grotesque death. Yes, he was perceived to be a political and religious threat. But as we'll see, *there's so much more to this picture*—the most important picture in history. In a world that sees only the ugly, we need to help our kids see the beauty. As the apostle Paul wrote, "The message of the cross is foolishness to those who are perishing, but to us who are being saved it is the power of God" (1 Cor. 1:18).[4]

Three Keys to Impactful Conversations about the Death of Jesus

1. *Make sure your child understands the seriousness of sin*. Kids sometimes think of sin simply as "bad stuff" we do, but the significance of the cross cannot be appreciated without an understanding of the seriousness of sin. As you talk about sin, be sure to emphasize that it's no small thing. It's what separates us from God and is the fundamental problem in our world.

2. *Talk about Jesus's death in a way that's appropriate for your child's age and sensitivities*. Some kids (especially younger ones) can be particularly sensitive to the subject of death. But there's no need to avoid this section if that's the case

in your family—it's too important. You can talk factually about Jesus's death without discussing the gruesome details of crucifixion. Remember, it's okay for kids to feel sad that Jesus had to suffer. We just don't want to leave them there. Simultaneously emphasize the *beauty* of what the cross represents and that death wasn't the end for Jesus (we'll discuss the resurrection in part 4).

3. *Explain why we need to understand the statement "Jesus died for our sins" more deeply.* Older kids may think they already know what they need to about Jesus's death because they understand that Jesus "died for our sins." However, they likely don't realize how much theological depth underlies that statement. Before beginning these conversations, explain how important a deeper understanding of Jesus's death is for your child's faith and how frequently this subject is misunderstood by both Christians and nonbelievers today.

13. Did Jesus Predict His Violent Death and Resurrection?

Although I grew up in a Christian family and spent a lot of time at church in my childhood, I never read the Bible much myself. I knew the major stories in it and had memorized verses to earn Sunday school reward stickers, but I hadn't really *read* it. At some point after I graduated from college, I realized that was a problem and set out to read the New Testament.

I don't remember which Gospel I read first, but I remember being blown away when I encountered something I had never heard about in church: Jesus repeatedly predicted his violent death and resurrection. Wow! I thought this was incredible evidence that the resurrection was true and not simply made up by his followers. After all, if Jesus predicted his resurrection and then wasn't raised from the dead, it would have proved his claims to deity were false, and Christianity never would have started. Predicting something miraculous like a resurrection leaves no wiggle room for pretenders! But there's an assumption embedded in that logic that I didn't realize until I began engaging with skeptics: *that Jesus actually predicted his resurrection.*

The Gospels were written decades after Jesus's death, so critical scholars have long argued that these predictions were invented by the early church to support their claim that Jesus was raised from the dead. This, of course, assumes the resurrection didn't happen. If it *did*, Jesus was who he claimed to be (God) and would have had the supernatural foreknowledge to make such predictions. There would be little reason to question them.

Ultimately, therefore, the question of whether Jesus predicted his violent death and resurrection is closely related to the question of whether he was raised from the dead (we'll look at evidence for the resurrection in part 4). That said, we can also look at the prediction texts from the perspective of a historian. Aside from worldview assumptions about the plausibility of a resurrection, what evidence of historicity, if any, do these written accounts of Jesus's predictions have? (Note that this chapter is necessarily a bit more academic in nature, but the conversation guide will help you discuss the important points in a kid-friendly way.)

Marks of Historicity in the Prediction Texts

New Testament scholar and historian Michael Licona wrote a helpful study on Jesus's predictions for the *Journal for the Study of the Historical Jesus*.[1] In his article, Licona analyzes four of Jesus's predictions and shows how they exhibit specific marks of historicity. We'll look at those texts in a moment, but first we need to understand what "marks of historicity" are. Licona discusses several kinds, but in the interest of space, we'll focus on three:

1. *Multiple attestation.* An event is more likely to be historical when it's reported by multiple independent sources. Determining independence in the New Testament can be difficult, however. We have four different Gospels, but scholars don't

consider everything in them to be from four independent sources. For example, almost all scholars believe that Matthew and Luke drew some of their material from Mark. In those cases, the material is considered to be from a single source (Mark), even if it's contained in multiple Gospels. Let's say, however, that an event is reported in both Matthew and Mark, but it differs significantly in some respect. Scholars may then conclude that the accounts came from two independent sources (and Matthew wasn't just borrowing from Mark). Historians give more credibility to accounts that are "multiply attested" in this way.

2. *Early attestation.* The closer in time a source is to the event it relays, the more credibility historians give it. Something written hundreds of years after an event (with no evidence that it was based on a much earlier source) would not have this mark of historicity.

3. *Embarrassment.* When people lie or invent stories, they usually don't include material that causes them to look bad or lose credibility. If something embarrassing is included in an account, historians consider it more likely to be true.

With these criteria in mind, let's look at the four prediction texts Licona analyzes.

1. Jesus's Words after Peter's Confession (Matt. 16:21–25; Mark 8:31–35; Luke 9:22–24)

In chapter 2, we learned about the importance of Peter's confession that Jesus is the Messiah. Jesus's response to that confession was a warning about and a prediction of his coming suffering, death, and resurrection:

He then began to teach them that the Son of Man must suffer many things and be rejected by the elders, the chief priests and the teachers of the law, and that he must be killed and after three days rise again. He spoke plainly about this, and Peter took him aside and began to rebuke him. But when Jesus turned and looked at his disciples, he rebuked Peter. "Get behind me, Satan!" he said. "You do not have in mind the concerns of God, but merely human concerns." (Mark 8:31–33)

This prediction exhibits two key marks of historicity. First, it's multiply attested. The above quote is from Mark, but scholars believe that the accounts of the event contained in Matthew and Luke are from an independent source. Second, it meets the criterion of embarrassment. Peter rebuked Jesus, and Jesus rebuked Peter. If early Christians made this up, they wouldn't want to portray Jesus rebuking the man who was to become an important leader of the church.

2. Jesus's Conversation with the Disciples While Passing through Galilee (Matt. 17:22–23; Mark 9:30–32; Luke 9:44–55)

Another prediction occurred soon after the one we just looked at, as Jesus and the disciples passed through Galilee:

Jesus did not want anyone to know where they were, because he was teaching his disciples. He said to them, "The Son of Man is going to be delivered into the hands of men. They will kill him, and after three days he will rise." But they did not understand what he meant and were afraid to ask him about it. (Mark 9:30–32)

Scholars believe that these words of Jesus in Mark come from an even earlier source (for linguistic reasons that are more complex than what we can address here). This is an example of early attestation supporting the historicity of the account. It's from a source even closer in time to the event than Mark, and Mark is usually considered to be the earliest written Gospel.

3. The Last Supper (Matt. 26:21–32; Mark 14:18–28; Luke 22:15–20; see also 1 Cor. 11:24–25)

At the Last Supper, Jesus told the disciples that his body and blood were going to be broken and poured out for them—a prediction of his coming death (and its sacrificial nature). This is another event that is multiply attested, as scholars believe that Mark and Luke had independent sources for what they wrote. In addition, Paul references the event in 1 Corinthians. This is important because Paul wrote 1 Corinthians several years before Mark and Luke wrote their Gospels. This means that the event also meets the criterion of early attestation.

4. Jesus's Prayer in the Garden of Gethsemane (Matt. 26:36–46; Mark 14:32–40; Luke 22:39–46)

Jesus's prayer and discussion with his disciples in the garden of Gethsemane show that he knew a violent death was coming. He was "deeply distressed and troubled" (Mark 14:33), saying that his soul was "overwhelmed with sorrow to the point of death" (Matt. 26:38). He prayed, "Abba, Father . . . everything is possible for you. Take this cup from me. Yet not what I will, but what you will" (Mark 14:36). The nature of this account would have been embarrassing to the early church—not something they would have invented—because it wouldn't inspire others to "take up their own cross and follow him if they wanted to be his disciples."[2] The account, therefore, given the criterion of embarrassment, has a mark of historicity.

Several other passages contain predictions of Jesus's violent death and/or resurrection, but they don't have specific marks of historicity. That doesn't imply they're *not* historical; they just don't meet the kinds of criteria historians like to have to corroborate an account. However, the historical support we have for at least *some* of the predictions lends credibility to the others. For further research, I encourage you to look up the following additional texts:

- Jesus says he will give his life as "a ransom for many" (Mark 10:45).
- Jesus implies he will die in Jerusalem, as prophets do (Luke 13:32–33).
- Jesus says the Son of Man must be "lifted up" (predicting his death on a cross; John 3:13–14; 8:28; 12:32–34).
- Jesus tells the disciples not to share about the transfiguration until the Son of Man has "been raised from the dead" (Matt. 17:9; see also Mark 9:9–10).
- Jesus tells the parable of the tenants, which foretells his death, resurrection, and vindication (Matt. 21:33–46; Mark 12:1–12; Luke 20:9–19).
- Jesus says he will be in "the heart of the earth" for three days and three nights, just as Jonah was in the belly of a fish for that amount of time (Matt. 12:38–40; 16:2–4; Luke 11:29–30).
- Jesus speaks of himself as a temple that will be destroyed but raised again in three days (John 2:18–22; see also Matt. 26:61–62; Mark 14:58; 15:29).

So Why Didn't Jesus's Followers Expect His Death and Resurrection?

Before we conclude, we should acknowledge that these predictions raise an important question. If Jesus repeatedly told his followers what was going to happen, why were they so confused leading up to the crucifixion and shocked when the risen Jesus appeared to them?

The most likely reason is that they had a very different idea in mind for what would happen to the Messiah (see chapter 2). Their expectations didn't include a violent death and/or a resurrection three days later. Most Jews believed in a *general* resurrection of the righteous at the end of time, but they didn't expect the resurrection of individuals before then. The writers of the texts even admit the confusion of the disciples regarding the predictions. After the transfiguration, for example, Jesus ordered the disciples not to tell anyone what they had seen until "the Son of Man had risen from the dead." The text then says that the disciples "kept the matter to themselves, discussing what 'rising from the dead' meant" (Mark 9:9–10; see also 9:32). We see this even more explicitly in John 2:18–22. After Jesus cleared the temple courts, the people asked him for a sign that he had the authority to do so. Jesus replied, "Destroy this temple, and I will raise it again in three days" (v. 19). The text explains that the temple he spoke of was his body and says, "After he was raised from the dead, his disciples recalled what he had said. Then they believed the scripture and the words that Jesus had spoken" (v. 22). In other words, the resurrection clarified many things Jesus had said that the disciples hadn't necessarily understood before, given their expectations. Many things made sense in *retrospect*.

In this chapter, we've seen that there's good reason to believe that Jesus predicted his violent death and resurrection. This has particular importance for the discussion we'll have in chapter 15: Did Jesus die willingly? But before we get there, we need to look at one more question for context. We'll turn now to the relationship between Old Testament animal sacrifices and Jesus.

KEY POINTS

- Historians use criteria such as multiple attestation, early attestation, and embarrassment to help determine the historicity of reported events.

- Four prediction texts that exhibit specific marks of historicity include (1) Jesus's words after Peter's confession, (2) Jesus's conversation with the disciples while passing through Galilee, (3) the Last Supper, and (4) Jesus's prayer in the garden of Gethsemane.
- The historical support we have for at least some of Jesus's predictions lends credibility to the others.
- Despite Jesus's predictions, the disciples were confused leading up to the crucifixion and shocked when the risen Jesus appeared to them. This is most likely because they had very different expectations for what would happen to the Messiah.

CONVERSATION GUIDE

Open the Conversation

- If a friend predicted they were going to throw a ball in the next ten seconds, then they did so, would you be impressed with their prediction? Why or why not? *(No, because they could choose to fulfill that prediction.)*
- If a friend predicted there would be a car accident in the world tomorrow, then there was one, would you be impressed with *that* prediction? Why or why not? *(No, because car accidents regularly happen, so there was an extremely high chance the prediction would come true in the chain of normal events.)*

Advance the Conversation

- According to the Gospels, Jesus predicted his resurrection multiple times. How is that different from the two kinds of predictions we just talked about? *(A resurrection is a miracle—something extraordinary God would have to cause—so no mere human could simply choose to make it happen.)*

- If Jesus predicted his resurrection and wasn't resurrected, what would that have told his followers? *(He wasn't God, because he had been wrong.)*
- Because the Gospels were written years after Jesus's death, some people think that the early Christian church invented Jesus's predictions. But read Mark 8:27–33. Historians point out that the early church wouldn't have *wanted* to invent this account. Why do you think that is? *(Discuss the criterion of embarrassment and how it applies here. Explain the other two criteria and that multiple prediction texts have these marks of historicity. For deeper discussion, look up several prediction texts listed in this chapter.)*
- When the risen Jesus first appeared to the disciples, they were shocked. If Jesus really had predicted his resurrection, why do you think they were still so surprised? *(Read Mark 9:30–32. The disciples didn't fully understand what Jesus had meant until after the resurrection had taken place.)*

Apply the Conversation

- An atheist blogger wrote, "I believe that the only reason that conservative Christians believe [Jesus predicted his death and resurrection and it wasn't later invented] is because conservative Christians so desperately want these 'prophecies' to be true. In any other situation, not involving their faith, I would bet they would never believe any prediction written in a book published years after the event predicted had already taken place."[3] How would you respond?

14. What's the Relationship between Old Testament Animal Sacrifices and Jesus's Death?

Children's Bibles all tend to feature the same stories—usually the ones that are easy to understand and correspond nicely with glossy pictures. You'll surely find Adam and Eve, Noah's ark, Joseph with his multicolored coat, and Daniel in the lions' den. But what you probably won't find is an explanation of animal sacrifices in the Old Testament and how they relate to Jesus's death on the cross.

I understand why this is the case, of course. Kids can find the whole idea of God commanding the killing of animals to be quite disturbing. In fact, I remember when my animal-loving daughter first heard about these sacrifices, because her reaction was one of shock and sadness. She responded, "That's terrible! Doesn't God love animals? He created them!" Avoiding the subject isn't the solution, however, for two reasons. First, this topic is important. Many of the ways that Jesus's death is explained in the New Testament don't make sense without a basic understanding of the Old Testament sacrificial system. Second, this isn't an intuitive subject that kids will just "get" on their own. And when kids don't have an accurate understanding of the meaning and the role of sacrifice in the Bible, it can lead to all kinds of unfortunate interpretations. The internet, for example, is filled with articles on how God is a crazy, bloodthirsty deity who ultimately sought a human sacrifice in Jesus. We'll come back to that idea and deal with related challenges in the next chapter. But first, in this chapter, we'll establish an understanding of the sacrificial system within a biblical context.

Sin Is the Big Problem

In Genesis 1, we read that God created everything and that it was "very good." By Genesis 3, however, things had gone south. God had told Adam and Eve they could enjoy everything in the garden of Eden except for fruit from the tree of the knowledge of good and evil (Gen. 2:16–17). If they ate from it, they would die. We all know how that story ended. Eve was tempted by the serpent and ate from the tree, and then Adam did as well. This is when sin entered the world—an event known as the fall. The story of the fall is so familiar to most kids that it's easy for them to lose sight of its theological importance: the fall is *the* event that sets the stage for understanding everything that follows. The rest of Scripture is the story of God's plan to redeem humankind from slavery to sin and ultimately restore creation.

Despite this biblical emphasis, today's culture greatly trivializes the idea of sin, and it's important to understand why. Recall from chapter 7 that the definition of sin is the transgression of God's moral law. *If God didn't exist, the concept of sin would be meaningless—there would be no divine moral law to transgress.* For Christians, the sin that separates us from our Creator and Sustainer is the fundamental problem of human existence. For a secular, godless society, sin doesn't even exist. It's not hard to see why biblical solutions to the problem of sin are seen as foolishness in the eyes of skeptics: they don't believe there's a problem to begin with. Therefore, any sacrifices for sin—in the Old *or* the New Testament—sound unnecessary at best and ridiculous at worst. But within the biblical context (discussed in chapter 7) that (1) God exists; (2) God is holy, loving, and just; (3) God gave us a moral law; (4) all people have that law written on their hearts; (5) all people are guilty of breaking that law; (6) this has resulted in our relational separation from God; and (7) the punishment for sin is death, *sacrifice in order to pay for sin and restore relationship with God is both coherent and meaningful.* To see why, let's start with the Old Testament.

Sacrifice in the Old Testament

Moses led the Israelites to Mount Sinai after their escape from Egyptian slavery. There God gave them the Ten Commandments, directed them to build a tabernacle, and instructed them on the rules of sacrificial worship. The primary purpose of the sacrificial system was to *atone* for the sins of the people. To make atonement is to satisfy someone or something for an offense committed. In this case, sacrifices were to satisfy God for the offense of sin. (The importance of atonement was discussed in chapter 7.)

There were five types of sacrifices, each used for a different purpose throughout the year. Most of them involved animals, though some involved grains or breads. The burnt offering was used as a general atonement for sin and required the sacrifice of a bull, sheep, goat, dove, or pigeon (Lev. 1:1–17). The animal's blood was drained, and the priest sprinkled the blood on the sides of the altar. The body was then cut into pieces and consumed in a fire. The sprinkled blood symbolized that the life of an innocent animal had been taken to pay for the sins of a guilty human (Lev. 17:11)—a payment required because God had established the penalty for sin as death (Gen. 2:17). God's mercy and love allowed this substitute so humans wouldn't have to give their own lives. It was a vivid reminder of both the severity of sin and the goodness of God.

An important part of the sacrificial system was the annual Day of Atonement (Lev. 16). On this day, the high priest washed himself, wore special clothing, burned incense, and brought sacrificial blood to atone for the sins of himself, his family, and the people of Israel. It was the only time during the year that he was allowed to enter the Holy of Holies—the sacred space for God's presence in the inner chamber of the tabernacle (and later of the temple in Jerusalem). In addition to making sacrifices, the high priest would place his hands on the head of a goat, symbolically transfer the sins of the community to the goat, and send it into the wilderness to "remove" sin from Israel (this is where we get the term *scapegoat*). With this action, the Israelites were assured that their sins were forgiven (Lev. 16:30).

All of this admittedly sounds quite strange to us today, but animal sacrifices were common throughout the ancient Near East. God used a familiar practice and transformed its meaning for the Israelites. Whereas other cultures typically believed they were offering food to capricious gods to gain favor, the Israelites sacrificed for atonement and reconciliation with God. The practice may have *looked* similar, but it had a very different purpose. Still, most of us are happy we don't have to kill goats today. And there is a good reason we don't have to anymore: Jesus.

How Do Old Testament Sacrifices Relate to Jesus?

The Old Testament sacrificial system served as a remarkable foreshadowing of the purpose and effects of Jesus's death. Hebrews 10 offers a beautiful commentary on this relationship. We'll use selected passages from it to highlight three points to understand.

1. The Law and Sacrificial System Was a Temporary Plan That Existed to Point Forward to Jesus

The sacrificial system was never intended to be permanent. Its inadequacy is seen in the fact that sacrifices had to be repeated each year. That's because animal sacrifices don't actually remove sin. They were only a placeholder in history until a permanent sacrifice could be made:

> The law is only a shadow of the good things that are coming—not the realities themselves. For this reason it can never, by the same sacrifices repeated endlessly year after year, make perfect those who draw near to worship. Otherwise, would they not have stopped being offered? For the worshipers would have been cleansed once for all, and would no longer have felt guilty for their sins. But those sacrifices are an annual reminder of sins. It is impossible for the blood of bulls and goats to take away sins. (Heb. 10:1–4)

2. Jesus Was the Perfect and Therefore Final Sacrifice

Jesus lived a sinless *human* life, so he was able to become a perfect substitute for us in his death—something an animal could never do. This is why we no longer sacrifice animals. The blood Jesus shed on the cross was the first perfect sacrifice, making it the *final* sacrifice needed for the cleansing of sin:

> We have been made holy through the sacrifice of the body of Jesus Christ once for all. Day after day every priest stands and performs his religious duties; again and again he offers the same sacrifices, which can never take away sins. But when this priest had offered for all time one sacrifice for sins, he sat down at the right hand of God, and since that time he waits for his enemies to be made his footstool. For by one sacrifice he has made perfect forever those who are being made holy. (Heb. 10:10–14)

3. We Now Have Full Access to God

Recall from earlier in this chapter that only the high priest could approach God through the Holy of Holies and only once per year on the Day of Atonement. This room was separated from the outer chamber by a heavy veil, representing the barrier that existed between humankind and God. Jesus's death removed that barrier so we can now approach God directly:

> Therefore, brothers and sisters, since we have confidence to enter the Most Holy Place by the blood of Jesus, by a new and living way opened for us through the curtain, that is, his body, and since we have a great priest over the house of God, let us draw near to God with a sincere heart and with the full assurance that faith brings, having our hearts sprinkled to cleanse us from a guilty conscience and having our bodies washed with pure water. (Heb. 10:19–22)

At the moment Jesus died, "the curtain of the temple was torn in two from top to bottom" (Matt. 27:51). The symbolism of this event was powerful: the final sacrifice had been made, and a veil no longer separated people from God. Jesus, as the ultimate high priest and through the perfect sacrifice of his own body, permanently gave us direct access to God himself (see also Heb. 9:11–14).

Now that we have a basic understanding of sacrifice in its biblical context, we can go on in chapter 15 to address some common challenges and misunderstandings regarding Jesus's death.

KEY POINTS

- Without a proper understanding of the existence and severity of sin, biblical solutions to that problem (such as sacrifice) will not make sense.

153

- The primary purpose of the sacrificial system in the Old Testament was to atone for the sins of the people.
- The sprinkled blood of sacrifices symbolized that the life of an innocent animal had been taken to pay for the sins of a guilty human—a payment required because God had established the penalty for sin as death. God's mercy and love allowed this substitute so humans wouldn't have to give their own lives.
- The sacrificial system was a temporary plan that pointed forward to Jesus.
- Jesus lived a sinless *human* life, so he was able to become a perfect, final substitute for us in his death—something an animal could never do. This is why we no longer sacrifice animals.

CONVERSATION GUIDE

Open the Conversation

- One of the first things the Bible tells us about is the creation of Adam and Eve and how they disobeyed God's command not to eat from a tree in the garden of Eden. Do you think this account is an important part of the Bible? Why or why not? *(Review the details of the fall and explain that the entry of sin into the world provides the backdrop for the rest of the Bible.)*

Advance the Conversation

- After Moses led the Israelites out of Egyptian slavery, God gave them laws for how to live as a new nation. Some of these laws instructed them on how to sacrifice animals to pay for their sins. Why do you think God asked them to do that? *(Explain how the sacrificial system worked. The penalty for sin is death, but God in his mercy and love allowed an animal substitute so humans wouldn't have to give their own lives.)*

- Read Hebrews 10:10. The Bible tells us that Jesus's death was a perfect, *final* sacrifice—we no longer need to sacrifice animals to pay for sin. What do you think made Jesus's death different from an animal's death for sin? *(Jesus lived a sinless human life, so he was able to become a perfect substitute for us in his death—something an animal could never do. Explain that animal sacrifices were always meant to be temporary and that Jesus's death gave us full access to God.)*

Apply the Conversation

- Someone asked online, "Why [do] many religions require a sacrifice (an animal, a lamb, a cow, [etc.]) in God's name? Is he happy that we kill another creature that he created?"[1] How would you respond from the Christian perspective?

15. Did Jesus Die Willingly?

In the previous chapter, we learned how Jesus's death provided a needed sacrifice to make us right with God. That's certainly good news for us! But was it good news for *Jesus*—the one who had to suffer so much on the cross? Or was he a victim, like the innocent animals killed for hundreds of years, with no choice but to die for the sins of others? If so, what does that say about the character of God?

These are questions that have come to the forefront of discussion among skeptics and even some Christians today. For example, William Paul Young, author of the bestselling book *The Shack*, says in his lesser-known book, *Lies We Believe about God*:

> Who originated the Cross? If God did, then we worship a cosmic abuser, who in Divine Wisdom created a means to torture human beings in the most painful and abhorrent manner. Frankly, it is often this very cruel and monstrous god that the atheist refuses to acknowledge or grant credibility in any sense. And rightly so. Better no god at all, than this one.[1]

This kind of argument can be found in many forms. Among skeptics, the type of "cosmic abuse" is typically alleged to be human sacrifice. They claim that if Jesus's death was sacrificial in nature, as Christians believe, then it implies that God likes human sacrifice and isn't worthy of worship (if he exists). We'll start by answering this specific challenge from skeptics, then we'll address the theological problems that Christians sometimes have with the idea that Jesus's death was a sacrifice for sin.

What God Says about Human Sacrifice

The nations that surrounded ancient Israel practiced human sacrifice in the worship of their deities. *But God explicitly, repeatedly, and clearly condemns all such activity in the Bible.* Deuteronomy 12:31 states, "You must not worship the LORD your God in their way, because in worshiping their gods, they do all kinds of detestable things the LORD hates. They even burn their sons and daughters in the fire as sacrifices to their gods" (see also Deut. 18:10). Unfortunately, the Israelites didn't always listen to God's commands, and we later see that child sacrifice in *Israel* was one reason God exiled them from the land (Ezek. 16:20–22). Although God's stance on human sacrifice is clear from passages like these, skeptics often take other passages out of context to suggest otherwise. In most cases, the passages they point to are merely *describing* something that happened historically, not *prescribing* the practice (see 2 Kings 17:17; 21:6; 23:10; Ps. 106:37–38; Isa. 57:5–6; Jer. 7:31).[2]

Perhaps the most frequently misunderstood account related to human sacrifice in the Bible is that of God asking Abraham to sacrifice his son Isaac (Gen. 22:1–18). At first glance, those words appear to contradict everything I just wrote. Yes, God asked Abraham to sacrifice his son. *But he didn't allow him to actually do it.* The request was a test of Abraham's faith because Isaac was his only son and God had promised a multitude of descendants *through* that son (v. 1). Willingly offering Isaac for sacrifice would demonstrate Abraham's faith that God wouldn't break his promises, even if their fulfillment sounded impossible given what God was asking.

But when Abraham was about to sacrifice Isaac, God stopped him and instead provided a ram caught by its horns in a thicket (v. 13). God ultimately showed Abraham that he didn't want a human sacrifice. He tested Abraham's faith, then provided a substitute. At the time, that substitute was an animal. Two thousand years later, it was God's own Son. Far from condoning human sacrifice, the story of Abraham and Isaac is a remarkable foreshadowing of the death of Jesus.

Jesus *Willingly* Gave His Life

We can now turn to the theological concerns progressive Christians often have with Jesus being a sacrifice for our sins. They sometimes specifically label this idea cosmic *child* abuse, referring to the relationship between God the Father and Jesus his son. To understand the nature of Jesus's death—and why the charge of "cosmic child abuse" doesn't hold up—it's helpful to remember three P's: Jesus's death was *planned*, *purposeful*, and *personal*.

Planned: Jesus Knew That He Would Suffer and Die

In chapter 13, we saw that Jesus predicted his violent death and resurrection multiple times; he said he "must" suffer and die. This shows that Jesus didn't just happen to end up in the wrong hands. There was no stroke of bad luck or shocking surprise. He knew that his death was part of the plan, even announcing on the way to Jerusalem that his "appointed time" was near (Matt. 26:18). When Jesus was arrested and Peter attempted to defend him by the sword, Jesus responded, "Do you think I cannot call on my Father, and he will at once put at my disposal more than twelve legions of angels? But how then would the Scriptures be fulfilled that say it must happen in this way? . . . But this has all taken place that the writings of the prophets might be fulfilled" (vv. 53–54,

56). Jesus clearly viewed the cross as part of a necessary plan for the prophesied Messiah.

Purposeful: Jesus Knew Why He Would Suffer and Die

Jesus knew not only *that* he would die but also *why* he would die: "The Son of Man did not come to be served, but to serve, and to give his life as a ransom for many" (Mark 10:45). A ransom is a payment to release someone from something. *Jesus came to release us from sin by paying our debt* (see also Rom. 5:8–9; 1 Pet. 2:24; 3:18). In saying that he came to give his life as a ransom for many, he identified himself with the suffering servant of Isaiah 53:4–6 who was "pierced for our transgressions"—a messianic prophecy:

> Surely he has borne our griefs
> and carried our sorrows;
> yet we esteemed him stricken,
> smitten by God, and afflicted.
> But he was pierced for our transgressions;
> he was crushed for our iniquities;
> upon him was the chastisement that brought us peace,
> and with his wounds we are healed.
> All we like sheep have gone astray;
> we have turned—every one—to his own way;
> and the LORD has laid on him
> the iniquity of us all. (ESV)

This shows that the idea of Jesus being a sacrifice for sin wasn't some tangential add-on to Christian belief over the centuries. It was Jesus's self-identified *purpose* for coming.

Personal: Jesus Chose to Die

Just because Jesus knew (1) it was the plan for him to die and (2) why he would die, this doesn't necessarily mean he died *willingly*. But the Bible clearly shows that this was indeed the case. Jesus wasn't forced to do something by an "abusive Father" but rather *personally chose* to "lay down" his life:

- "I am the good shepherd. The good shepherd lays down his life for the sheep. . . . Just as the Father knows me and I know the Father—and I lay down my life for the sheep" (John 10:11, 15; see also 15:13).
- "The reason my Father loves me is that I lay down my life— only to take it up again. No one takes it from me, but I lay it down of my own accord. I have authority to lay it down and authority to take it up again. This command I received from my Father" (John 10:17–18).

People sometimes press the abuse point further and say that those who "choose" to be victims are still victims. But that brings us to a final, crucial point that requires theological clarity about who Jesus is. Recall from chapter 6 that the Bible affirms (1) there is one God, (2) God is three distinct persons, and (3) each person is fully God. This means that God didn't sacrifice a random human being who happened to be a willing victim. Jesus is fully God, so he sacrificed his *own* life as payment for sin. Yes, Jesus is fully human, and, yes, he's the Son in the Trinity, but to compare his death to child abuse is to disregard this essential point and turn God's great act of love for the world into something morally atrocious.

But Why Did Jesus Think He Was Forsaken by God?

When Jesus took his last breaths on the cross, he cried out, "My God, my God, why have you forsaken me?" (Matt. 27:46). This initially seems to contradict what we've discussed. Despite how this sounds, however, something much deeper is going on here.

Jesus's cry quoted the first words of Psalm 22. King David had written those words of anguish a thousand years earlier, and Jesus intentionally identified with them on the cross. David wrote how his enemies pierced his hands and feet, how his bones were on display, and how lots were cast for his garments. The same things happened to Jesus. But, importantly, the psalm ends with victory.

> You who fear the LORD, praise him!
>   All you offspring of Jacob, glorify him,
>   and stand in awe of him, all you offspring of Israel!
> For he has not despised or abhorred
>   the affliction of the afflicted,
> and he has not hidden his face from him,
>   but has heard, when he cried to him. . . .
> All the ends of the earth shall remember
>   and turn to the LORD,
> and all the families of the nations
>   shall worship before you.
> For kingship belongs to the LORD,
>   and he rules over the nations. (vv. 23–24, 27–28 ESV)

Jesus's cry wasn't one of confusion or a search for answers he didn't have. It wasn't the mark of someone being victimized by a cruel father. It was a scriptural reference to let us know that despite the anguish he *willingly* took on, the Messiah's story ends in victory.

KEY POINTS

- God explicitly, repeatedly, and clearly condemns human sacrifice in the Bible.
- Jesus's death was planned, purposeful, and personal. He knew *that* he would die, he knew *why* he would die, and he *chose* to die.

- Jesus is fully God, so he sacrificed his *own* life as payment for sin.
- Jesus's cry on the cross was a reference to Psalm 22. It showed that despite his anguish, the story ends in victory.

CONVERSATION GUIDE

Open the Conversation

- In the previous chapter, we learned why God asked for animal sacrifices in the Old Testament and how Jesus's death was a perfect, final sacrifice for us. But do you think that Jesus *wanted* to sacrifice himself for sin? Why or why not? *(Help your child consider why the question matters. If Jesus didn't go to the cross willingly, it means he was a helpless victim like animals were.)*

Advance the Conversation

- Do you think it's possible that Jesus ended up dying on the cross because of bad luck—for example, because he was in the wrong place at the wrong time? *(No. Jesus predicted his death multiple times and claimed that it was part of a plan with a purpose—to give his life for us. Read Mark 10:45.)*
- Read John 10:11, 15, and 17–18. What do these verses tell us about Jesus's willingness to go to the cross? *(It was his choice.)*
- In ancient cultures, people killed their own children as a sacrifice to keep the gods they believed in happy. Some people today compare Jesus's sacrifice on the cross to those ancient child sacrifices and claim that Jesus's death means God is cruel. How are these two kinds of sacrifices different? *(Jesus wasn't a victim of someone else's choice because he's God himself; he chose to sacrifice his own life. Review the nature of the Trinity if*

needed. Read the passages condemning human sacrifice in the Bible and explain the account of Abraham and Isaac.)

- When Jesus took his last breaths on the cross, he cried out, "My God, my God, why have you forsaken me?" (Matt. 27:46). Why do you think he said that if he willingly died for us? *(Explain that this was a reference to Psalm 22, which begins with anguish—as in the cross—and ends in victory—as in the resurrection. Read the psalm together.)*

Apply the Conversation

- How would you respond to William Paul Young's quote from the beginning of this chapter?

16. What Did Jesus's Death Accomplish?

A few weeks ago, I decided to introduce my kids to the movie *The Sound of Music*. Yes, it's a bit cheesy, but I thought they would enjoy the music, scenery, and real-life story. My son made it only through the first song before deciding the movie would be as enjoyable as getting teeth pulled (understandable, I suppose, for a ten-year-old boy). But my daughters soaked it up.

What I hadn't realized going into it, however, was that there's a lot of background information that needs explaining in order for a ten-year-old and an eight-year-old to comprehend what's going on. First, they had no idea what an abbey is, and that's where the movie opens. That alone required a ten-minute discussion. From there we had to stop multiple times to discuss things such as what World War II was, the relationship between Germany and Austria during that time, how Hitler could come to power, the courtship process of the upper class, and why some people would be embarrassed by their kids playing in clothes made out of curtains.

Fast-forward to last week. My younger daughter watched *The Sound of Music* in her second-grade music class. I laughed when she told me, given our experience watching it a few weeks earlier. I asked her, "How on earth did you guys do that? There's no way second graders would understand that movie without constantly stopping for explanation like we did!" She replied, "Oh, they all understood it. Well, kind of. I don't think they *really* understood what was going on, but they understood it in their own ways."

I can only imagine what some of those interpretations of *The Sound of Music* must have been like! But no matter what any given second grader *thought* was going on, an objective reality exists. Someone may have *thought* World War II was a battle between unicorn armies, but the fact remains that it was something very different. In the same way, Christians today sometimes reduce the significance of Jesus's death on the cross to whatever it means to *them*. They don't necessarily believe that his death had an *objective* meaning that's true for all people. But the Bible tells us that Jesus's death indeed accomplished some very specific, objective things.

What Did Jesus's Death Accomplish?

When people treat the cross as an open-to-interpretation historical event, they usually do so at the expense of foundational biblical truths such as the existence and severity of sin, the nature of God, and the need for atonement. One pastor (who identifies herself as a "21st Century Progressive Christian Pastor"), for example, says:

> We are not fallen creatures. We are evolving creatures. Jesus did not die upon the cross to save us from God's wrath, Jesus died on the cross because he threatened the powers that be and because he was willing to live for what he believed in. Because he chose love over hate, good over evil, and refused to take up the sword, Jesus threatened the status quo and the powers that be chose to execute him. Jesus didn't die for our sins. Jesus lived for the things he believed in. Jesus lived for love and loved so greatly that he was willing to die for that love and in dying Jesus showed us that love never dies.[1]

These words ignore and misconstrue what the Bible explicitly states about Jesus's death. Much could be said in this chapter, but we'll focus on six particularly important things to understand about what Jesus's death accomplished.

1. Jesus's Death Atoned for Our Sins

The atonement for sin is primarily what we've discussed so far in part 3. Jesus's death accomplished many things, but our understanding of it must start with the atonement, as other truths flow from this reality. As we learned in chapter 14, the need for atonement was established long before Jesus with the Old Testament sacrificial system. God put that system in place to teach people that sin is real, sin is serious, and sin separates us from him, leading to death. But God, in his mercy and love, allowed animals to die in place of sinful humans. As we saw, this entire system pointed forward to Jesus's death on the cross as the final, perfect sacrifice. To say that Jesus didn't die for our sins is to ignore (1) this core biblical story line, (2) the planned, purposeful, and personal nature of Jesus's death that we learned about in chapter 15, (3) large sections of the book of Hebrews, and (4) Jesus's own words: "The Son of Man did not come to be served, but to serve, and to give his life as a ransom for many" (Mark 10:45).

2. Jesus's Death Removed Us from the Curse of the Law

In Galatians 3:10, Paul writes that those who rely on the works of the (Old Testament) law for their justification before God are cursed by it (see Deut. 27:26). He says this because a person must follow the law perfectly to be justified by it, and *no one* can follow the law perfectly, leaving us all condemned. Because Jesus atoned for our sins, however, we are no longer under this "curse" of the need for perfection. Galatians 3:13–14 says:

Christ redeemed us from the curse of the law by becoming a curse for us, for it is written: "Cursed is everyone who is hung on a pole." He redeemed us in order that the blessing given to Abraham might come to the Gentiles through Christ Jesus, so that by faith we might receive the promise of the Spirit.

Thankfully, we don't have to keep the law to become right with God. We are now justified by our faith in Jesus (Gal. 2:16; see chapter 28 for more on salvation).

3. Jesus's Death Reconciled Us to God

Our sins separated us from God, but now that our sins have been paid for, that relationship can be restored. Paul explains this reconciliation in Colossians 1:19–22:

For God was pleased to have all his fullness dwell in him, and through him to reconcile to himself all things, whether things on earth or things in heaven, by making peace through his blood, shed on the cross. Once you were alienated from God and were enemies in your minds because of your evil behavior. But now he has reconciled you by Christ's physical body through death to present you holy in his sight, without blemish and free from accusation.

Similarly, Paul writes in Romans 5:10 that "while we were God's enemies, we were reconciled to him through the death of his Son." By God's initiative, the work of the cross made peace between us possible.

4. Jesus's Death Demonstrated God's Love

I went through a time in my life when I really questioned whether God loves us. After all, Scripture doesn't talk about God's love on page after page, yet God's love is often the primary message we hear about in church. I struggled to reconcile those facts until I was reading the book of John one day. The most famous verse in the Bible suddenly jumped off the page:

> For God so loved the world that he gave his one and only Son, that whoever believes in him shall not perish but have eternal life. (John 3:16)

For God so loved the world . . . Those words caught my attention in a way they never had before. The answer to my searching became clear for the first time based on how that sentence ends. God's love for us was ultimately demonstrated by Jesus's death on the cross—a sacrificial act that enabled us to have eternal life with him (see also Rom. 5:8). I had never really seen Jesus's death as an act of *love* before, just a fact of what he had done. It was life changing to internalize that the God of the universe loved us so much that he wanted to be with us forever and was willing to humble himself to the point of death on a cross to make that possible (Phil. 2:8). If we're looking for a cutesy, Valentine's Day kind of love in the Bible, we won't find it. But if we're looking for the love of a holy God, we'll find it on the cross.

5. Jesus's Death Defeated the Power of Satan

When Jesus began his earthly ministry, he faced Satan's temptations in the wilderness (Luke 4:1–13). In obeying his Father rather than succumbing to sin, Jesus dealt a blow to the powers of darkness. This battle continued throughout his ministry, culminating in victory:

> He forgave us all our sins, having canceled the charge of our legal indebtedness, which stood against us and condemned us; he has taken it away, nailing it to the cross. And having disarmed the powers

and authorities, he made a public spectacle of them, triumphing over them by the cross. (Col. 2:13–15)

Satan remains active in the world because the kingdom of God is not yet fully present (1 Pet. 5:8), but the cross ensured the end to Satan's story: the lake of fire (Rev. 20:10). When Jesus died for our sins, Satan lost the ability to accuse us of guilt before God. No one who puts their trust in Jesus will perish with him.

6. Jesus's Death Gave Us Eternal Life

God has set "eternity in the human heart" (Eccles. 3:11); we know this life is brief and we long for something more. Jesus's death is what made that "something more" possible for us. John 1:12 says, "To all who did receive him, to those who believed in his name, he gave the right to become children of God." As children of God, we will not perish but will have an eternal life more wonderful than we can imagine: "'What no eye has seen, what no ear has heard, and what no human mind has conceived'—the things God has prepared for those who love him" (1 Cor. 2:9).

What Jesus accomplished on the cross is too important to leave to our subjective interpretations. Those interpretations are meaningless if not rooted in what actually happened. The Bible makes it clear that Jesus accomplished several very important, *objective* things through his death.

KEY POINTS

- Christians today sometimes reduce the significance of Jesus's death on the cross to whatever it means to *them*. But the Bible tells us that Jesus's death accomplished some very specific, objective things.

169

- Jesus's death atoned for our sins, removed us from the curse of the law, reconciled us to God, demonstrated God's love, defeated the power of Satan, and gave us eternal life.

CONVERSATION GUIDE

Open the Conversation

- Based on what we've learned so far in part 3, what is one major thing Jesus accomplished on the cross? *(His death atoned for our sins. Review how the Old Testament sacrificial system pointed forward to Jesus.)*

Advance the Conversation

- Describe a time when you felt like you had to be more perfect than you were able to be—at home, school, church, or somewhere else. How did it make you feel? *(Read Galatians 3:10. Explain that Jesus's death removed the "curse" of needing to follow the Old Testament law perfectly in order to be made right with God. No one can do that.)*
- Read Colossians 1:21–22. This tells us something else that Jesus accomplished on the cross. What is it? *(Explain what reconciliation means and why it matters that we can now be at peace with God.)*
- If a friend asked you to explain how Jesus's death on the cross shows God's love for us, what would you say? *(The God of the universe loved us so much that he wanted to be with us forever and was willing to humble himself to the point of death on a cross to make that possible.)*
- The Bible tells us that Jesus's death defeated Satan. How do you think it did that? *(When Jesus died for our sins, Satan lost the ability to accuse us of guilt before God. Read 1 Corinthians*

2:9 and discuss how those who put their trust in Jesus will have eternal life.)

Apply the Conversation

- How would you respond to the pastor quoted at the beginning of this chapter regarding her beliefs about the meaning of Jesus's death?

17. If Jesus Is God, How Could He Die?

A few months ago, my kids and I were talking about the hope we have as Christians for eternal life. I was asking them various questions about why this hope even matters and what makes it possible. Even though these are fairly basic points, I find it helpful to periodically ask these kinds of questions to see where my kids are in their understanding. It's been encouraging to watch their answers develop depth over time—and it's been helpful to see where some clarification is needed.

When I asked what makes eternal life possible, my daughter answered, "Because God died on the cross for us!" Without much consideration, I restated her answer with a correction. "Yes, because *Jesus* died on the cross for us." She quickly countered, "Well, Jesus is God, so God died on the cross."

Admittedly, I wasn't sure how best to respond at that moment. Technically, she was right—Jesus is fully God, so in some sense, God died on the cross. But at the same time, that statement can lead to some theological confusion. I didn't have the mental energy to flesh out the issues in our conversation, so I let the subject lie. There are good reasons, however, to make sure kids understand why it's important to be precise with our language about Jesus's death on the cross.

Did God Die on the Cross?

The problem with my daughter's statement was that she didn't qualify what she meant by *God*. Most of the time when we say "God" in everyday language, we're referring to the Triune God in his entire being. In this sense, it's inaccurate to say that God died on the cross. *Neither God the Father nor God the Holy Spirit took on a human nature and lived on earth.* Only God the Son—Jesus—lived a human existence and could, therefore, die a human death.

We can't leave our understanding there, however. In what *sense* did Jesus die, given that he's fully human and fully God? First, regarding his humanity, it's important to remember that Christians believe death is only a transition. When we die, our soul separates from our body and we continue living, albeit in a different state; our human nature continues to exist. Similarly, when Jesus died, he said, "It is finished," then bowed his head and "gave up his spirit" (John 19:30). Since Jesus had a human nature, that human nature continues to exist just as ours does after physical death (more on what the Bible says about his continued humanity in a moment). Second, Jesus's physical death had no impact on his *divine* nature. He didn't cease to be fully God just because he physically died. This means that his divine nature continues to exist as well. Jesus will remain fully God and fully human forever.

With that said, we can now understand the problem with saying that God—in an unqualified sense—died on the cross. God, as the necessary, eternal, Triune being, can never die (1 Tim. 1:17). If God (the Triune being) ceased to exist, the universe would cease to exist as well! But God the Son could *physically* die as the one member of the Trinity who became incarnate. This is why it's important to state more specifically that *Jesus*—not "God"—died for our sins.

Yes, Jesus Is Still Human

Though we just briefly established that Jesus will remain fully human forever, we shouldn't gloss over that point too quickly. It's something many Christians have never thought about—including me, until just a few years ago. I had always assumed that Jesus temporarily acquired his humanity for life on earth but dropped it after he returned to heaven. Then one day I stumbled across an article that mentioned Jesus is *still* human. I thought, *Wait, what? Is that what the Bible really says, or did I just land on a site written by a fringe Christian sect with bizarre ideas?* The idea felt *that* foreign to this lifelong Christian. But the Bible does indeed indicate that Jesus continues to have a human nature. We can base this on two points.

First, Jesus was bodily raised from the dead; he didn't shed his physical nature and move on. The Gospel writers tell us that the risen Jesus ate food (Luke 24:42–43; John 21:1–14; Acts 1:4), was touched (Matt. 28:9), showed his bodily wounds (Luke 24:39–40; John 20:20), accepted an invitation to visit a home (Luke 24:29), and had conversations (Matt. 28:8–10, 18–20; Luke 24:13–39; John 20:11–29). Jesus himself said to the disciples, "Look at my hands and my feet. It is I myself! Touch me and see; a ghost does not have flesh and bones, as you see I have" (Luke 24:39). That said, Jesus's resurrection body isn't the same as the human bodies we have right now. It's a glorified body designed for eternity (1 Cor. 15:50). Paul tells us that we will eventually have glorified bodies as well (Phil. 3:20–21).

Second, Jesus ascended to heaven in bodily form and will return in the same way:

> After he said this, he was taken up before their very eyes, and a cloud hid him from their sight. They were looking intently up into the sky as he was going, when suddenly two men dressed in white stood beside them. "Men of Galilee," they said, "why do you stand here looking into the sky? This same Jesus, who has been taken from you into heaven, will come back *in the same way* you have seen him go into heaven." (Acts 1:9–11, emphasis mine)

This implies that Jesus didn't have a resurrection body only for temporary purposes. He will eventually return in the same (bodily) way in which he left (see also 1 Tim. 2:5; Rev. 1:13). Jesus's human and divine natures are permanently united.

Was the Cross a Defeat for God?

We've now answered this chapter's specific question, but with a little space remaining, we can take a brief detour into a related subject that's raised by Muslims today: Was the cross a defeat for God? Whereas Christians sometimes struggle to understand in what sense Jesus could die if he's God, Muslims struggle to understand how God would let Jesus die *at all*. Some background is necessary to understand why.

Islam has a high regard for Jesus, though Muslims don't believe he was in any way divine or the Son of God. Rather, they believe he was a great prophet and was given an important message to share—that Muhammad would be coming. Because of this unique role, the Quran (Islam's holy book) speaks of Jesus on multiple occasions. Regarding our current subject, Sura 4:157 says that Jesus was neither killed nor crucified:

> And they did not kill him, nor did they crucify him; but [another] was made to resemble him to them. And indeed, those who differ over it are in doubt about it. They have no knowledge of it except the following of assumption. And they did not kill him, for certain. Rather, Allah raised him to Himself.

So what happened to Jesus according to these verses? Muslim scholars vary in their answers. The most common interpretation is that it wasn't Jesus who was crucified but rather someone whom Allah (the Islamic name for God) made to look like him. In other words, the Jews believed they were crucifying Jesus, but it was only someone who *looked* like Jesus. The real Jesus went free (his eventual fate is debated). In connection with this understanding, Muslims believe that death on a cross would have been beneath Jesus, as a prophet of God. As one Muslim said, "We honor [Jesus] more than you [Christians] do. . . . We refuse to believe that God would permit him to suffer death on the cross."[1]

Let's consider two points in response.

First, regarding the historical credibility of the claim that Jesus wasn't crucified, it's important to know that the Quran was written about six hundred years after Jesus's life. The four Gospels, which all agree that Jesus was crucified, were written within about sixty-five years of Jesus's life. Paul's letters, which also agree that Jesus was crucified, were written as early as twenty years after his life. As we learned in chapter 1, early non-Christian historical sources also reference the crucifixion of Jesus, including writings by Josephus (a Jewish writer) and Tacitus (a Roman writer). *All of these sources were written hundreds of years before the Quran.* While this doesn't automatically mean that the earlier sources are accurate, historians overwhelmingly accept the crucifixion as a historical fact based on the consistent witness of these early, diverse sources.

Second, the difference in how Muslims and Christians view Jesus's death on the cross is ultimately a result of our different understandings of atonement. Islam doesn't teach a concept of atonement, so there's no need for Jesus to die in Islamic theology. Since the Quran claims that he wasn't crucified anyway, Muslims conclude that the cross was "beneath" him—such a death would have been the defeat of God. Christians, however, believe that sin requires atonement, as we've already discussed. Within this theological context, the fact that God chose to make atonement for us is a beautiful demonstration of his love and mercy. For Christians, there's no defeat of God on the cross *because the cross was God's own plan all along.* The crucifixion is a historical event that represents victory (1 Cor. 15:55–57).

We're coming to the end of part 3, but we have one more aspect of Jesus's death to discuss before moving on to conversations about the resurrection. It's a subject that doesn't receive much attention, but it's an important (and often misunderstood) link between parts 3 and 4: Where was Jesus between his death and resurrection?

KEY POINTS

- Most of the time when we say "God" in everyday language, we're referring to the Triune God in his entire being. In this sense, it's inaccurate to say that God died on the cross.
- Neither God the Father nor God the Holy Spirit took on a human nature and lived on earth. Only God the Son—Jesus—lived a human existence and could, therefore, die a human death.
- Jesus will continue to have both his human and his divine nature forever.
- The Quran claims that Jesus didn't die on the cross. Muslims believe that the cross was "beneath" him and would have represented the defeat of God.
- For Christians, there's no defeat on the cross because the cross was God's plan all along. The crucifixion is a historical event that represents victory.

CONVERSATION GUIDE

Open the Conversation

- Do you think it's equally correct to say, "God died on the cross" and "Jesus died on the cross"? Why or why not? *(Help your child think through what it would mean if God—the Triune being—died. Clarify that only Jesus died on the cross.)*

Advance the Conversation

- In chapter 6, we learned that Jesus is fully human and fully God. When Jesus died on the cross, do you think he stopped being human? Why or why not? *(Explain that we sometimes think Jesus "dropped" his humanity after he died on the cross, but the Bible indicates that he will have both divine and human natures forever. Discuss the two points from this chapter that show his continued humanity, and read Acts 1:9–11 together.)*

- *(For older kids)* Muslims believe that Jesus was a great prophet of God (though not God himself) and that he didn't actually die on the cross. They believe that if Jesus, God's prophet, had been crucified, it would have been the defeat of God. Why, from a Christian perspective, was Jesus's death not a defeat? *(The cross was God's own plan. Take time to share more background about Muslim beliefs from this chapter.)*

Apply the Conversation

- In an atheist internet forum, a person commented, "Jesus, according to the trinity is the immortal, eternal and omnipotent god. There's nothing to add. Jesus couldn't die if he was god, and if he wasn't, the trinity flies out the window."[2] Where does this person's misunderstanding of Christian theology lie? How would you respond?

18. Where Was Jesus between His Death and Resurrection?

As we saw in the previous chapter, John 19:30 tells us that Jesus's spirit departed his body at death. We remember this event on Good Friday. On Easter Sunday, we celebrate Jesus's physical resurrection. But where was Jesus's spirit on Saturday? That might sound like an inconsequential question at first, but some elaborate speculations have been offered, leading to some questionable theological conclusions. For example, prominent pastor and bestselling author Joel Osteen once said in a sermon:

> The Bible indicates that for three days, Jesus went into the very depths of hell. Right into the enemy's own territory. And He did battle with Satan face to face. Can you imagine what a show down that was? It was good vs. evil. Right vs. wrong. Holiness vs. filth. Here the two most powerful forces in the universe have come together to do battle for the first time in history. But thank God. The Bible says Satan was no match for our Champion. This was no contest. Jesus crushed Satan's head with His foot. He bruised his head. And He once and for all, forever defeated and dethroned and demoralized our enemy.[1]

That's a vivid portrait! The problem is that the Bible doesn't say anything about Jesus fighting Satan in hell after he died. There's absolutely *nothing* about the cosmic battle Osteen described. Yet many people similarly believe that Jesus went to hell before his resurrection (at least in some sense, even if not in the full "cosmic battle" sense). Where does the idea come from? That takes some explanation.

"He Descended into Hell"

For centuries, Christians have recited what's known as the Apostles' Creed, which is a statement of Christian faith dating back to the second century AD. Part of the creed affirms that Jesus "was crucified, died, and was buried. He descended into hell. The third day he rose again from the dead." This is recited by millions of Christians each week (including my own kids, who say it in their school chapel every Wednesday). A key reason why many people assume that Jesus went to hell is because they've learned this line in the Apostles' Creed. The phrase "he descended into hell," however, is not in the Bible, and theologians today aren't certain of its original intended meaning in the context of the creed.

At first, the meaning might sound obvious, because today we immediately associate the word *hell* with the place of judgment described in chapter 8. However, more than one Greek word is translated as "hell" in the New Testament, and sometimes the original word referred only to the grave or the general realm of the dead. The phrase "he descended into hell" doesn't appear in the earliest surviving versions of the creed, but the one person who included it before AD 650 understood it to mean only that Jesus was *buried*—not that he visited the hell we think of today.[2] These words were eventually added more consistently to the Apostles' Creed, but we don't know what sense the later editors intended them to have—hell as a grave, the realm of the dead, or a place of judgment. Because the phrase was added so late, and because it's not clear what the intended meaning was, some people and churches today omit it from the creed they recite.

While this explains why many Christians believe Jesus went to hell between his death and resurrection, it doesn't explain how the idea got into the Apostles' Creed in the first place. If the phrase was only meant to refer to Jesus going to the grave, no more explanation is needed; of course Jesus went to the grave when he died. However, those who believe something more was intended trace the idea to two passages in 1 Peter. First Peter 3:18–20 says:

> For Christ also suffered once for sins, the righteous for the unrighteous, to bring you to God. He was put to death in the body but made alive in the Spirit. After being made alive, he went and made proclamation to the imprisoned spirits—to those who were disobedient long ago when God waited patiently in the days of Noah while the ark was being built.

This passage certainly raises some big questions. Who were these imprisoned spirits? Where were they imprisoned? What kind of message did Jesus proclaim to them? What was the outcome? We don't know. Peter doesn't elaborate, and the answers aren't clarified elsewhere. First Peter 4:6 is thought to be related, however:

> For this is the reason the gospel was preached even to those who are now dead, so that they might be judged according to human standards in regard to the body, but live according to God in regard to the spirit.

There's no consensus on what these obscure verses from 1 Peter mean. A few of the most common interpretations include the following:

- Jesus went to the realm of the dead to preach to the Old Testament saints so they could be set free for heaven (some

181

tie this to the "captives" set free in Eph. 4:8–10). This is the Roman Catholic view.

- Jesus went to a part of hell to preach to angels, humans, or evil spirits (see also Jude 6).
- Jesus figuratively suffered the pains of "hell" while on the cross.
- Jesus went to hell to declare his victory over Satan. (Note that Jesus defeated the power of Satan by conquering death, but the Bible doesn't say he had to literally descend to hell to do so.)
- Jesus spoke through Noah in the past; the verses are referring to something that already happened long ago.

We're obviously not going to resolve the mystery in this chapter (see this endnote for a further reading recommendation).[3] Instead, let's conclude by looking at what we *can* affirm about Jesus between his death and resurrection, given the rest of Scripture.

Between Death and Resurrection: What We Do Know

Jesus Was Still Alive

As we saw in the previous chapter, Jesus didn't cease to exist after his physical body died. He didn't yet have a *resurrection* body (that happened on Sunday), but his spirit was alive.

Jesus Went to "Paradise" the Day He Physically Died

The most explicit information we have about where Jesus was immediately after death comes from the account of his conversation with the thieves who died next to him on the cross. Luke 23:39–43 says:

One of the criminals who hung there hurled insults at him: "Aren't you the Messiah? Save yourself and us!" But the other criminal rebuked him. "Don't you fear God," he said, "since you are under the same sentence? We are punished justly, for we are getting what our deeds deserve. But this man has done nothing wrong." Then he said, "Jesus, remember me when you come into your kingdom." Jesus answered him, "Truly I tell you, *today you will be with me in paradise.*" (emphasis mine)

Based on this passage, we know that Jesus's spirit specifically went to heaven the same day he died. Is it possible, based on the other passages we looked at, that he did something in hell, *then* went to paradise the same day, making both ideas true? Yes. This just isn't clearly outlined in Scripture.

Jesus Was Finished Atoning for Our Sins

Some popular teachers have suggested that Jesus took on more suffering for our sins when "he descended into hell." But nothing in Scripture indicates that he continued to suffer for our sins after his physical death, even *if* he did something in hell. Jesus anticipated paradise, not suffering. In addition, just before Jesus died, he said, "It is finished" (John 19:30). This is the translation of the Greek word *tetelestai*. *Tetelestai* was written on business documents and receipts in New Testament times to show that a bill had been paid in full. Similarly, Jesus paid the debt of our sins in full *on the cross*. His words were an affirmation that the atonement was finished.

Jesus Wasn't Giving People a Second Chance for Salvation

Some have also suggested that Jesus visited hell to preach to those who had died in order to give them a second chance for salvation. While that theoretically could be consistent with the passages we looked at, this interpretation would contradict the clear teaching of Scripture in other places. Hebrews 9:27 says, "People are destined to die once, and after that to face judgment." There's little reason to believe that the obscure passages from 1 Peter teach something contradictory.

Encountering verses in the Bible that we're not sure how to interpret can sometimes be frustrating. In such cases, however, it's important to focus on what we *can* affirm, given the whole witness of Scripture, and not speculate excessively. Speculation can lead to theological errors that are far more problematic than the original verses.

KEY POINTS

- The meaning of the phrase "he descended into hell" from the Apostles' Creed has long been debated because it's not found in the Bible. The author may have meant that Jesus went to hell as a grave, the realm of the dead, or a place of judgment.
- The Bible doesn't tell us where Jesus was between his death and resurrection, though much speculation has taken place. That speculation is primarily based on two passages from 1 Peter (3:18–20; 4:6).
- There is no consensus on what these passages mean. However, we can affirm that (1) Jesus was still alive, (2) Jesus went to "paradise" the day he physically died, (3) Jesus was finished atoning for our sins, and (4) Jesus wasn't giving people a second chance for salvation.

CONVERSATION GUIDE

Open the Conversation

- Jesus died on a Friday and was resurrected on the following Sunday. Where do you think he was on Saturday? *(Help your child think through the distinction between where his physical body was and where his spirit was. Affirm that we know he was alive in spirit, based on the prior chapter's discussion.)*

Advance the Conversation

- *(If you attend a church that recites the Apostles' Creed, read the creed and stop after the phrase "he descended into hell." Ask your child what they think that means. Explain some of the history of the phrase and why we're not sure of the original intended meaning. If you have a younger child who is not familiar with the creed, this may not be a necessary discussion. Older kids, however, can benefit from it.)*

- Read Luke 23:39–43. What information does this passage give us about where Jesus was between his death and resurrection? *(Jesus went to "paradise"—heaven with his Father—the day he died.)*

- Read Jesus's last words on the cross in John 19:30. What do you think he was saying was "finished"? *(Explain the meaning of the word tetelestai. Jesus had finished paying the debt of our sins. Discuss how people sometimes think that Jesus went to hell to suffer further, but this contradicts what the Bible says.)*

- *(For deeper study with an older child, read the passages from 1 Peter and touch on the interpretations people have offered.)*

Apply the Conversation

- Read the quote from the pastor at the beginning of this chapter. The scene he describes implies that Jesus fought for our salvation with Satan after he died on the cross. Is this consistent with what the Bible says? Why or why not?

PART 4

The Resurrection
of *Jesus*

Overview

My daughter was born with an extremely generous heart. She constantly thinks of ways to help others and to raise money for charity. Most recently, she decided to save all of her allowance money for a year so she can buy more shoeboxes for the Operation Christmas Child program run by Samaritan's Purse.[1]

She recruited a friend to join her, and the two of them decided they were going to take orders for baked goods to raise money from classmates. They printed pictures of the items, wrote prices on each picture, and glued them to a sign-up sheet. My daughter showed it to me before school one morning and said that she and her friend were going to announce the sale in class that day. While I know some parents would give a nice nod of approval and send their child to school, I went into business mode.

"I love that you are doing this! But I think there's a lot we should think about in order for you to meet your goals. For example, did you consider the cost of ingredients before pricing the items? Have you thought about how much time each item will take to bake and how many orders you can reasonably do each weekend? Will kids have their own money to purchase these, or will they need to ask their parents? If they need to ask their parents, you'll need to create a flyer explaining that it's a fundraiser. And if kids are supposed to pay after they receive the order, how do you know they'll actually give you the money?"

My daughter looked at me like a deer in headlights. Then she burst into tears.

"Mommy, you have ruined EVERYTHING! You just made it all SO COMPLICATED!"

The fact is I knew from looking at the items she was offering and the prices she had chosen that she would spend her entire weekend baking just to make a few dollars that her friends probably wouldn't even have upon delivery. She would have been devastated. My questions may have sounded complicated to her, but in reality, they were just the questions that needed to be considered if her plan was going to work for the purposes she had in mind.

As parents, we can empathize with my daughter's feelings. We've got a lot on our plates, so we don't love things that are more complicated than we think is necessary either. If you're new or somewhat new to apologetics (how to make a case for and defend the truth of Christianity), I want to acknowledge that the following chapters on the resurrection may seem to raise questions that are more "complicated" than you feel are necessary to discuss with your child. Historical evidence? Burial theories? Conspiracy claims? Hallucination hypotheses? Is all this really necessary? Isn't the resurrection just a matter of faith?

Yes. The resurrection is a matter of faith. But it's important to understand what biblical faith is. Biblical faith is putting our trust in what we have *good reason* to believe is true.[2] The question is, What evidence do we have to support the biblical claim that Jesus was raised from the dead? This isn't a minor point. If Jesus *wasn't* raised from the dead, our faith is useless (1 Cor. 15:14).

The truth of Christianity, therefore, rests on the truth of the resurrection, but kids will frequently hear today that it's ridiculous to believe what the Bible says about Jesus being raised from the dead—and those challenges will come from all directions. The popular magazine *Scientific American*, for example, featured an article titled "What Would It Take to Prove the Resurrection?" and explained that any natural explanation is more probable than a miracle explanation, so miracle claims (such as the resurrection) should be rejected.[3] Or search for "resurrection memes" online, and you'll see thousands of photos mocking the resurrection as some kind of zombie event. You might even hear these challenges in church. Many "progressive" Christian churches today deny the plausibility of a physical resurrection and teach that Jesus was resurrected only in "hearts and minds."[4]

The following six chapters will help you talk with your child about the resurrection in ways that will equip them to confidently engage with challenges like these. While these conversations may feel more "complicated" than how you've thought about the resurrection in the past, remember that our kids are growing up in a complicated world. We need to have the conversations with them that *they* need, regardless of what *we're* comfortable with. Like addressing the deeper questions concerning my daughter's bake sale, addressing deeper questions about the resurrection can make a critical difference, even if these questions feel like more than we (or they!) want to work through.

That said, the main ideas of part 4 are actually quite straightforward:

- The truth of the resurrection is central to Christianity (chapter 19).
- Historical facts surround the resurrection that even most critical (non-Christian) scholars accept. The question is, What is the best explanation for the facts we have? (chapters 20–21).

- The explanations skeptics offer either do not account well for these facts or cannot account for them at all (chapters 22–24).
- A supernatural resurrection is the best explanation for the historical data we have, assuming a person doesn't rule out the possibility of a miracle before considering the evidence.

Bestselling atheist author Richard Dawkins was once asked what he thinks happened to the body of Jesus. Dawkins replied, "Presumably what happened to Jesus was what happens to all of us when we die. We decompose. Accounts of Jesus's resurrection and ascension are about as well-documented as Jack and the Beanstalk."[5] If we don't want our kids to think the resurrection is comparable to a fairy tale, we need to give the subject the depth of attention it deserves. When we do, they'll know that their faith is grounded in a historical event—not an author's fanciful imagination.

Three Keys to Impactful Conversations about the Resurrection of Jesus

1. *If you're new to this subject, read all of part 4 before beginning these conversations.* Doing so will help you best understand how the details fit into the bigger picture before talking with your child.

2. *Keep the big picture in focus.* Prior to having these conversations, talk through the four bullet points in this overview with your child. This will give them a mental road map so that even if they don't retain every detail, they'll understand the overarching approach to investigating evidence for the resurrection.

3. *Consider a detour into the evidence for God's existence.* Chapter 24 briefly discusses how the plausibility of the resurrection depends on whether God exists. If you've previously

discussed the evidence for God's existence with your child, this is a good time to review it. If not, this is a good time to introduce it! Chapter 1 of *Keeping Your Kids on God's Side* highlights three key points to discuss. For extended study, see chapters 1–6 in *Talking with Your Kids about God*.

19. Why Does It Matter If Jesus Was Resurrected?

Like many families, we have kids who are involved in activities that keep our Saturdays busy on an ongoing basis. The luxury of sleeping in on weekends is a dream we had to let go of once baseball, soccer, and dance took an extracurricular place of importance in our kids' lives. Occasionally, however, schedules align in order for us to have a leisurely Saturday morning. And everyone in our family agrees on what that means.

Pancakes.

My husband is the pancake chef in the house. My sole responsibility for pancake mornings is ensuring that the cupboard is stocked with syrup. This minor obligation has been more challenging than it sounds, however. What we *can't* all agree on is which syrup to buy. I've been through all the "healthier" natural options, but the kids (and husband) have all concluded that it's not even worth eating pancakes if they have to put something healthy on top. I finally broke down and bought a less healthy but more popular brand. It was a hit with everyone.

The winning syrup has become a running joke, however, because of what it represents. The front label prominently says, "Butter Rich Syrup." But the line under it says, "Natural Butter Flavor . . .

Contains No Butter." It *tastes* buttery. It *smells* buttery. It even *looks* buttery! But it isn't *actually* buttery. A butter imposter won the stomachs of my family.

The central "ingredient" in Christianity is the resurrection. As the apostle Paul says in 1 Corinthians 15:14, "If Christ has not been raised, our preaching is useless and so is your faith." In chapters 20–24, we'll look at how we can be confident that Jesus was, in fact, raised from the dead. But kids must first have an appreciation for how important this investigation is. They need to understand that a belief in Jesus without a belief in the resurrection might as well be labeled "Christianity Flavor . . . Contains No Christianity." Such a faith might look and smell like Christianity, but it's missing the central ingredient.

What *Kind* of Resurrection Is Central to Christianity?

If you've been a Christian for a while, you probably already have a specific idea in mind of what the word *resurrection* means in the context of Jesus: he died, was buried, and was then raised to life again in bodily form. It's becoming increasingly popular, however, for people to redefine the resurrection in symbolic terms, with an emphasis on what the resurrection means to *them*. New York University professor Scott Korb, for example, says, "The miracle of a bodily resurrection is something I rejected without moving away from its basic idea. What I mean is that we can reach the lowest points of our lives, of going deep into a place that feels like death, and then find our way out again—that's the story the resurrection now tells me."[1] There is a vast difference, however, between a resurrection that's physical and one that's merely symbolic of finding our way out of "the lowest points of our lives." It's important that we clarify what *kind* of resurrection is central to Christianity.

If the resurrection accounts in the Bible amounted to not much more than "Jesus died, but we saw him alive, and now we feel transformed!" one might rightly question what, exactly, the disciples meant by "saw him alive." With such a limited report, a case could be made that the disciples were using those words only as a figure of speech. But that's not the type of biblical accounts we have. The Gospels repeatedly include details that either implicitly or explicitly demonstrate that the reported resurrection event was *bodily* in nature. For example:

- Jesus predicted the resurrection of his body. He said, "Destroy this temple, and I will raise it again in three days" (John 2:19). John 2:21 explains that "the temple he had spoken of was his body."
- All four Gospels report that Jesus's tomb was empty (Matt. 28; Mark 16; Luke 24; John 20). If the resurrection was intended to be only a symbolic story, there would be no need to emphasize that Jesus's body was no longer in the tomb. The empty tomb was reported as evidence that Jesus's *body* had been raised to life.
- The Gospel writers report that the risen Jesus interacted with people in physical ways. Recall from chapter 17 that he ate food, was touched, showed his bodily wounds, accepted an invitation to visit a home, and had conversations. A symbolic resurrection account would have no need for so many details that explicitly portray the risen Jesus in physical form.
- Jesus himself emphasized the bodily nature of his resurrection, saying, "Look at my hands and my feet. It is I myself! Touch me and see; a ghost does not have flesh and bones, as you see I have" (Luke 24:39).

In addition to evaluating the biblical accounts, we can look at the cultural context of the first-century world in which the resurrection claim was made. If the word *resurrection* was known to refer to some kind of nonbodily return to life, there might be reason to reassess our conclusions about what appears to be the plain meaning of the text. However, that's not the case. New Testament scholar N. T. Wright, in *The Resurrection of the Son of God*, explains:

> The meaning of "resurrection," both in Jewish and the non-Jewish world of late antiquity, was never that the person concerned had simply "gone to heaven," or been "exalted" in some way which did not involve a new bodily life. Plenty of disembodied post-mortem states were postulated, and there was a rich variety of terminology for denoting them, which did not include "resurrection." "Resurrection" meant embodiment; that was equally so for the pagans, who denied it, as it was for the Jews, at least some of whom hoped for it.[2]

When we consider both the biblical accounts and the cultural context, it's clear that the claimed resurrection of Jesus was bodily in nature.

Why Is the Resurrection So Important to Christianity?

Now that we've clarified the nature of the resurrection, we can return to the question of *why* the resurrection is so important to Christianity. While much theological ground could be covered in response, here are three basic points to understand.

1. Jesus's Resurrection Validated His Predictions and Claims to Divinity

No mere human could choose to be resurrected. Only someone who is truly God, and therefore has power over death, could do so. The resurrection was the ultimate validation of Jesus's divinity, and from that validation flow the critical implications of the truth of his teachings and his authority over our lives.

2. Jesus's Resurrection Confirms We Are No Longer in Our Sins

Acts 17:30–31 says that the resurrection is "proof" that God has "set a day when he will judge the world with justice by the man he has appointed." Those who trust in Jesus's sacrifice as payment for their sins will be found righteous on that day (Rom. 8:1).

3. Jesus's Resurrection Assures Us That We, Too, Will Be Raised

Jesus's resurrection is God's pledge that we, too, will be raised from death to eternal life (Rom. 8:11). Paul says in 1 Corinthians 15:20–23 (see also Phil. 3:21):

> Christ has indeed been raised from the dead, the firstfruits of those who have fallen asleep. For since death came through a man, the resurrection of the dead comes also through a man. For as in Adam all die, so in Christ all will be made alive. But each in turn: Christ, the firstfruits; then, when he comes, those who belong to him.

With these points in mind, it's evident why Paul said that our faith is useless if Jesus has not been raised. We would be putting the trust for our eternal life in someone who was neither able to conquer death himself nor able to validate his claims to divinity in the ways he said he would. Conversely, if Jesus *was* raised from the dead, we can place our faith in him as Lord and Savior with the full confidence that we will inherit eternal life.

The truth of the resurrection changes *everything*.

This, of course, should lead us to ask how we can be so confident that Jesus really was raised from the dead. We'll explore that question in the next five chapters.

KEY POINTS

- The truth of Christianity hinges on the truth of the resurrection. If Jesus has not been raised, our faith is "useless" (1 Cor. 15:14).

- The Gospels repeatedly include details that either implicitly or explicitly demonstrate that the reported resurrection event was *bodily* in nature—not merely symbolic. Jesus predicted his bodily resurrection, the Gospels emphasize that the tomb was empty, the Gospel writers report that the risen Jesus interacted with people in physical ways, and Jesus himself emphasized the bodily nature of his resurrection in his words to the disciples.

- The resurrection is central to Christianity for three key reasons: (1) it validated Jesus's predictions and claims to divinity, (2) it confirms we are no longer in our sins, and (3) it assures us that we, too, will be raised.

CONVERSATION GUIDE

Open the Conversation

- If a friend asked you what it means when people say Jesus was "resurrected," how would you explain what a resurrection is? *(Discuss how some people today believe the resurrection was only a "symbol" of something like hope when things are bad. However, there's a big difference between a symbolic resurrection and a bodily resurrection. Make sure your child understands the difference.)*

Advance the Conversation

- The Bible tells us about many things Jesus did after he was raised from the dead (and before he went to heaven). For example, he had conversations with several of the people he appeared to. What other things can you think of that Jesus did after the resurrection? *(Read the verses in this chapter that recount how he ate food, touched people, showed his wounds, and visited a home. Ask your child what this means about the nature of the resurrection—was it bodily or symbolic?)*

- All four Gospels (the books of Matthew, Mark, Luke, and John) report that people found Jesus's tomb empty. Why do you think this is an important detail for figuring out whether the Gospel writers were telling a symbolic story or were reporting something that actually happened? *(The body was gone because it had been raised back to life.)*

- Read Luke 24:39. What do Jesus's own words tell us about the nature of the resurrection? *(Jesus showed the disciples he was bodily raised from the dead.)*

- Read what the apostle Paul wrote in 1 Corinthians 15:14. Why do you think the resurrection is so important in Christianity that if it didn't happen, our faith is *useless*? *(Walk through the three points discussed in this chapter. Emphasize the main idea that the truth of Christianity rests on the truth of the resurrection.)*

Apply the Conversation

- A pastor wrote online, "I think that human beings have always turned to the use of metaphor when they've had an experience that words alone cannot express. For example, 'I was scared to death!' or 'She's so happy that she's walking on air' or 'The news truly broke her heart.' None of these statements is literally true, yet each one of them gives expression to a sentiment or an experience that is nonetheless profoundly true. I believe that there is a similar dynamic of truth in the concept of Christ being raised from the dead. So, no, I don't think that to be a Christian we have to believe that Christ literally, bodily rose from the dead."[3] How would you respond to her claim that the resurrection of Jesus might be a metaphor like "I was scared to death!"?

20. What Historical Evidence Is There for Jesus's Resurrection?

I joined millions of Americans this year in making a New Year's resolution to lose weight. On December 31, I prepared by downloading an app to track my day-to-day progress. If you've never used an app like this before, the idea is that you weigh yourself each morning, you input the weight, and the app creates a helpful chart that connects the data points to show how your weight is trending over time. This is really cool . . . until you forget to weigh yourself one day. Then your tidy little chart suddenly contains a glaring hole to forever commemorate the day you failed. Those of us who are perfectionists can hardly gaze at such a thing. I forgot to weigh myself just sixteen days into January and hated the missing data point so much that I deleted the app.

Although I had no way of knowing with certainty what I weighed that day, I *could* have input my best estimate. Anything within a three-pound range of what I weighed the days before and after would have been fair. But if I entered a weight that was twenty pounds more than what I weighed the day before, you'd say that's unreasonable. Fifty pounds more? Even more unreasonable, unless you're assuming I weighed myself holding a small anvil that day. And if I tried to convince you that the missing data point was five thousand pounds, you'd say that's not just unreasonable—that's impossible.

We make judgments like this all the time when we don't have complete information. We use what we know to best determine what we don't know. Contrary to popular thinking, belief in the resurrection isn't a blind leap in the dark, as if we're just filling in the blanks of history with nothing to go on other than untethered hope. There are generally accepted historical facts related to the claimed resurrection of Jesus that provide us with "before and after" data points.[1] By looking at these facts, we can evaluate what the best explanation is for what happened two thousand years ago. We'll use this chapter and the next to learn about the facts, then we'll use chapters 22–24 to consider explanations.

Four Historical Facts Almost All Scholars Agree On

In chapter 21 of *Keeping Your Kids on God's Side*, I explain what is known as "the minimal facts approach to the resurrection." This approach, developed by New Testament scholars Gary Habermas and Michael Licona in *The Case for the Resurrection of Jesus*, identifies the "data that are so strongly attested historically that they are granted by nearly every scholar who studies the subject, even the rather skeptical ones."[2] In other words, the authors' goal was to strip away any religious assumptions about the events surrounding the resurrection to determine what historical facts the vast majority of scholars would still agree on. Through this process, they identified four such facts that are (mostly) uncontroversial. Since I discuss their approach and the four facts in *Keeping Your Kids on God's Side*, I'm not going to repeat the details of the discussion here. Instead, I'll provide a very brief review of these facts, and then we'll use the remainder of this chapter to dig more deeply into new content regarding what is arguably the most important fact of the four: Jesus's disciples *believed* that he rose and appeared to them after his death.

Fact 1: Jesus Died by Crucifixion

Crucifixion was a common form of Roman execution, so there is nothing historically suspicious about the claim that Jesus died on a cross. As we already saw, his crucifixion is even referenced by non-Christian historical sources, including writings by Josephus and Tacitus.

Fact 2: The Church Persecutor Paul Was Suddenly Changed

Paul wrote several books of the New Testament and is one of the most influential Christians who has ever lived. But he first was an enemy of the church, responsible for persecuting many early believers (Acts 7:58; 8:1, 3; 1 Cor. 15:9; Gal. 1:13; Phil. 3:6). Paul suddenly became a passionate Christian, however, after the risen Jesus allegedly appeared to him (Acts 9:4–6), and he spent the rest of his life preaching the resurrection throughout the world, eventually being martyred for his claim.

Fact 3: The Skeptic James, Brother of Jesus, Was Suddenly Changed

The Bible tells us that Jesus's brothers were not believers during his earthly ministry (Mark 3:21, 31; 6:3–4; John 7:5). However, after Jesus's alleged resurrection, his brother James is unexpectedly described as a leader of the church (Acts 15:12–21; Gal. 1:19). What happened? First Corinthians 15:7 claims that the risen Jesus appeared to him. James was eventually martyred as well.

Fact 4: Jesus's Disciples Believed That He Rose and Appeared to Them after His Death

Habermas says there is "virtual consensus" among scholars who study Jesus's resurrection that his disciples truly believed he appeared to them risen from the dead.[3] Scholars agree that the historical data suggests that (1) the disciples claimed the risen Jesus appeared to them, and (2) after Jesus's death, they were transformed from fearful individuals who abandoned him at his arrest and execution into bold proclaimers of the resurrection.

To be clear, facts 2, 3, and 4 do not mean that these scholars all believe that Paul, James, and the disciples actually saw a resurrected Jesus. But there is strong scholarly consensus that these individuals all *believed* that they did and lived transformed lives in response to that belief. How can we be so confident of this? Let's look more closely at what we know of the disciples' lives.

How Do We Know the Disciples Believed the Risen Jesus Appeared to Them?

If all we knew today about the disciples is that they said a resurrected Jesus appeared to them, it would be an interesting fact of history. There would certainly be speculation as to why they would claim such an extraordinary thing and whether they actually believed it. But what if we knew they continued making that claim for the rest of their lives knowing they might be killed for it—and that some of them *were* killed for it? That wouldn't prove their claim was accurate, but it would certainly demonstrate the *sincerity* of their belief; people are rarely willing to suffer and/or die for what they *know* to be a lie. It turns out this doesn't need to be a hypothetical question—it's exactly the kind of historical information we have.

Biola University professor Sean McDowell has conducted extensive research on what happened to the apostles after Jesus's death.[4] In his book *The Fate of the Apostles*, McDowell examines the historical evidence for each apostle's fate and rates the likelihood of his martyrdom on a ten-point probability scale (0 being not possibly true to 10 being the highest possible probability). He concluded the following:

- Highest possible probability (9–10): Peter, Paul, James (Jesus's brother), and James (son of Zebedee)
- More probable than not (7): Thomas
- More plausible than not (6): Andrew
- As plausible as not (5): Philip, Bartholomew, Matthew, James (son of Alphaeus), Thaddeus, Simon the Zealot, Matthias
- Improbable (3): John

We don't know for sure how many of the apostles were killed for their testimony, but based on McDowell's analysis, it's almost certain that several were. There are early church traditions that tell of the martyrdoms of other apostles but only in sources from a much later time (those sources may contain historical truth, but there is no way to verify it). That said, it's important to understand that the strength of the evidence for the sincerity of the apostles' claim that Jesus rose from the dead doesn't rest on proving they all died as martyrs. It rests on their *willingness* to suffer and die. Both early Christian and non-Christian writings tell of the first-century persecution of Christians, indicating that the apostles would have known they were preaching the resurrection at risk of their lives, whether they were ultimately killed for it or not.[5] This willingness to put their lives at risk strongly suggests that they truly believed what they preached and weren't concocting an elaborate lie.

People sometimes raise the objection that the apostles may have *tried* to recant but were killed anyway. McDowell offers three reasons why such an objection is not compelling.[6] First, there's no evidence this ever happened (with the exception of Judas). Second, the apostles died over a period of about sixty years, hundreds of miles apart, and in diverse ways. It's highly improbable that they all tried to recant in the last minutes of their lives but were killed anyway—and there is no evidence that even *one* did. Third, if one of them did recant, it would be shocking to find no mention of it in history. Later enemies of the church would have seized upon the opportunity to reference it and discredit Christianity.

While the four facts described in this chapter are the ones accepted by almost all scholars who study the resurrection, there's one more fact that's supported by such strong historical evidence that it's accepted by roughly 75 percent of them (including the majority of critical scholars): the empty tomb.[7] We'll turn now to the evidence for this important additional fact.

KEY POINTS

- There are four historical facts related to the resurrection of Jesus that are granted even by the vast majority of non-Christian scholars: (1) Jesus died by crucifixion; (2) the church persecutor Paul was suddenly changed; (3) the skeptic James, brother of Jesus, was suddenly changed; and (4) Jesus's disciples believed that he rose and appeared to them.

- With respect to fact 4, both early Christian and non-Christian writings tell of the first-century persecution of Christians, indicating that the apostles would have known they were preaching the resurrection at risk of their lives. It's almost certain that several were killed for their testimony.

- The apostles' *willingness* to suffer and die demonstrates they weren't being deceptive with their message. They truly believed what they preached whether they were ultimately killed for it or not.

- No evidence exists that any of the apostles ever recanted their claim about the resurrection.

CONVERSATION GUIDE

Open the Conversation

- Imagine that you walked into the kitchen and found giant puddles of water on the floor. What are some reasonable explanations for what caused them to be there? What are some less reasonable explanations? *(Discuss how we make these kinds of judgments all the time. Introduce the idea that historical facts can be like these puddles—we can use what we know to infer what best explains them.)*

Advance the Conversation

- If you decided to search for historical evidence that Jesus was resurrected, what kinds of things would you look for? *(Brainstorm and discuss what evidence would be reasonable to look for— written testimony, for example—and what would be unreasonable— photographs, for example. Then walk through the four historical facts explained in this chapter. If your child is old enough, take the discussion of fact 4 deeper with Sean McDowell's analysis.)*
- Many people in history have been willing to die for their religious beliefs. For example, people have risked their lives in wars to defend what they believe to be true about God. Do you think that's different from Jesus's apostles being willing to die in order to tell others about the resurrection? Why or why not? *(It's different because the apostles would have known if they were risking their lives for a lie—they knew whether they had actually*

208

seen a risen Jesus. Many people would die for what they believe to be true, but few would die for what they know to be a lie. This is why the apostles' willingness to die demonstrates the sincerity of their belief.)

Apply the Conversation

- A Christian wrote in an online forum, "Even though we have the testimony of the apostles, they would be a [moot] point . . . when you look at it objectively. Ultimately, the belief in the resurrection is a leap of faith."[8] How would you respond to the idea that the testimony of the apostles doesn't matter? *(Hint: Consider what we learned in this chapter about the historical evidence that lends credibility to their claim.)*

21. Was Jesus's Tomb Really Empty?

As we learned in chapter 19, the accounts of the empty tomb were central to the testimony that Jesus was bodily raised from the dead. An empty tomb wouldn't necessarily mean that Jesus *was* resurrected, but a tomb containing his body would mean that he *wasn't*. This makes the historicity of the empty tomb a pivotal question.

The empty tomb is accepted as a historical fact by the majority of critical (non-Christian) scholars. But because it's not *as* universally accepted as the four facts described in chapter 20, we'll use a full chapter now to extend the discussion and consider the historicity of the empty tomb in more depth.

First Things First: Was Jesus Even Buried?

The empty tomb accounts assume two essential facts: (1) Jesus's body was placed in a tomb to begin with, and (2) the location of that tomb was known. If these points are in doubt, so too are the accounts of finding Jesus's tomb empty. It's crucial, therefore, to understand how we know that Jesus was buried and that the location of the tomb was known.

All four Gospels report that a man named Joseph of Arimathea—a member of the Jewish council—requested Jesus's body and laid it to rest in a tomb cut from rock (Matt. 27:57–60; Mark 15:42–46; Luke 23:50–53; John 19:38–42). Some critical scholars believe, however, that these reports were based on stories invented many years after Jesus's death and that Jesus was most likely *never buried at all*. New Testament scholar Bart Ehrman popularized this idea in his book *How Jesus Became God: The Exaltation of a Jewish Preacher from Galilee*.[1]

Ehrman argues that the biblical accounts are historically implausible because the Romans didn't allow those who were crucified to receive a proper burial (it was by Roman authority that Jesus was put to death). A key reason why Ehrman says that Jesus's burial was a legendary development is that one of the earliest creeds we have—part of 1 Corinthians 15 and dated to within a decade of Jesus's death—doesn't explicitly mention his burial *in a tomb*. Paul writes, "For what I received I passed on to you as of first importance: that Christ died for our sins according to the Scriptures, that he was buried, that he was raised on the third day according to the Scriptures, and that he appeared to Cephas, and then to the Twelve" (vv. 3–5). Furthermore, Ehrman points out that this creed doesn't mention Joseph of Arimathea by name. He reasons that if Cephas (Peter) was mentioned by name, Joseph of Arimathea would have been too—had the burial story existed by the early year in which the creed was written. Ehrman's conclusion is that Christian communities probably invented the story many years later.

Why does Ehrman care to press the point? He acknowledges that his conclusion means that "historians who do not believe that Jesus was raised from the dead should not feel compelled to come up with an alternative explanation for why the tomb was empty."[2] Ehrman correctly understands the importance of the empty tomb accounts to the resurrection testimony. If he's right—that Jesus was never buried or that his body remains buried in some unknown place—then we no longer need to talk about explanations for all the historical facts. Jesus wasn't bodily raised from the dead.

New Testament scholar Craig Evans wrote a detailed critique of Ehrman's burial claims in *How God Became Jesus: The Real Origins of Belief in Jesus' Divine Nature—A Response to Bart D. Ehrman*.[3] Let's look briefly at his responses to Ehrman's two major arguments against the historicity of Jesus's burial.

Crucified People Not Buried in the Roman Empire?

We know from ancient writings that the Romans often left crucified people on the cross to be devoured by animals as a deterrent for would-be criminals. However, other ancient writings and archaeological finds of *buried* crucifixion victims show that this was not always the case. Evans says, "Roman justice not only allowed for the executed to be buried, but it even encouraged it in some instances. . . . It is simply erroneous to assert that the Romans did not permit the burial of the executed, including the crucified. Bodies were in fact released to those who requested them."[4] In addition, because Jesus was crucified in Jewish lands (as opposed to other parts of the Roman Empire), there's an even greater likelihood that he was buried. Jewish law required that those hung for a capital offense were to be buried the same day (an application of Deut. 21:22–23), and historical writings show that the Roman administrators in the area generally respected Jewish laws and customs in peacetime—including burial customs. In short, there is no reason to conclude that the account of Jesus's burial is inconsistent with Roman practices, especially in Jewish areas.

Lack of Empty Tomb Details in 1 Corinthians 15?

Recall that the early creed embedded in 1 Corinthians 15 says that Jesus was buried but doesn't specifically say that he was buried in a tomb or by Joseph of Arimathea. Does this imply that those details were invented later?

Evans points out that saying Jesus was buried *in a tomb* would have been redundant for Jewish people of the time; they would have *assumed* that burial meant the body was placed in a tomb. If Jesus had been left hanging, the creed wouldn't have said anything about burial at all. There's nothing suspicious about the absence of the words "in a tomb." The same can be said about the lack of reference to Joseph. It's reasonable to assume that naming the person who saw the risen Jesus was more important than naming the person who buried him, especially given that the mention of Cephas is followed by a list of other resurrection appearances. The resurrection was clearly the emphasis in this passage. Many other well-supported historical details are not mentioned in the creed as well—such as Jesus's death in *Jerusalem*, at the time of *Passover*, and so on—but the lack of these descriptors in this one passage doesn't imply their nonhistoricity. The Gospels simply provide more detail than the creed in 1 Corinthians. The fact that they were written later in no way necessitates the conclusion that their additional details were invented.

Interestingly, there's actually a good historical reason why Joseph would have been involved in this event. Because the Jewish council delivered Jesus to Roman authorities for execution, it was their legal responsibility to arrange for his burial (and executed people were not allowed to be buried in their own family's tomb).[5] Joseph was a member of the council, so the Gospel writers may have simply been naming the specific council member who handled Jesus's burial. Importantly, Joseph's involvement is also evidence that Jesus was buried in a known location. Joseph obviously knew where his own tomb was located, and all four Gospels make it clear that Jesus's followers knew where it was as well. There's no historical reason to doubt these accounts.

But Was the Tomb *Empty*?

Based on our analysis so far, we can go forward with confidence that Jesus was buried and that he was buried in a known tomb. So let's return to our original question: How do we know the tomb was empty?

As with Jesus's burial, all four Gospels explicitly report that there was an empty tomb (Matt. 28; Mark 16; Luke 24; John 20). Three key pieces of evidence support this claim.

1. Jesus's Burial in Jerusalem Would Have Made an Empty Tomb Claim Easy to Disprove

The disciples first preached about Jesus's bodily resurrection in Jerusalem (Luke 24:47; Acts 2–8; Gal. 1–2). Since Jesus was buried there (and in a known location), those who opposed the spread of Christianity could have easily produced his body and discredited the entire resurrection story. Christianity would never have gotten off the ground.

2. The Jewish Response to the Resurrection Claim Assumed the Tomb Was Empty

Matthew 28:11–15 says that the chief priests challenged the disciples' preaching by claiming the disciples had stolen Jesus's body. This is very telling. They didn't argue that the tomb wasn't empty or that no one knew where Jesus was buried—only that there was another explanation as to *why* the tomb was empty. No surviving historical writings challenge the Gospels' claim that the tomb was empty; they only debate the reason it was.

3. Women Were Reported to Be the First Witnesses at the Empty Tomb

The Gospels all report that women were the first people to find the tomb empty. This might not seem significant, but in first-century

214

Jewish culture, women were not considered to be reliable witnesses. If early Christians wanted to invent the story of an empty tomb, it's highly unlikely they would have *chosen* to highlight women as the first witnesses. Few would have believed them.

We've now identified five well-supported historical facts surrounding the resurrection of Jesus. The pivotal question we're ready to ask is, What's the best explanation for those facts? That will be our focus for the next three chapters.

KEY POINTS

- An empty tomb assumes that (1) Jesus's body was placed in a tomb and (2) the location of that tomb was known.
- Some skeptics claim that the Romans didn't permit crucified people to be buried, so Jesus wouldn't have been buried. However, Jewish law required that those hung for a capital offense were to be buried the same day, and historical writings show that the Roman administrators in Jewish areas generally respected Jewish laws and customs in peacetime. There is no historical reason to doubt that Jesus was buried.
- Because the Jewish council delivered Jesus to Roman authorities for execution, it was their legal responsibility to arrange for his burial. This is consistent with the biblical account that a member of the council—Joseph of Arimathea—buried Jesus in a (known) tomb.
- Three key pieces of evidence support the empty tomb accounts: (1) Jesus's burial in Jerusalem would have made an empty tomb claim easy to disprove, (2) the Jewish response to the resurrection claim assumed the tomb was empty, and (3) women were reported to be the first witnesses at the empty tomb.

CONVERSATION GUIDE

Open the Conversation

- We learned in the last chapter about four historical facts related to Jesus's resurrection. Another historical fact that's very important to establish is that Jesus's tomb was empty. Why do you think this is so important when we talk about the resurrection? *(The disciples professed a bodily resurrection, so if Jesus's body was still in the grave, it would disprove their claim.)*

Advance the Conversation

- *(For older kids)* Some people say they don't think Jesus was even buried—that his body was left on the cross to be eaten by animals. If that were the case, how would it undermine the truth of the resurrection? *(If Jesus's body was never placed in a tomb, then there was no tomb to find empty, and a key part of the disciples' testimony would be proven false. Explain the historical context for Jesus's burial discussed in this chapter.)*

- The disciples first preached that Jesus's body was raised from the dead in Jerusalem—the same town where he was crucified and buried. If people didn't believe them, what is one way they could have proven that what the disciples were saying wasn't true? *(They could have gone to the tomb where Jesus was buried and shown that it wasn't empty.)*

- Read Matthew 28:11–15. What did the chief priests (who were opposed to Jesus) want people to believe happened to Jesus's body? *(They wanted people to think the disciples stole it.)*

- If Jesus's body was still in the tomb, do you think the chief priests would have told people the same story? Why or why not? *(No. They didn't want people to believe that Jesus was raised from the dead, so they would have shown everyone that the tomb wasn't empty to discredit the claim.)*

- All four Gospels tell us that the first people to find the tomb empty were women. In the culture of that time, however, people often didn't think women could be trusted to tell the truth. Why do you think the disciples were willing to tell everyone that Jesus's tomb was first found empty by women? *(They were committed to telling the truth despite cultural suspicions.)*

Apply the Conversation

- A person asked online, "Is Jesus's empty tomb evidence for his resurrection? If not, why?" A man replied, "We do not know where the body of Jesus was laid. Conclusion: we do not know whether the [tomb] is empty. The Jews had a custom to bury their deceased [outside] the walls of the town. Unfortunately we do not have the coordinates of all the locations where the deceased were buried."[6] Use what you learned in this chapter to explain why there is evidence that Jesus's tomb was empty—even if we're not certain today *where* Jesus's tomb was.

22. Did Jesus's Disciples Lie about the Resurrection?

When I was in first grade, my teacher accidentally put another child's drawing in my take-home folder. It didn't have a name on it, but it was a *really* good drawing—certainly not something I could have created, given my complete lack of artistic ability. My mom found it in my backpack one afternoon and gasped.

"Natasha! You did this? It's fantastic! This is your best drawing ever! This is a keeper."

She proudly hustled off and tucked it into my childhood souvenir folder.

I don't know how much time I had at that moment to admit that her pride was misplaced . . . but I didn't. Nor did I in the thirty-five-plus years that have since passed. And she *still* remembers how good that drawing was. For some reason, I've never had the heart to tell her it wasn't mine.

If I hadn't just confessed it in this book (sorry, Mom), I could have taken that lie to my grave. After all, I was the only one who knew the truth, and the lie had almost no repercussions in my life other than occasional guilt. Lies like that are easy to maintain. Others are almost impossible.

We've already seen that there's overwhelming evidence the disciples truly believed Jesus appeared to them, given that they were willing to suffer and die for their message (see chapter 20). Skeptics sometimes insist, however, that there are plenty of reasons why they would have been willing to suffer and die for what they knew was a lie. For example, historian and atheist activist Richard Carrier says:

> It's also possible for people to die for what they know is a lie—simply because they value something more. If someone believes a lie is essential for persuading the world to morally reform itself for the greater good . . . and that person values that greater good more than their own life, they will certainly die for the necessary lie.[1]

We could psychoanalyze the disciples to debate Carrier's claim that they had sufficient *motive* to risk their lives for a known lie (something highly questionable), but instead we're going to focus on a more fundamental question: *Could* the disciples have carried out such a lie? If there's not good reason to believe they had the ability to carry out a resurrection conspiracy given what would have been required to do so, an evaluation of their motives becomes a moot point; they *couldn't* have lied even if they had *wanted* to.

If the disciples lied about the resurrection, they would have had to do two major things: (1) steal Jesus's body (the tomb had to be empty to support the claim of a bodily resurrection) and (2) carry out a long-lasting and complex conspiracy to convince people everywhere of their lie. As we'll see, that's a tall order.

Could the Disciples Have Stolen the Body?

As background for the question of whether the disciples could have stolen Jesus's body, it's important to understand that anyone attempting to steal a corpse faced capital punishment in the Roman Empire.[2] Both the Romans and the Jews took grave robbery very seriously, and the disciples would have known they were risking their lives by tampering with a tomb.

Let's say, however, that for whatever reason, they were willing to risk their lives to steal Jesus's body. To do so, they first would have had to get past the guard put in place by Pilate (Matt. 27:65–66; the "guard" may have included multiple people). There's scholarly debate as to whether the guard was Roman or Jewish, but in neither case would the guard have been sympathetic to the disciples' plan or willing to aid them in the theft; the guard's life depended on keeping the body in the tomb. But what if the guard fell asleep while the disciples waited nearby? The disciples would still have had to sneak past the guard and move a stone from the tomb entrance that weighed hundreds to thousands of pounds without being caught. They would then have had to meticulously remove Jesus's burial cloths (John 20:5–7) and slip away with the body unnoticed. This is a highly unlikely scenario.

Since the account of the guard is in only one Gospel (Matthew), skeptics sometimes respond by saying there wasn't a guard at all—it was just a story fabricated by Matthew to support the disciples' claim that they couldn't have stolen the body. But even if there wasn't a guard, the disciples would still have had to stealthily move a huge stone and carry off the corpse without anyone noticing, all while risking capital punishment if caught. This remains a very unlikely scenario.

For the sake of argument, however, let's assume the disciples somehow managed to pull off the theft. Could they then have successfully carried out a resurrection conspiracy for the rest of their lives? Doing so would not have been as easy as you might think.

Could the Disciples Have Continued the Conspiracy?

Cold-case homicide detective J. Warner Wallace was an atheist until age thirty-five. At that time, he decided to investigate the reliability of the Gospels using the same detective skills he used professionally. Wallace initially believed the apostles had lied. He says:

> Maybe it was just my skeptical nature or my prior experience with people on the job. I understand the capacity people have to lie when it serves their purpose. In my view, the apostles were no different. . . . But as I learned more about the nature of conspiracies and had the opportunity to investigate and break several conspiracy cases, I started to doubt the reasonable nature of the alleged "Christian conspiracy."[3]

Wallace became a Christian as a result of his investigation and went on to write several books about the evidence for the truth of Christianity. In *Cold-Case Christianity*, he explains five "rules" for a successful conspiracy—and why, given these rules, it's so improbable that the disciples carried one out:[4]

1. *Small number of conspirators.* Lies are hard to uphold, so the fewer the number of people involved, the higher the likelihood of success.

2. *Thorough and immediate communication.* When conspirators can't readily communicate with one another, they can't determine if the others have confessed the truth. They're more likely to break the conspiracy to save themselves from punishment.

3. *Short time span.* Lies are difficult to maintain consistently over a long period of time, so the shorter the time the conspiracy requires, the better.

4. *Significant relational connections.* When conspirators are connected in deep and meaningful ways (family, for example), they're less likely to give one another up.

5. *Little or no pressure.* Unless they're pressured to confess, most conspirators will continue lying.

With these criteria in mind, let's consider how the circumstances of the disciples stack up. First, we're talking about twelve people at a minimum. The Bible speaks of many more eyewitnesses to the resurrection (for example, Acts 1:15–26), but we'll conservatively look at just the apostles (the original disciples plus Matthias, Judas's replacement). Wallace says that this number is "already prohibitively large from a conspiratorial perspective, because none of the other characteristics of successful conspiracies existed for the twelve apostles."[5] How were these characteristics lacking?

- The disciples didn't have thorough and immediate communication because they were dispersed from Jerusalem, scattered across the Roman Empire, and interrogated and martyred far from one another. They couldn't have communicated quickly enough to determine if someone else had confessed the lie because they didn't have the modern methods of communication necessary to make that happen.

- They would have had to protect the lie for a very long time. Several of the apostles lived for *decades* after the resurrection.

- While some of the apostles were brothers, the rest apparently had no relationship with one another and came from diverse backgrounds.

- They would have been under great pressure to confess the lie, given that they were risking their very lives to tell people about the resurrection (see chapter 20).

Wallace concludes, "I can't imagine a less favorable set of circumstances for a successful conspiracy than those that the twelve apostles faced. . . . These men and women either were involved in the greatest conspiracy of all time or were simply eyewitnesses who were telling the truth."[6]

If a person is going to suggest that the resurrection was a lie created and carried out by the disciples, they have much explaining to do. That doesn't mean it's not *possible* the disciples lied, but we're looking for the *best* explanation for the historical data. Note, too, that a conspiracy would not explain the historical facts that Paul and James suddenly transformed into followers of Jesus (recall that Paul said Jesus appeared to him and that 1 Corinthians says Jesus appeared to James); an additional explanation would still be needed for these conversions. In short, the lying disciples theory raises more questions than it answers.

KEY POINTS

- If the disciples lied about the resurrection, they would have had to (1) steal Jesus's body (the tomb had to be empty to support the claim of a bodily resurrection) and (2) carry out a long-lasting and complex conspiracy to convince people everywhere of their lie.
- Both the Romans and the Jews took grave robbery very seriously; it was punishable by death. The guard at the tomb would not have been sympathetic to the disciples' plan or willing to aid them in the theft.
- Even if the guard was asleep or not present at all, the disciples would still have had to move a stone weighing hundreds to thousands of pounds and carry off the body without being noticed.
- Successful conspiracies typically require (1) a small number of conspirators, (2) thorough and immediate communication, (3) a short time span, (4) significant relational connections, and (5) little or no pressure. None of these characteristics describe the disciples' circumstances.

CONVERSATION GUIDE

Open the Conversation

- What is a lie you could easily keep forever without anyone figuring it out? What would make that lie easy to keep?
- Let's say you told your mom or dad that you have a hamster in your dresser drawer (but you don't actually have one). Would that lie be easy or hard to keep? Why? *(Hard. A parent could easily disprove the claim by opening the drawer.)*

Advance the Conversation

- We already learned that the disciples were willing to suffer and die to tell others about the resurrection of Jesus. People still sometimes think they would have done so *knowing* they were lying. So let's think about what that lie would have required. First, the disciples would have had to steal Jesus's body. Why? *(If the body was still in the tomb, anyone could have pulled it out to show that the claim of bodily resurrection was untrue.)*
- *(Draw a simple picture of a stick figure guard in front of a tomb, a large rock covering the tomb, and stick figure disciples to the side.)* Imagine that this is the scene after Jesus was buried. What steps would the disciples have had to take to steal his body? *(Think through what it would take to get past the guard, remove the stone, and take the body using the details from this chapter.)*
- Let's say that somehow the disciples *did* manage to steal Jesus's body. Do you think the resurrection lie would have been the kind of lie that's easy or hard to keep telling? Why? *(Talk through J. Warner Wallace's criteria for a successful conspiracy and how they don't match the disciples' circumstances.)*
- Think back to the five historical facts surrounding the resurrection that we learned about earlier. Which ones would

not be explained by lying disciples? *(The transformations of Paul and James.)*

Apply the Conversation

- How would you respond to the following quotation from a skeptic? "The disciples probably stole the body and hid it somewhere in order to keep [getting benefits]. Most of them were fishermen, etc. who didn't have a whole lot going for them, but as disciples they were getting room and board for no work. Since Jesus claimed to be the Messiah, it wasn't enough to honor his gravesite. Being killed proved he was a phony. They had to claim he wasn't really dead, and would come back soon to fulfill the prophecies. Matthew 27:64 tells you what the skeptics were saying at the time it was written. Matthew tries to refute this with a story about the Jews placing a guard at the tomb, which is obviously fake because none of the other gospels mentions it."[7] *(Challenge older kids to reply to each claim individually using what they've learned so far. For younger kids, read the quote up to "getting room and board for no work" and ask them to respond.)*

23. Were Jesus's Disciples Mistaken about the Resurrection?

I've always had a fondness for old diners. Not diners *trying* to be old but diners that are actually old because no one has bothered to update them. These charming restaurants usually have orange carpet, clashing curtains, half-empty pie displays, turkey dinners, and lots of senior specials. They make my old-fashioned self feel like all is right in the world again. But these places also tend to have every parent's enemy . . . the claw machine.

If "claw machine" doesn't immediately ring a bell for you, it's that game with dozens of stuffed animals inside and a metal grabber that you lower onto an item of your choice in an attempt to hook it. If you hook it, you keep it. But the claw is made not to hold on very tight, so just as you think that slightly creepy tiger is yours forever, it mischievously slips back into the pile. You must then exit the restaurant pulling a devastated child who thinks you're the worst parent ever for refusing to put *more* money into the creepy tiger pit.

I have to report, however, that my daughter did actually pull a toy out one time. It was a spiky purple rubber ball. She fell in love with it. She thought the spikes looked like eyes, so she named it Purple Friend and continues to sleep with it (I know that sounds really sad, but I assure you she has many real friends!). To her, the ball is not an *it*; it's a *he*. And she's protected "him" fiercely ever since.

Purple Friend took on a life of its own because my daughter saw something in a ball that wasn't there. Of course, she knows in her head that it's an impersonal object, but emotionally she's attached to it as something much more.

There are many ways people experience something powerfully based on something they "see" that isn't really there. You wouldn't say they're being deceptive but rather that they're mistaken. In the same way, skeptics have offered numerous explanations for how the disciples may have believed Jesus rose from the dead based on some kind of mistaken interpretation of a visual experience. Yes, that would have to mean the disciples, Paul, James, and everyone else who reported seeing the risen Jesus *all* mistakenly saw something that led to the same belief. And the empty tomb would have to remain an unsolved mystery, because visions wouldn't explain a missing body. Nonetheless, people as far back as the second century have suggested that the resurrection "appearances" were really just hallucinations or other visionary mistakes.

Did the Disciples Hallucinate?

A hallucination is an experience involving the apparent perception of something not actually there. How would hallucinations explain what happened to the disciples? People vary on what they propose, but as one example, New Testament scholar Gerd Lüdemann suggests that Peter was so consumed with grief and guilt that it led to him having a vision of Jesus that convinced him Jesus was resurrected. Others got caught up in the frenzy, and the resurrection "appearances" became contagious—a "shared hallucinatory fantasy."[1]

While hallucination hypotheses have long abounded, it wasn't until recently that a medical doctor evaluated them in light of modern psychiatric knowledge. Joseph Bergeron, who conducted the research, explains the significance of this medical analysis:

These [hallucination-related] hypotheses . . . are primarily proposed by nonmedical writers and found in debates or theological books by New Testament scholars, rather than being subjected to a more appropriate, specialized medical readership. As a result, the analysis of potential medical causes for these hallucinatory symptoms is generally flawed and often absent. . . . Psychiatric hypotheses for the disciples' postcrucifixion experiences of Jesus are not to be found in peerreviewed medical literature. This is noteworthy since these hypotheses propose hallucinatory symptoms which imply an underlying medical pathology.[2]

From a medical perspective, therefore, hallucination hypotheses cannot be casually asserted without considering whether they're medically consistent with the known facts of a given case. With that in mind, let's look at two key medical characteristics of hallucinations that are relevant for this particular discussion.

First, a hallucination is a symptom of an underlying medical condition. Bergeron says that these conditions fall into one of three categories: *psychophysiological* (changes in brain structure or function, such as in the case of a brain tumor); *psychobiochemical* (chemical derangement, such as in the case of alcohol withdrawal); and *psychodynamic* (psychiatric illnesses, such as schizophrenia). These are all serious medical conditions. It's extraordinarily unlikely that the disciples, Paul, James, and others who reportedly saw the risen Jesus all suffered from underlying mental conditions that predisposed them to hallucinations. And even *if* that were reasonable to believe, no one would have accepted the testimony of a troop of mentally ill people!

Second, hallucinations are private experiences. Hallucination hypotheses can't account for the events when the disciples (and others) reportedly experienced what they believed was the risen Jesus *at the same time* (for example, John 20:19–20). Bergeron explains:

> While some may consider the disciples' post-crucifixion group encounters with the resurrected Jesus as collective simultaneous hallucinations, such an explanation is far outside mainstream clinical thought. What are the odds that separate individuals in a group could experience simultaneous and identical psychological phenomena mixed with hallucinations? . . . Concordantly, the concept of collective-hallucination is not found in peer reviewed medical and psychological literature.[3]

That said, religiously inspired group *visions* have been documented. For example, you may have heard about visions of Mary (mother of Jesus) that groups have reported at certain times and places. Independent scholar Jake O'Connell reviewed the best documented reports of collective visionary experiences and concluded that they share the following characteristics: (1) there's a heightened sense of group expectation to experience the vision, (2) not everyone in the group experiences it, (3) those who do experience it have varied visions relative to one another, and (4) the apparitions do not carry on conversations.[4]

While O'Connell believes, based on these reports, that collective "hallucinations" are possible (contrary to current medical understanding), he concludes that the resurrection accounts still do not fit this profile. In particular, if first-century Jews had held any expectation that would have influenced the nature of a vision, it would have been that Jesus would be assumed into heaven in some kind of glorified state. As Christian philosopher William Lane Craig explains, "An assumption [into heaven] is a wholly different category from a resurrection. To infer from heavenly visions of

Jesus that he had been resurrected ran counter to Jewish thinking . . . whereas Jesus's assumption into heaven would have been the natural conclusion."[5] Resurrection claims, therefore, don't fit the profile of collective visions because they ran *counter* to expectations; collective visions typically *align* with expectations. Also contrary to the profile of collective visions, the Gospels report that Jesus carried on conversations with multiple people (Matt. 28; Luke 24; John 20; Acts 1:3).

Even if a person accepts the medical legitimacy of collective hallucinations, the resurrection accounts don't fit the profile of any known cases.

Did the Disciples Have Visions Because They Were Grief-Stricken?

It might sound far-fetched that grief alone could lead to visionary experiences, but it's actually well documented that people mourning the loss of a loved one sometimes report having an experience with the deceased person—most commonly a spouse. The nature of the experience is typically described as "a sense of closeness."[6] *Visual* experiences of the deceased are rare but do happen. Unlike hallucinations, however, they're considered to be within the bounds of normal grief processes and are not symptomatic of underlying illness.

Given what we know about these grief-based experiences, is it possible they account for the disciples' resurrection beliefs? If just one (or even two!) disciples reported visions of Jesus, they *could* be consistent with a grief explanation, but such visions involving a friend rather than a spouse would be rare. In addition, grief-based experiences cannot account for all we know because (1) it wouldn't be expected that *all* the disciples would have such visions (either individually or simultaneously), and (2) whoever did have such a vision would not have concluded it was an actual encounter with a physically resurrected Jesus (grief-related visions are not prolonged or interactive). Grief also can't explain Paul's reported experience with Jesus because he was an enemy of the church at the time Jesus reportedly appeared to him, not a grieving friend or family member.

Given the strong evidence that the disciples truly believed the risen Jesus appeared to them (see chapters 20 and 22), it's tempting for skeptics to casually explain away their beliefs as mistaken conclusions based on visionary experiences. However, if such an explanation is going to be offered, a kind of visionary experience that could actually account for what we know needs to exist. As we've seen, there isn't one.

KEY POINTS

- A hallucination is a symptom of an underlying medical condition. There's no reason to believe that the disciples, Paul, James, and others who reportedly saw the risen Jesus all suffered from underlying mental conditions.
- Hallucinations are also private experiences. Hallucination hypotheses, therefore, can't account for the times when the disciples (and others) simultaneously experienced what they believed was the risen Jesus.
- If just one (or even two!) disciples reported visions of Jesus, they *could* be consistent with a grief-induced experience, but it wouldn't be expected that *all* the disciples would have such visions or that they would have conversations with the visions.
- Hallucination theories do not account for why the tomb was empty.

CONVERSATION GUIDE

Open the Conversation

- When you think of optical illusions you've seen, which ones come to mind? *(If your child doesn't know what an optical illusion is or can't think of one, do the rubber pencil trick.[7] Hold the end of a pencil loosely between your thumb and first finger, then move your hand up and down vertically so the loose end bounces. This makes the pencil appear wavy.)*

Advance the Conversation

- An optical illusion is something that tricks our eyes so that what we *think* we see is different from what is really there. Optical illusions can trick anyone! Sometimes, however, people have a mental condition that causes them to see things that aren't there. People have suggested that the disciples experienced hallucinations that led them to believe Jesus was alive. Do you think this is a good explanation for the historical facts we've looked at? Why or why not? *(There's no evidence that those who claimed to see Jesus alive suffered from a mental condition. Even if one person did actually hallucinate, this wouldn't explain why everyone else claimed to see the same thing. Explain that science also shows that groups of people don't hallucinate together. If your child is old enough, raise the subject of collective visions and how they differ from the resurrection claims.)*

- Another reason people sometimes see something that isn't there is because they're experiencing a lot of grief—such as when their spouse dies. Some grieving people report that they believe they heard or saw the loved one who passed away. Do you think grief might be a good explanation for the historical facts surrounding Jesus's resurrection? Why or why not? *(The disciples would have grieved Jesus's death, but it's highly doubtful they all experienced visions because of it. Explain that grief-induced visions also don't have conversations with people as the disciples claimed Jesus did. Such visions also wouldn't explain the conversion of Paul, who wasn't grieving, or the empty tomb.)*

Apply the Conversation

- In response to a person asking what could have caused the disciples to hallucinate, a man replied, "Perhaps one or a few of Jesus's grief-stricken followers had [a grief hallucination] experience shortly after he died. After a few days or weeks or months of 'did you experience it too?' it's not strange that Paul could think that Jesus appeared to 'the twelve,' and with fifty years of oral retelling and elaboration you get the stories where he hung around bodily for a while."[8] How would you respond?

24. Did People Invent the Resurrection Many Years Later?

My younger daughter loves reading mysteries. She recently discovered Nancy Drew and the Clue Crew, which is a series of short mystery books for younger elementary-age kids. A couple of nights ago she asked me to read one aloud to her. It was about a famous cat named Fluffington who suddenly disappeared from a Hollywood movie set while the Clue Crew (a group of kid sleuths) was visiting. As I read, I had to smile at the simplicity and predictability of the story. The reader learns a few very basic facts about the case, meets three possible suspects, and evaluates which one is the best "explanation" for the mystery at hand. The case is quickly solved, then it's time for parents to shell out another five dollars for the next mildly captivating book in the series.

Some skeptics would say that solving a fictional mystery is no different from what we've been doing by looking at resurrection "facts" and possible explanations in the last few chapters. They believe we're spinning our mental wheels analyzing the details of a fictional story made up long after Jesus's death. For example, popular atheist blogger Bob Seidensticker wrote, "I don't imagine a sinister mastermind behind the creation of Christianity, just like there is no reason to imagine one behind Zoroastrianism or Mithraism, and there is none behind the corruption of a message in the game of Telephone. It's just a story—a legend that grew over time."[1] For skeptics such as Seidensticker, the question of a resurrection is no more historically relevant than the question of what happened to Fluffington.

Those who believe the resurrection is a legendary tale often acknowledge that Jesus existed and had followers (see chapter 1), but they claim that as Christian communities told and retold the stories of Jesus's life, history became distorted. Fact and fiction were mixed to the point that they were indistinguishable. And the early church eventually started believing a very tall tale: Jesus had been physically raised from the dead.

There's a big problem with this theory, however: no evidence exists that this is the case. In fact, all the evidence points to the contrary.

Was the Resurrection a Legendary Addition to Christianity?

The subject of New Testament reliability is quite complex, as it involves multiple levels of questions (questions that are far outside the scope of what we can cover here).[2] We don't have to be New Testament experts, however, to address the specific question of whether the resurrection was a legend that developed long after Jesus's death. It turns out the answer is fairly simple.

While scholars vary widely on their dating of the Gospels (and, respectively, how historically reliable they believe them to be), they're almost unanimous in dating Paul's letters to AD 50–60. *And Paul wrote repeatedly of the resurrection as central to the truth of Christianity* (for example, Rom. 1:4; 1 Cor. 15:4; Phil. 3:10). This means we know that the resurrection was already preached within twenty to thirty years of Jesus's death and within the lifetime of eyewitnesses. This is hardly the kind of time and circumstance needed for a complex legend to develop—something typically requiring the passing of several generations.

But we can get even closer to Jesus's life.

Recall from chapter 21 that scholars have determined that Paul was quoting an early Christian creed in part of 1 Corinthians 15 (a creed is a formalized statement of faith).[3] While there's debate over where the creed ends and Paul's own writing begins, at a minimum the creed includes verses 3–5: "For what I received I passed on to you as of first importance: that Christ died for our sins according to the Scriptures, that he was buried, that he was raised on the third day according to the Scriptures, and that he appeared to Cephas, and then to the Twelve." Note that Paul says he *received* this creed. Most scholars agree that he received it in the early to mid-30s AD when, according to Galatians 1:18, he "went up to Jerusalem to get acquainted with Cephas [Peter] and stayed with him fifteen days." *This means that a creed proclaiming the resurrection was already formulated and being transmitted within four to six years of Jesus's death.*

To be clear, this understanding isn't affirmed only by Christian scholars. Critical scholars acknowledge it as well. Atheist New Testament scholar Gerd Lüdemann (whom we met in the last chapter) says, "The elements in the tradition are to be dated to the first two years after the crucifixion of Jesus . . . not later than three years after the death of Jesus."[4] Michael Goulder, another atheist New Testament scholar, writes, "[It] goes back at least to what Paul was taught when he was converted, a couple of years after the crucifixion."[5] Robert W. Funk, founder of the highly critical Jesus Seminar, states, "The conviction that Jesus had risen from the dead had already taken root by the time Paul was converted about 33 CE. On the assumption that Jesus died about 30 CE, the time for development was thus two or three years at most."[6]

Put simply, there is little doubt that the resurrection was proclaimed from the very beginning of the Christian movement, and there is no indication that any early Christian community ever existed *without* a belief in the resurrection. This doesn't mean, of course, that the resurrection is true. But it does mean we're not spending our time trying to make sense of something in the realm of Nancy Drew and the Clue Crew. There really are historical facts surrounding the resurrection, people really did make resurrection claims, and the facts really do demand an explanation.

A Resurrection Is the Best Explanation (Unless You've Already Ruled It Out)

It's time now to ask, "What if Jesus actually *was* raised from the dead?" It's not hard to see that this explanation would account for all the data: Jesus was crucified (and died), the tomb was empty *because he was bodily raised from the dead*, Paul was transformed from a church persecutor into a bold proclaimer of the resurrection *because Jesus appeared to him*, James was transformed from a skeptic into a leader in the church *because Jesus appeared to him*, and the disciples were willing to suffer and die to proclaim the resurrection *because Jesus appeared to them*.

A resurrection undoubtedly makes sense of the historical data in a way no other explanation does. But many people will never consider it possible. Why? Because they *assume* God doesn't exist. As we saw in chapter 4, if God doesn't exist, then miracles aren't possible (nothing can have a supernatural cause if nothing supernatural exists). We should agree with atheists that *if* God doesn't exist, then it's *not* possible that Jesus was supernaturally raised from the dead—explanation off the table! But it's important to understand that this rejection of the resurrection as a *possibility* has nothing to do with the historical evidence. It has everything to do with a philosophical commitment to an atheistic worldview.

If a person is willing to consider the possibility of God's existence, however, the door opens to a thoughtful evaluation of the historical data. God's existence doesn't automatically mean that Jesus rose from the dead, of course. For any given miracle claim, we must look at the evidence. If I told you my coffee mug walked around my computer on its own this morning, you would rightly question the truth of that claim, even if you believe God exists and can choose to move mugs. But the resurrection is no case of a walking coffee mug. As we've seen, it's a miracle claim with significant *evidence*. In addition, whereas a walking coffee mug would be a miraculous event with no apparent purpose, the resurrection would be a miraculous event in a context where we might *expect* God to act.[7] For hundreds of years, the Jewish people claimed that God had revealed himself to them. They believed that he validated human messengers of his truth by miraculous signs. They professed that he had promised a Messiah. And they waited. Eventually, Jesus came along and claimed to be that Messiah. But how could they be sure he was the Messiah? If God exists, had promised a Messiah, and wanted to confirm that Jesus was that person, a miraculous sign—such as the resurrection—would not only be possible but also expected.

I think we can all agree that the resurrection sounds extraordinary—something far outside anything we've personally witnessed. *But just because something sounds crazy doesn't mean it isn't true, and not all miracle claims are equally valid.* As skeptics always emphasize, we have to consider the evidence. And that's exactly what we've done. The evidence has led us to the truth of the resurrection.

KEY POINTS

- Some skeptics claim that the resurrection is a legend that grew over time and was added to Christian belief as the early church retold stories of Jesus's life.
- To the contrary, the dating of Paul's letters (and the previously composed creed quoted in 1 Corinthians 15) demonstrates that Christians were proclaiming the resurrection within four to six years of Jesus's death. Far more time would be required for a legend to develop.
- There's no evidence of any early Christian community that didn't have a belief in the resurrection.
- The rejection of the resurrection as a *possibility* has nothing to do with historical evidence. It's a philosophical commitment to an atheistic worldview.
- A supernatural resurrection is the best explanation for the historical facts unless you've already ruled it out by assuming that God doesn't exist.

CONVERSATION GUIDE

Open the Conversation

- What is the best mystery book you've ever read?
- In the last few chapters, we've been looking at the "mystery" of the resurrection. We've learned facts of the case and looked at why certain explanations don't fit those facts well. How is the resurrection similar to or different from mystery books you've read? *(Explain how some people think that everything we've looked at is no different from a fictional mystery—the "facts" are all part of a resurrection story made up many years after Jesus's death.)*

Advance the Conversation

- Read 1 Corinthians 15:3–5. This was written by the apostle Paul. We know from Bible scholars (both Christians and non-Christians) that the information he says he "received" was given to him within four to six years of Jesus's death. What does this tell us people were already saying about Jesus at that time? *(He died for our sins and was resurrected. Explain how this shows that the resurrection wasn't a legend added to Christian belief decades later. Unlike with a mystery novel, we can know we're dealing with historical facts that demand an explanation.)*

- *(Write down the five historical facts studied in chapters 20 and 21.)* Here are the historical facts we've learned. Do you think the idea of a resurrection fits the facts worse, the same as, or better than the other explanations we've considered? Why? *(Talk through each point and show how the resurrection makes sense of the historical data in a way no other explanation does.)*

- Jesus's resurrection sounds pretty extraordinary—we don't normally see a person come back from the dead! Why do you think Christians believe that's even possible? *(Remind your child of the chapter 4 conversation on miracles and how their possibility depends on the existence of God. Explain that people who say the resurrection isn't possible are assuming God doesn't exist.)*

- If I told you that my coffee mug got up by itself and walked around my computer this morning, would you believe me? Why or why not? *(Get your child to think beyond "that sounds crazy!" Explain how the context of the resurrection claim sets it apart from a claim like this.)*

Apply the Conversation

- The author of an article on a news website wrote, "There is not one proven case of a human being rising from the dead.

So believing in the resurrection involves a leap of faith that many people are unwilling to make. But they may still believe in the fundamental precepts of Christianity, and in the message of the resurrection itself."[8] Using all you've learned in part 4, how would you respond?

PART 5

The Difference Jesus MAKES

Overview

When my son was younger, he loved Legos and was really good at building sets on his own. In fact, he was a little *too* good, given how much those sets cost. He could build even the most complex ones within a couple of hours. Unfortunately, he never wanted to build the same thing twice, so buying Legos was like burning cash (though burning cash is far less painful than unexpectedly stepping on a Lego piece).

As he got older, his interest in Legos was replaced with an interest in something called K'Nex. K'Nex sets tend to have more sophisticated designs, so they're a great next step for a Lego-loving child. They do, however, suffer from the same longevity issue; unless you have a kid who likes rebuilding, those beautiful designs are quickly constructed, then pushed to the corner of the room to sit indefinitely.

For a long time, my son wanted a particular K'Nex roller coaster set, but it was expensive for what it was. Then one day I stumbled upon what I thought was the perfect solution: a K'Nex set with almost a thousand pieces that could be used to make a hundred models. Instead of buying a single-use set for a roller coaster, I assumed this would be an opportunity to get him a set he could use to build a roller coaster plus many other things. I happily purchased it and gave it to him for his birthday.

A few weeks passed, and I noticed he hadn't built much with it—including a roller coaster. I asked him why. He replied, "The roller coaster? Oh, you can't make that with this set. It doesn't have all the pieces and connectors you need. You have to get the set specifically designed for that. Also, this set only came with detailed instructions for a few of the pictured models, so there's not a lot I know how to build."

I then realized the flaw in my logic. I had assumed that as long as he had hundreds of pieces to work with, he could build whatever he wanted, *including* specific designs like the roller coaster. But, as is obvious to me now, certain models need specific pieces that don't necessarily come in any other set—even one with hundreds of other pieces to choose from.

If we want our kids to build a robust understanding of Christianity—a specific "roller coaster"—we have to make sure they have the right pieces. A key purpose of this book has been to help you identify the pieces of understanding about Jesus that kids need today, given the difficult world in which they're growing up. This is a hugely important first step that's missed by parents who assume their kids will develop a thorough and accurate understanding of Christianity by putting together whatever pieces they happen to gather at church. Having the conversations in this book (as well as those in *Keeping Your Kids on God's Side* and *Talking with Your Kids about God*) will go a long way toward giving your child the specific pieces of understanding they need to work with.

That said, we can't stop there. Just as with the K'Nex set, kids need guidance on how to put those pieces together accurately. Without instructions, they can build *some* thing but not necessarily the *intended* thing. A distorted roller coaster isn't a big deal, but a distorted understanding of Christianity is.

The purpose of part 5 is to take all the pieces we've looked at and ask, "Now what? What *should* an understanding of Christianity look like when we put all the pieces together and apply them to our lives?" We'll start by establishing what it means to be a Christian (yes, that's a simple question, but it can have surprising complexity). Then we'll look at how Christians view the Bible and God differently than non-Christians do. This will lead to a discussion of what it means to be saved and what our resulting trust in Jesus should look like. Finally, we'll conclude the book with a conversation on why knowing the truth about Jesus means *sharing* that truth with others—a connection often misunderstood and resented by a secular world.

C. S. Lewis famously said, "I believe in Christianity as I believe that the sun has risen, not only because I see it but because by it, I see everything else."[1] Through these final conversations, we'll similarly see that the difference Jesus should make in our lives is . . . everything.

Three Keys to Impactful Conversations about the Difference Jesus Makes

1. *Use the K'Nex story to explain the importance of having specific pieces of understanding about Christianity and knowing how to put them together.* Before beginning the chapters in part 5, read this overview to your child, stopping after my son's statement. Ask, "What was wrong with what the mom assumed?" (I—the mom—assumed that if my son had hundreds of pieces, he had the right pieces to make whatever he wanted.) Reflect with your child on all the important "pieces" of Christianity they've learned so far and the need for guidance on how to put them together for their life in a biblically faithful way.

2. *Explain that Christians can have varied understandings of the answers to the questions in this section.* Although the subjects covered in part 5 sound basic, Christians sometimes

understand them in very different ways. In fact, if your child is older, they've likely already experienced this, and it can be quite confusing—especially when the answers they hear contradict one another. (Think of how many different things Christians can mean when they say they "trust in Jesus," for example.) Discuss how familiar answers to basic questions aren't always biblically accurate or adequately nuanced.

3. *Emphasize that knowing truth is not the same as living truth.* We've focused so far in this book on *knowing* truth. In this final section, we're transitioning to *living* truth. It's not enough to know what's true if that truth doesn't transform us. Take time to share how knowing the truth of Jesus has made the difference in your own life. Consider having your child interview other Christian family members or Christian adults to learn how knowing Jesus has made the difference in their lives as well.

25. What Is a Christian?

I recently wrote a blog post about the fact that research shows committed Christians are now a minority.[1] I contrasted this with the environment in which I grew up: a small town where everyone I knew fit into one of four buckets: (1) committed Christians, (2) nominal Christians, (3) those who didn't call themselves Christians but accepted Judeo-Christian values, and (4) Mormons. Soon after I published the post, I received the following email:

> I wondered if there was a reason why Mormons were labeled separately from the other three buckets. I'm a Mormon myself, but I'm very much a committed Christian. . . . I just know many people aren't aware that we follow Jesus Christ due to the misleading nature of our accrued nickname after the Book of Mormon, [which] testifies of Christ and His mission and gospel.

Of all the chapter titles in this book, "What Is a Christian?" is surely the question that sounds easiest to answer. It seems obvious that Christians should be able to define what a Christian is! However, people today can mean vastly different things when they use the word. For example, the woman who emailed me seemed to define a Christian as anyone who "follows" Jesus. However,

Mormons deny the Trinity, affirm that Jesus, Satan, and humans are spirit siblings, and believe that humans can progress toward being gods themselves—some very different beliefs than Christians have historically held, given what the Bible teaches. You can see the problem. If we define a Christian as anyone who "follows" Jesus, that can mean almost anything, because a person can define "following" in any number of ways. Describing a Christian simply as someone who "believes in," "trusts in," or "accepts" Jesus has similar problems of ambiguity. To more meaningfully define what a Christian is, we need to look at what the word originally meant. But before we do so, let's examine more closely why this discussion matters.

How Important Are Definitions Anyway?

According to the latest research, about 70 percent of Americans are Christians (based on people's self-identification and how researchers group religions).[2] However, research also shows that just 9 percent of Americans have a biblical worldview—accepting core truths taught in the Bible.[3] These statistics show that there's a major disconnect between the popular use of the word *Christian* and the beliefs you might assume that word represents. *This lack of clarity can lead to much confusion for our kids.* A brief analogy can help us see why.

My daughter used to love penguins. For a long time, she would point out cute penguin shirts, penguin stuffed animals, and penguin toys. When our family went to Sea World one summer, I assumed she would go crazy over the penguin exhibit. But while walking through it, she was totally uninterested. When I asked why, she replied, "I don't like the real ones that much. The ones on things at the store are much cuter."

Because the word *Christian* is used so loosely in today's culture, kids can easily become confused about what being a Christian actually means—to the point of preferring a cute, toy penguin version of Christianity over the real thing. And when kids develop their spiritual identity around an incomplete or inaccurate replica, it's easy for them to eventually end up in the statistical gap of those who identify as a Christian but don't hold a biblical worldview (we'll talk more about why having a biblical worldview is important in the next chapter).

We can help them gain clarity by looking at what it *first* meant to be a Christian and how that meaning still applies today. To be clear, the purpose of the following discussion is not to label people as "in" or "out" of some kind of Christian club, as is sometimes alleged when conversations on this subject arise. It's also not to place ourselves in judgment of who is or isn't saved; that role belongs to God alone. But words mean something. If we're going to call ourselves Christians, we need to have a solid understanding of what we're claiming for *ourselves*—and how that claim should affect our lives.

What Is a Christian according to the Bible?

The first time the word *Christian* is found in the Bible is in Acts 11:26, which says, "The disciples were called Christians first at Antioch" (see also Acts 26:28; 1 Pet. 4:16). In the ancient world, a disciple was someone with an all-encompassing dedication to a teacher—someone who trusted their teacher, adhered to what the teacher taught, and followed the teacher's ways. A disciple was much more than a student in the modern sense. Christians, therefore, were those who dedicated their lives to Christ in this comprehensive way.

Just before Jesus ascended to heaven, he instructed his disciples, "Go and make disciples of all nations, baptizing them in the name of the Father and of the Son and of the Holy Spirit, and teaching them to obey everything I have commanded you" (Matt.

251

28:19–20). *Discipleship was to continue.* That means Christians today should still be those who are fully devoted to the teachings and ways of Jesus (as given to us in the Bible) and who, in turn, make disciples of others.[4] Being devoted to the teachings and ways of Jesus isn't some kind of detached intellectual process, however. In Luke 14:27, Jesus says, "Whoever does not carry their cross and follow me cannot be my disciple." That's a strong statement. Jesus calls those who are his disciples to *die* to their old selves, not coldly study his words and actions from afar. This is why he connects making disciples to the command to baptize (Matt. 28:19–20); baptism symbolizes burying the old self and resurrecting to new life (Rom. 6:3–4)—a full surrender to Jesus himself.

People sometimes think that being a Christian is only about how you live, while others think it's only about what you believe. But it should be clear from this brief discussion that either extreme is in error. Being a disciple of Jesus involves what we believe *and* how we live. We see this inseparable connection throughout Jesus's teachings (see parts 1–4) as well as in the rest of the New Testament. The apostle Paul, for example, uses the first eleven chapters of Romans to explain correct belief about who God is and who we are in Christ. Then in Romans 12:1, he transitions to explaining correct living *in light of* correct belief. Belief and behavior are inextricably linked parts of discipleship.

Putting this all together, we might say that a Christian is a disciple of Jesus who has died to oneself in order to find new life in him (Rom. 6:3–4), who seeks to obey Jesus's commands (Matt. 28:20), and who is called to make disciples of others. Of course, much more could be said. This is not *only* what a Christian is, and there are many other biblically faithful ways a definition could be articulated. But it's a starting point for conveying the biblical sense of the word.

The Difference Jesus Makes

Our discussion so far gives us the necessary background to see why the following commonly used ways to define what a Christian is fail to do biblical justice to the word.

Definitions Based on Belief in God

A belief in God, in and of itself, doesn't necessarily mean a person is a Christian. Some believe in a distant God who set the world in motion but doesn't intervene in it. Some believe in a God described by holy books other than the Bible. Others believe in a God of their own conception. But Christians believe that God revealed himself in the person of Jesus, and as we saw in this chapter, that has many specific implications for what we believe and how we live.

Definitions Based on Moral Behavior

People sometimes identify themselves or others as Christians based on their general agreement with Christian values. However, many different beliefs can underlie behavior that's consistent with Jesus's teachings. Anyone with any worldview can dedicate their life to serving the less fortunate, for example. But a person who does so while rejecting Jesus would not be a Christian.

Definitions Based on Christian Practices

While it may *look* as if a person who engages in certain spiritual practices is a Christian, that's not necessarily the case. There are, for example, many people who attend a Christian church each week yet reject what Jesus taught. Some today even identify themselves as "religious fictionalists"—people who "practice a religion even though they think the core beliefs associated with that religion are false."[5] Attending church, praying, and reading the Bible are important spiritual practices for Christians, but merely doing those things doesn't necessarily mean a person *is* a Christian.

Definitions Based on Any Kind of Acceptance of Jesus

This brings us full circle to the question raised at the beginning of this chapter. Are Mormons Christians because they love Jesus? What about Jehovah's Witnesses? And what about New Agers who see Jesus as an enlightened master? If a person were to ask you if these or other groups are Christian, the best thing to do is ask, "What do you mean by Christian?" Oftentimes a person is asking because they want to know if you think adherents to other religions are saved. If that's the underlying reason for the question, then a conversation about what the Bible says regarding salvation is more relevant (see chapter 28). But if a person is really asking what you believe it means to be a Christian, it's worth taking the time to give a nuanced answer. Acknowledge that people define the word *Christian* differently, but explain what the Bible says it means and why that meaning should still matter to us today.

As I said earlier, so much more could be said about what a Christian is. We still have a lot to unpack! Next up is a particularly important conversation on how Christians should view the Bible.

KEY POINTS

- If we define a Christian as anyone who "follows," "believes in," "trusts," or "accepts" Jesus, that can mean almost anything, because a person can define those words in any number of ways.
- For a more meaningful definition, we need to look at what the word *Christian* originally meant. Christians were disciples

of Jesus, fully dedicated to his teachings and ways and living transformed lives in surrender to him.

- Jesus commanded his disciples to continue making disciples, baptizing them and teaching them to obey all his commands.
- Being a Christian involves both what we believe and how we live.
- Defining a Christian based only on a person's belief in God, moral behavior, Christian practices, or general acceptance of Jesus fails to do justice to the biblical sense of the word.

CONVERSATION GUIDE

Open the Conversation

- If someone asked you what it means to be a Christian, what would you say? *(If your child says it's someone who "believes in Jesus," "accepts Jesus," etc., challenge them to see how that can mean a variety of things.)*

Advance the Conversation

- Read Acts 11:26. What does this tell us about who the first Christians were? *(Disciples of Jesus. Explain what it meant to be a disciple at that time.)*
- Read Jesus's words to his disciples before ascending to heaven in Matthew 28:19–20. How are these words important for understanding what it means to be a Christian today? *(We should still be disciples, fully dedicated to Jesus. Jesus also connects discipleship to baptism—representing the transformation of a disciple's life—and obedience. Read the definition offered in this chapter as one example of a more specific description of a Christian.)*
- Do you think being a Christian is about what you believe, how you live, both, or neither? *(Both. This connection is inseparable*

for a disciple of Jesus because Jesus's teachings include both. Explain that this is why you can't tell if someone is a Christian based only on moral behavior.)

- If a person attends a Christian church, prays, and reads the Bible, do you think that means they're a Christian? Why or why not? *(There's no way to know based only on actions. For older kids, extend the discussion by asking how your child would respond if someone asked them whether a Mormon is a Christian.)*

Apply the Conversation

- A person asked online, "Can I be a Christian but not believe in God?"[6] How would you respond? *(For deeper discussion, visit the webpage and evaluate the varied responses people offered.)*

26. How Is a Person's View of the Bible Different as a Christian?

Last year one of my daughters joined the American Heritage Girls (AHG) troop at her school. AHG is a Christian alternative to Girl Scouts that includes badge work, service projects, leadership opportunities, and outdoor experiences.[1] Just as you would expect from a scout-type program, membership comes with a cute outfit and giant membership book that provides organizational rules and detailed requirements for completing the dozens of available badges.

My daughter had the opportunity to look through her friend's book at one of the first meetings before she had received her own in the mail. She couldn't wait to get started. I found her in her room the next evening working hard on something that involved cotton balls and sticks. When I asked her what she was doing, she told me she was working on a badge. Here's how the rest of the conversation went.

Me: "Did you read all the requirements for that badge?"

Daughter: "No. I came up with my own idea."

Me: "But to complete the badges, you have to do what the handbook tells you. You can't just do whatever you want."

Daughter: "Yes, I can!"

Me: "Well, you *can*, but if you're not doing what's outlined by AHG, it's not AHG badgework anymore; it's just your own creation."

Even if my daughter *thought* what she was doing was part of AHG and *said* what she was doing was part of AHG, it *wasn't* part of AHG. It should be recognized that there are limits to what can reasonably be considered part of a group's identity, purpose, and work. For AHG, those things are defined in its handbook. For Christians, those things are defined in the Bible.

The Bible as the Inspired Word of God

To be sure, many people identify as Christians today who don't consider the Bible to be their definitive "handbook," because they don't consider it to be the fully true Word of God (for any number of reasons). As a result, their spiritual beliefs and practices can vary widely because they don't feel those beliefs and practices are necessarily constrained by what the Bible says. Recall, however, how we defined what a Christian is in the last chapter—we looked at the original sense of the word in the *Bible*. Why start there? Almost everything we know about Jesus is from the Bible, so if a person is going to claim a Jesus-related identity, it will have to at least partly come from what the Bible says about him. Those who don't fully accept the Bible as God's Word, then, must pick and choose what they personally believe to be true from it. Like my daughter working on her own creations, they're forging their own spiritual path. We won't use this chapter to debate whether such a view should still fit within the definition of Christianity but rather to focus on why Christians *should* fully accept the Bible as God's Word and what it means to do so. We'll start with what Jesus himself thought of Scripture. After all, if we're his disciples, we should affirm what he affirmed.

Jesus referred to Scripture on many occasions in the Gospels. It's important to remember, however, that "Scripture" in Jesus's time didn't refer to the Bible as we currently know it—the New Testament hadn't been written yet. Scripture was what we now call the Old Testament. Jesus clearly affirmed its divine origin and authority in multiple ways:

- He referred to Scripture as "the word of God" that cannot be set aside (John 10:35).
- He frequently used the words "it is written" to emphasize the importance of scriptural teachings (the phrase is used over ninety times in the New Testament).
- He repeatedly rebuked his critics for their lack of scriptural understanding, saying, "Have you not/never read?" (Matt. 12:1–8; 19:3–6; 21:14–16, 42–44; 22:23–33).
- He cited Scripture in response to Satan's temptations (Luke 4:1–13).
- He saw himself as the fulfillment of Scripture (Luke 24:44–49; see chapter 2).
- He indicated that the words of Scripture are imperishable (Matt. 5:18).

As we learned in chapter 12, the New Testament claims the same scriptural status for itself. And 2 Timothy 3:16 says, "All Scripture is God-breathed and is useful for teaching, rebuking, correcting and training in righteousness." Theologians use the word *inspiration* to capture this idea. Inspiration means Scripture is "God-breathed" in the sense that God guided its human authors through the Holy Spirit (2 Pet. 1:21). The Bible doesn't detail *how* God guided them, but we do see examples of many types of processes at work, including historical research (Luke 1:1–4), observation of life (Ecclesiastes), Spirit-assisted memory (John 14:26), miraculous revelation (2 Cor. 12:1–4), dictation (Rev. 2–3), and personal discernment (1 Cor. 7:25–26, 39–40).[2]

Multiple implications flow from this understanding that Scripture is the inspired Word of God. Three of the most important to understand are these:

1. The Bible is *truthful* because God cannot lie (Heb. 6:18).
2. The Bible is *authoritative* because its words originate from God himself. God, as our sovereign Creator, clearly has the knowledge and the right to tell us what we should (and shouldn't) believe and do.
3. The Bible is *sufficient* for teaching us what we need to know for salvation and living godly lives (2 Tim. 3:15–17). This doesn't imply that other sources cannot be helpful in our spiritual development but rather that other sources aren't *necessary* for these purposes.

Theologians have written extensively on and debated the meanings of words such as *truthful*, *authoritative*, and *sufficient*; there is certainly much more that could be said on this subject.[3] However, these basic points will give your child a solid foundation from which to learn more.

When Christians Disagree about What the Bible Teaches

All of this being said, we all know that even Christians who agree that the Bible is the inspired Word of God can have significant disagreements over some of what it teaches, and we've all seen this play out in unfortunate ways. Historically, such disagreements led to the development of Christian denominations, as entire groups divided over topics such as baptism, church governance, the relationship between God's sovereignty and human free will, and more.[4] Even *within* churches, individuals differ in their views on things such as the age of the Earth, end-times events, and the role of spiritual gifts today.

There are many legitimate reasons why Christians who agree that the Bible is the inspired Word of God still vary in their interpretation of certain texts. As such, we should remember that the Bible itself is inspired, not our interpretations. This should call us to humility in theological conversations with our brothers and sisters in Christ. At the same time, we should also acknowledge that not every biblical interpretation is equally sound. We should always seek to interpret a text in a way that's as faithful as possible to the full witness of Scripture.

Despite our varied interpretations, it's crucial to understand that Christians are united on what are often called the *essentials* of the faith—those things that are central to the message proclaimed by the apostles. While more could be added, the essentials at a minimum include a belief in the following:

- one God (Deut. 4:35; see also 6:4; Exod. 20:3; Isa. 43:10; 44:6) in three persons (see chapter 6)
- the deity of Jesus (John 8:58; 10:30; 20:28; Phil. 2:5–8; Col. 2:9; see chapter 3)
- the resurrection (John 2:19–21; 1 Cor. 15:14, 17; see part 4)
- salvation by grace (Rom. 3:20; Gal. 2:21; 5:4; Eph. 2:8–9; see chapter 28)
- the basic gospel message (1 Cor. 15:3–4; see also Gal. 1:8–9)

These beliefs alone form a unique and life-changing worldview that sets Christians apart from non-Christians. Christians are united by far more than we're divided.

The Difference Jesus Makes

For those who reject any kind of supernatural worldview (atheists and other skeptics), the Bible is simply an ancient book written by men who were attempting to explain a world they didn't understand. They see it as a book filled with myths, errors, contradictions, and implausible stories. Far from being an authoritative source for their lives, it's the subject of mockery.

For those who believe in some concept of God, the Bible might be anything from a purely human book that happens to contain some useful insights on life (the view of many who are "spiritual but not religious") to a book that holds important truths but was corrupted over time and required new revelation (the view of Mormons and Muslims).

For Christians, however, the Bible is the unique written revelation of God himself that has full authority for our beliefs and practices. Truth is not necessarily what we prefer to be true, what we're most familiar with, what costs us the least, what our friends think, or what society accepts. Truth is what the God of the universe—who, by definition, has all knowledge and authority—has revealed in his Word.

In this chapter, we've focused on why Christians should accept the Bible as the inspired Word of God based on what the Bible itself says. For evidence supporting its reliability (why we should believe what the Bible claims) and how to respond to the challenges of skeptics, see part 4 in *Keeping Your Kids on God's Side*.

KEY POINTS

- Jesus clearly affirmed the divine origin and authority of the Old Testament.

- The New Testament claims the same scriptural status for itself.
- Theologians use the word *inspiration* to capture the idea that Scripture is "God-breathed"; God guided the Bible's human authors through the Holy Spirit.
- The Bible's divine inspiration implies that it's *truthful, authoritative*, and *sufficient*.
- Even Christians who agree that the Bible is the inspired Word of God can have significant disagreements over some of what it teaches, but Christians are united by far more than we're divided.

CONVERSATION GUIDE

Open the Conversation

- In the previous chapter, we discussed what a Christian is. Why do you think we used the Bible to define a Christian? *(Almost all we know about Jesus is from the Bible, so that's where we should look to define what a Christian is.)*

Advance the Conversation

- Read Matthew 12:1–8. What do you think Jesus was referring to when he asked the Pharisees, "Haven't you read?" *(He was referring to the Scriptures of his time—the Old Testament. Explain that Jesus repeatedly affirmed the Old Testament's divine origin and authority with phrases like this. Read Matthew 5:18 as another example.)*
- If Jesus affirmed the Old Testament's divine origin and authority, and Christians are disciples of Jesus, what should that mean for our own views regarding the Old Testament? *(We should affirm what Jesus affirmed.)*

263

- Read 2 Timothy 3:16. What do you think it means that Scripture is God-breathed? *(Explain the concept of inspiration and recall from chapter 12 that the New Testament claims for itself the same scriptural status as the Old. Discuss how God and humans were both involved in writing the Bible.)*
- Even when Christians agree that the Bible is the inspired Word of God, they still can disagree on how to interpret various passages. What is something you can think of that Christians disagree on? *(Discuss the difference between rejecting the Bible as the inspired Word of God and differing interpretations among those who accept it. Explain what essentials are and that Christians are united by more than we're divided.)*

Apply the Conversation

- Someone shared on the Whisper app, "I'm a Christian, but I don't believe in the Bible. I believe that there is a God, I just don't believe in a book written by man."[5] How would you help this person understand the importance of the Bible for defining a Christian's beliefs and practices?

27. How Is a Person's View of God Different as a Christian?

On my blog's Facebook page, I shared a news story one day that touched on multiple hot cultural topics. Many Christians commented with their concerns about the morality of the event involved. One commenter, however, was dismayed by those reactions. She wrote:

> Wow. Look how CERTAIN you all are. How SURE you are. You have convinced yourself that your understanding of God's love for humanity has been finalized. . . . Why not consider that others have experienced God in such a variety of ways that even if we wrote them in a book, they would only be scraping the surface to understanding God's love for us? Why not live out of a place of mystery—a place of love and acceptance of all people than live out of a place of all-knowing pride and righteous indignation?

Having read all the comments to which she referred, I can say the tone was not one of "all-knowing pride and righteous indignation." Everyone expressed themselves respectfully. It seems what she was *really* offended by was the view itself—that Christians believe God has revealed certain moral standards in the Bible.

It's common today for people to shoot the messenger when Christians share what God says in his Word; they think Christians *themselves* are claiming to be some kind of authority and effectively ask, "Who are *you* to tell me what God thinks?" Like the quoted commenter, they often appeal to "mystery" as a reason for dismissing any claims to knowledge about him.

As Christians who believe that the Bible is God's inspired Word (see chapter 26), however, we believe that God *chose* to reveal much about himself. Through the incarnation of Jesus and what is written in the Bible, many things that *would have been* mysterious have been made known. There is no need to "live out of a place of mystery," as the commenter suggested, where God himself has revealed what's true. If we do, we're choosing to live in the dark where God has given light.

How God Has Revealed Himself

Christians have traditionally recognized that God has revealed himself in two ways: through general revelation and special revelation. General revelation is the knowledge about God that all people can obtain through the natural world. For example, Psalm 19:1–2 says, "The heavens declare the glory of God; the skies proclaim the work of his hands. Day after day they pour forth speech; night after night they reveal knowledge." The apostle Paul says there is no excuse for not believing in God because he has so clearly revealed himself in nature (Rom. 1:18–20). He goes on to say that God has also given humans an innate knowledge of what's right and wrong (2:14–16). Because God has revealed himself through general revelation, there's significant evidence for his existence outside of the Bible itself. It's extremely important for kids to understand this evidence when growing up in a secular world that's quick to dismiss the Bible as God's Word. It helps them not only to share the good reasons for their faith with others but also to know how their own faith is grounded in evidence at multiple levels.[1]

General revelation can take us as far as establishing that a universe-creating, life-designing, and moral-lawgiving God exists. This view of God is not unique to Christians; anyone can have the same understanding. If this were all that God had revealed to us, we would know that a being of this kind existed, but we'd know very little about him. Thankfully, God chose to reveal himself further by *supernatural* means, intervening in the world through miracles, the incarnation, and the writing of Scripture. This is what we call special revelation. For Christians, therefore, God is not completely shrouded in mystery. He has revealed many important truths about himself, including (but not limited to) the following:

- his nature (for example, one God in three persons)
- his attributes (for example, his holiness, sovereignty, transcendence, omnipresence, omnipotence, faithfulness, goodness, lovingness, and justness)[2]
- his purposes (for example, to have a relationship with us)
- his moral requirements (for example, to love him and love others)

Think back to all the important areas of knowledge we've covered in this book. *Almost none of this information would be known had God not chosen to reveal it through his Word.* God chose to reveal a great deal about who he is, who we are, and what our lives should look like in response to those realities.

Acknowledging that there is much we can know about God doesn't imply, of course, that we can know *everything* about him. As Job 11:7–8 says, "Can you fathom the mysteries of God? Can you probe the limits of the Almighty? They are higher than the heavens above—what can you do? They are deeper than the depths below—what can you know?" Not everything we'd like to know has been revealed, nor could everything we'd like to know be understood by finite human beings. We have light but not complete illumination.

The Difference Jesus Makes

The fact that God has revealed himself through nature, Jesus, and the Bible means that a Christian's understanding of God is specifically shaped by those revelations. This is in contrast to many commonly heard sentiments that object to such an understanding. Let's look at four of the most popular ones. (People sometimes mean other things with these statements, but we're considering them from the perspective of the context described.)

1. "I don't want to put God in a box."

People often make the "God in a box" comment to suggest that when we make a claim about who God is and what he wants for us, we're somehow placing limits on him. But as we discussed, God himself is the one who chose what to reveal and what to limit our knowledge of. In other words, *God drew his own box* around how we should understand him. We're not the ones putting him there when we share what he said. We shouldn't claim to know *more* than what he revealed, of course, but we shouldn't claim to know less either.

2. "Why do you think you know more about God than I do?"

This kind of comment reduces to a charge of arrogance. If a Christian is simply passing on a biblical teaching, however, such a charge is misplaced. It's not arrogant to believe that objective truth exists and that God has revealed that truth in the Bible. A person who claims that God *didn't* reveal himself through the Bible is making as much of an objective truth claim as a Christian. When a Christian states what the Bible says, they're not claiming to be smarter or more insightful than anyone else (or at least they shouldn't be!). They're only claiming that the Bible is God's Word. We should be prepared, of course, to back up our claims with good reason, offered with gentleness and respect (1 Pet. 3:15).

3. *"I'll let God be the judge of that."*

This comment is often made by a Christian in the context of another Christian stating a biblical teaching on morality—usually for the purpose of suggesting that we shouldn't speak for God. As we learned in chapter 11, however, this is a misunderstanding of what Jesus said about judging sin and of the difference between discernment and condemnation. Jesus calls us to judge—discern—rightly. When it comes to biblical teachings on morality, God has already been "the judge of that" and has shared the verdict in his Word. When we speak the truth about biblical morality, we are communicating what God said, not attempting to speak on his behalf.

When this comment is made by a non-Christian, we're back to the assumption that we can't know anything meaningful about God. As Christians, we can share what the Bible says on the matter, point out that if the Bible is God's Word, then God has already shared his judgment on it, and offer to discuss why we have good *reason* to believe that the Bible is God's Word.

4. *"I know how I've experienced God, and that's all I need to know."*

This is both an extremely common attitude and a hard one to respond to. When people prioritize experience as their source of knowledge about God (over and against the Bible), having a

269·

fruitful conversation can be difficult. Pitting one person's experience against another's will only result in a stalemate; there's no tiebreaker for feelings alone.

That said, we can agree that knowledge about God is not confined to the Bible. As we saw, God has revealed himself through general revelation in nature. In addition, Christians have the Holy Spirit, who testifies to truth (John 15:26). And we also experience how God leads us in our own lives through our relationship with him. However, because we believe that the Bible is the inspired Word of God—and therefore fully truthful—nothing we experience that is actually from God will contradict his teachings in Scripture. This is one reason why it's so important for Christians to know that the Bible is God's Word. It provides an objective foundation for testing how our experiences line up with reality.

This chapter was fairly analytical, but let's not miss the incredible personal implication of all we just discussed: *the God of the universe wants us to know him.* Why is this so important to him—and to us? And how should that truth change our lives? Those questions bring us to the next chapter.

KEY POINTS

- Christians believe that God chose to reveal much about himself. There's no need to appeal to "mystery" where God has given light.
- God has revealed himself through general revelation (knowledge given to all through the natural world) and special revelation (knowledge given through supernatural means, such as miracles, the incarnation, and the writing of Scripture).

- Through these revelations, we are able to know important truths about God's nature, attributes, purposes, moral requirements, and more.
- Acknowledging that there is much we can know about God doesn't imply that we can know *everything* about him.

CONVERSATION GUIDE

Open the Conversation

- Do you think God wants us to know a lot about him? Why or why not?

Advance the Conversation

- Read Psalm 19:1–2; and Romans 1:20 and 2:14–16. According to these verses, what are some things we can know about God, even if we didn't have the Bible? *(Creation points to his existence, he has eternal power and a divine nature, and he gave us a moral conscience. This is called general revelation.)*
- While we can know some important things about God from nature, God chose to reveal much more about himself through Jesus and the Bible. What are some of the most important things we know about God from Scripture? *(Discuss the examples of his nature, attributes, purposes, and moral requirements. This is called special revelation.)*
- Read Job 11:7–8. What does this tell us about our knowledge of God? *(We can never understand everything about him. But God chose to reveal many important things.)*
- Imagine that a friend told you she doesn't need the Bible to know about God—she knows all she needs to through her experiences with him. What would you say? *(Talk about the*

value of experience with God in the life of a Christian, but explain the importance of the Bible providing an objective foundation for testing how our experiences line up with reality. For older kids, discuss the three other common sentiments from this chapter.)

Apply the Conversation

- How would you reply to the blog commenter quoted at the beginning of this chapter?

28. What Does It Mean to Be Saved?

For some reason, I don't remember many details from my elementary school years—just a random memory here and there, usually associated with some kind of strong feeling. One of those memories is from a time when I was nine and was jumping on a small trampoline in front of my house one afternoon.

A new family had moved in across the street that week. They had two girls about my age, which I was very excited about because we didn't have many kids in our neighborhood. While I was bouncing on my trampoline that afternoon, the girls came over to introduce themselves. Within five minutes, one asked, "Are you saved?"

I knew what she meant, and I knew that I was saved, but I was taken aback. A stranger had never asked me that question before. I replied with some hesitation, not knowing where this was going.

"Well, um, yeah, I'm saved . . ."

She looked at me more intently and asked, "But do you have the *Holy Spirit*?"

I didn't know much about the Holy Spirit at that point, so I asked, "What do you mean?" The two girls literally ran home at that moment. We never played together again because, as one of the girls later told me, their parents thought I would be a bad influence.

There's nothing in Scripture, of course, that suggests we shouldn't associate with people who aren't saved (otherwise, how could we obey Jesus's command to make disciples?). But if the girls detected uncertainty in my reply about what it *means* to be saved, they were right. I had made the decision to put my trust in Jesus at a young age, understanding that he in some sense "died for my sins" and that I needed to accept him as my Savior. I knew that in doing so I was "saved" and that I would go to heaven. But there was no depth beyond that to my understanding of salvation.

While it's appropriate for young kids to start with these basics, it's important to help our children develop a much fuller understanding of salvation as they grow in their spiritual maturity. When they gain that understanding, they'll have a much deeper appreciation for the beauty of what God has done—and all it means for their lives.

What Does It Mean to Be Saved?

To help our kids more fully understand salvation, it's helpful to break it down step by step.

The Problem

When we talk about people needing to be saved, we're implying that there's a problem—we need to be saved *from* something. A conversation about salvation, therefore, should start with a conversation about this presumed predicament in which we find ourselves.

You might recall that we already discussed this predicament in chapters 7 and 14, where we identified that the fundamental problem of human existence is sin. We saw that God gave us a moral law, all people have that law written on their hearts, all people are guilty of breaking that law, and God set the punishment for sin as death. *This is our grim situation—we are condemned.*

But people sometimes think that God is the one who unnecessarily *made* the situation so grim. After all, he's the one who set such a serious penalty. Why not simply forgive us? As we learned in chapter 7, it's because God isn't only loving—he's also just. To better understand why this matters so much, imagine there's a judge in your city who regularly lets murderers go free without penalty because of his "love" for them. There would be a public outcry at the *injustice*; we instinctively understand that love without justice is not love at all. If we understand this about an earthly judge, how much more we should understand it about a holy God! God *must* punish sin to remain consistent within his perfectly loving and just nature.

Our Inability to Save Ourselves

It's human nature to think that if we work hard enough, we can do anything we want. But the Bible is clear: no amount of human works is sufficient to earn our way back into God's good graces. Left to our own devices, we're stuck in our state of condemnation. Romans 3:10–12 says, "There is no one righteous, not even one; there is no one who understands; there is no one who seeks God. All have turned away, they have together become worthless; there is no one who does good, not even one." People who reject Christianity often assume that if there *is* some kind of heaven, they'll go there because they're basically "a good person." But as we can see, the Bible tells us that this assumption couldn't be further from the truth. Isaiah 64:6 says that "our righteous acts are like filthy rags." None of us are good. All of us have sinned and are unable to save ourselves from condemnation.

God's Provision for Forgiveness

Now for the *good* news.

There's an important difference between the imaginary judge who sets criminals free and God. God is both the judge and the

275

offended party. That means he's in the unique position to both set the penalty *and* absolve humans of their guilt as he sees fit within his just character—and he lovingly decided to make provision for our forgiveness. Payment for sin was required by his justness, but he made that payment *himself* through Jesus's death on the cross in our place (see part 3).

God's Offer of Salvation

The Bible doesn't teach that just because God made provision for the forgiveness of sin that everyone will be reconciled to him and inherit eternal life (see chapter 7). We must *respond*. Once again, the words of John 3:16 are instructive—as is the larger context of verses 17 and 18:

> For God so loved the world that he gave his one and only Son, that whoever believes in him shall not perish but have eternal life. For God did not send his Son into the world to condemn the world, but to save the world through him. Whoever believes in him is not condemned, but whoever does not believe stands condemned already because they have not believed in the name of God's one and only Son.

This, then, is God's offer of salvation: *those who believe in Jesus will have eternal life.*[1] We do not have to remain condemned. By putting our faith in Jesus—trusting that he is our Savior—we are forgiven of our sins (1 John 1:9), made right with God (Rom. 5:1), and able to live forevermore with him (John 3:16).

It's important to emphasize that this offer of salvation is the product of God's grace alone; he didn't have to make the offer, and there's no alternative through our own initiative. As the apostle Paul says, "For it is by grace you have been saved, through faith— and this is not from yourselves, it is the gift of God—not by works, so that no one can boast" (Eph. 2:8–9).

Our Response

So how, specifically, does a person accept God's offer of salvation? The Bible doesn't give us a step-by-step process to "officially" accept Jesus as our Savior, but Romans 10:9–10 tells us the basic idea of where our hearts and minds should be:

> If you declare with your mouth, "Jesus is Lord," and believe in your heart that God raised him from the dead, you will be saved. For it is with your heart that you believe and are justified, and it is with your mouth that you profess your faith and are saved.

People sometimes think that being saved is about praying a specific prayer. But words alone save no one. God knows and judges the heart.

The Difference Jesus Makes

It's natural for Christians to think about salvation in terms of what happens to us after we die, but we sometimes forget that salvation is also about having a transformed life now. Paul says, "If anyone is in Christ, the new creation has come: The old has gone, the new is here!" (2 Cor. 5:17; see also John 3:5–8; Gal. 2:20). When we're saved, our bodies become a temple of the Holy Spirit (1 Cor. 6:19; see also Rom. 8:9), and the Spirit produces fruit in our lives: love, joy, peace, patience, kindness, goodness, faithfulness, gentleness, and self-control (Gal. 5:22–23). Our identity in Christ necessarily changes the way we think and live.

This doesn't mean we no longer sin, of course. We're still human beings and will struggle with temptation. But our hearts are transformed so that we no longer *want* to sin. If we continue sinning in order that God's grace may abound, we have not fully understood the gospel (Rom. 6:1). We should continually strive to be in obedience to Jesus's commands and to avoid sin as much as we can (1 John 5:1–3; 2 Pet. 1:5–11).

While the Bible doesn't give us a lot of detail about eternity, we know that those who have put their trust in Jesus will be surrounded by the glory of God forever, never to experience the pains of this life again. One of the most beautiful pictures we have of eternity is from Revelation 21:3–4:

> God's dwelling place is now among the people, and he will dwell with them. They will be his people, and God himself will be with them and be their God. "He will wipe every tear from their eyes. There will be no more death" or mourning or crying or pain, for the old order of things has passed away.

What an amazing truth. Here especially we can see what an *eternal* difference Jesus makes.

KEY POINTS

- *The problem.* We are a condemned people because we're all guilty of breaking God's law, and the penalty is death.
- *Our inability to save ourselves.* No amount of human works is sufficient to earn our way back into God's good graces.
- *God's provision for forgiveness.* Payment for sin was required by God's justness, but he made that payment *himself* through Jesus's death on the cross in our place.
- *God's offer of salvation.* Those who trust in Jesus as their Savior will have eternal life.
- *Our response.* "If you declare with your mouth, 'Jesus is Lord,' and believe in your heart that God raised him from the dead, you will be saved" (Rom. 10:9).
- *What salvation means for this life.* Our identity in Christ changes the way we think and live.

- *What salvation means for eternity.* We will be surrounded by the glory of God forever.

CONVERSATION GUIDE

Note: The following questions assume that your child is familiar with what it means to be saved and will encourage them to think more deeply about it. If this is a new concept for them, introduce it by walking them through the key points in this chapter rather than using these questions.

Open the Conversation

- If someone asked you what it means that Christians are saved, what would you say?

Advance the Conversation

- When we talk about the need for a person to be saved, we're implying that there's a problem—we need to be saved *from* something. What do you think humans need to be saved from? *(Explain why we're in the grim situation of being a condemned people. Make sure your child understands how God's lovingness and justness require that guilty people can't simply go free.)*
- Do you think some people might be good enough to earn salvation on their own? Why or why not? *(No one can be good enough. Read Isaiah 64:6; Romans 3:10–12.)*
- Based on what you know about Jesus, how did his death on the cross give us the possibility of forgiveness? *(Recall what was learned in part 3. Payment for sin was required by God's justness, but he lovingly made that payment himself through Jesus's death on the cross in our place.)*

279

- Read John 3:16–18. What must people do to accept God's offer of salvation—to have eternal life? *(Believe in Jesus. By putting our faith in him—trusting him as our Savior—we are forgiven, made right with God, and able to live forevermore with him.)*
- How do you think being saved changes a person's life? *(Our identity in Christ changes the way we think and live. Discuss the points given in this chapter and explain how Christians should view sin.)*
- *(If your child has never made a decision to put their trust in Jesus, ask if they want to! Read Romans 10:9–10 and pray together.)*

Apply the Conversation

- A person asked online, "What does it mean to be saved?" Someone replied, "In religious terms, it means the religion's god of choice has accepted you into whatever paradise beyond the grave has been promised to its followers."[2] How would you reply to help the commenter more deeply understand salvation from the Christian perspective?

29. What Does It Mean to Trust in Jesus?

Because I write about apologetics on my blog, parents often find my articles through search engines when looking for help having conversations with a child who no longer thinks Christianity is true. Many will email me or leave a blog comment to share their heartbreak and seek advice. While every situation is unique, there are common threads I've seen over time.

One of those commonalities is for a child to walk away after experiencing some kind of significant suffering. The child either was surprised that God allowed it to happen or prayed for a different outcome and God "didn't answer."[1] They ended up feeling betrayed by the God they trusted in and decided that Christianity isn't true (or that God doesn't exist at all).

Of course, this doesn't happen just to kids. Adults can feel as if God has broken their trust as well. Consider the following comment from a Christian internet forum as one example: "I have come to realize that because I have seen so many wonderful people get sick and pray and believe for healing, NOT get healed and leave behind such grief and suffering, I no longer trust God to be in control."[2] What's tragic—about this story and the ones I've heard from many parents—is that people's relationship with

Jesus was damaged or undone by a *misunderstanding* of what it should mean to put our trust in him.

In this chapter, we'll look at three important ways the Bible tells us to trust in Jesus, then we'll look at three common misunderstandings about trust that can lead to spiritual brokenness.

Biblical Ways of Trusting in Jesus

When we discuss trust, we're talking about more than an intellectual affirmation of truth. For example, I've been hearing a lot lately about how great self-driving cars will be. Even if I believed the research showing they're reliable, however, there's no way I would ever let one drive me! I wouldn't *trust* it at all. You see, trust is when we *apply* what we believe to be true to our lives. In the same way, the following three biblical ways of trusting in Jesus aren't cold facts. They should represent a life-changing reality for Christians.

1. We Should Trust in Who Jesus Is

Trusting that Jesus is God means knowing that nothing and no one can stand against his perfect plan; he is in complete control, even when we don't understand the events that unfold around us. As the apostle Paul wrote in Romans 8:31, "If God is for us, who can be against us?" That's a question worth keeping close to our hearts. When we trust that Jesus is God and understand all he has *already* done (see part 3), we can be confident in all he *will* do.

2. We Should Trust in the Promises Given in the Bible

Because we can trust in who Jesus is, we have reason to trust in the promises given in the Bible (see chapter 26). It's important, therefore, to know *what* promises are given in the Bible. A few of the most important ones include:

- Those who believe in Jesus will be forgiven of their sins and will inherit eternal life (see chapter 28).
- Jesus will give wisdom to those who ask (James 1:5).
- Those who abide in Jesus will bear much spiritual fruit (John 15:5).
- Jesus will give rest to our souls (Matt. 11:28).
- Jesus will be with us always (Matt. 28:20).
- Jesus will come again (John 14:2–3).

3. We Should Trust That Whatever God Does Is Best

It goes without saying that we don't always understand God's ways. But when we know that God is all-good, all-knowing, and all-powerful, we can trust that whatever he does is best in view of eternity (a view we obviously don't have). Romans 8:28 says, "We know that for those who love God all things work together for good, for those who are called according to his purpose" (ESV). This doesn't mean that God will work things together for what *we* think is good or even what *seems* to be good. It means that God will work all things together for what *he knows* is good for those who love him.

When We Trust in Ways We Shouldn't

Let's now turn to three *unbiblical* ideas of trust that have worked their way into popular belief. All of these ideas can be highly destructive to a person's faith, so we should be intentional in teaching our kids why they're contrary to Scripture.

1. We Shouldn't Trust That Jesus Will Protect Us from All Harm and Suffering

When my kids were little, I picked up a book at a Christian bookstore about a girl who was being bullied. While the kids were bothering her, she prayed that Jesus would help. On the next page, one of the bullies suddenly decided to leave and take his friends with him. The story ended with the girl smiling, reminding us to trust that "Jesus protects us."

Honestly, I was angry that such a book would be printed. What happens when a young girl who is really being bullied comes to believe that as soon as she prays, her bullies will leave? If that doesn't happen, did Jesus abandon her? Does Jesus not love her? Should she no longer "trust" him? This kind of oversimplified (and inaccurate) theology is found throughout Christian books for kids. And it plants the seed of a dangerous idea—that we should trust that Jesus will protect us from all harm and suffering.

This couldn't be further from the truth of what the Bible says, however. The truth doesn't get clearer than Jesus's words in John 16:33: "In this world you will have trouble. But take heart! I have overcome the world" (see also Matt. 5:10–11). Equally obvious are Paul's words in 2 Timothy 3:12: "Everyone who wants to live a godly life in Christ Jesus will be persecuted." The list of verses could go on. Suffering is to be *expected*, but when it comes, Jesus will restore, confirm, and strengthen us in it (1 Pet. 5:10).

2. We Shouldn't Trust That Jesus Will Always Physically Heal

The idea that Jesus will always physically heal is related to the previous one but is specific to the suffering of personal illness. A number of Christians believe that Jesus will heal a person physically as long as they have enough faith. This seems to be the assumption behind the comment quoted at the beginning of this chapter. The woman concluded that because so many people pray and aren't healed, God isn't in control! Sadly, she has it backward. The Bible *does* tell us that God is "in control" (for example, Ps. 115:3), but it *doesn't* say that Christians will always be physically healed in this life.[3] There's nothing wrong with praying and hoping that Jesus will heal, but our *ultimate* hope must remain in what he did on the cross and his promises for eternity—when we will all be healed, both physically and spiritually.

3. We Shouldn't Trust That Our Prayers Will Be Answered in the Way We'd Like

The idea that our prayers will be answered in the way we'd like is really an extension of the previous point, just applied to prayer requests beyond healing. Sometimes when people say, "I'm trusting Jesus with this" in the context of prayer, they simply mean they're trusting in *who* Jesus is, knowing he will make the best decision in light of eternity. That's a biblical kind of trust, as we already discussed. But other times when a person says those words, they mean they're trusting that Jesus will answer their prayer according to their desired outcome. That's a trust the Bible *doesn't* say we should have and one that can lead to great resentment and a rejection of God. We simply don't have the full picture to understand why God answers prayers in the ways he does.

The Difference Jesus Makes

Paul's words in Romans 8:31–37 are worth quoting at greater length to help us more fully understand the difference that trusting in Jesus should make for a Christian's life:

> What, then, shall we say in response to these things? If God is for us, who can be against us? He who did not spare his own Son, but gave him up for us all—how will he not also, along with him, graciously give us all things? Who will bring any charge against those whom God has chosen? It is God who justifies. Who then is the one who condemns? No one. Christ Jesus who died—more than that, who was raised to life—is at the right hand of God and is also

interceding for us. Who shall separate us from the love of Christ? Shall trouble or hardship or persecution or famine or nakedness or danger or sword? As it is written:

> "For your sake we face death all day long;
>   we are considered as sheep to be slaughtered."

No, in all these things we are more than conquerors through him who loved us.

Victory belongs to the Lord—and to those who put their trust in him. *Nothing* can separate us from the love of Christ.

KEY POINTS

- Trust is more than an intellectual affirmation of truth. It's *applying* that truth to our lives.

- The Bible says that Christians should trust (1) in who Jesus is, (2) in the promises given in the Bible, and (3) that whatever God does is best in view of eternity.

- The Bible does *not* say, however, that we should trust that (1) Jesus will protect us from all harm and suffering, (2) Jesus will always physically heal, or (3) our prayers will be answered in the way we'd like.

CONVERSATION GUIDE

Open the Conversation

- *(Explain what a self-driving car is if your child doesn't know.)* If enough research was done to demonstrate that self-driving

286

cars are reliable, would you let one drive you somewhere? Why or why not? *(Explain that trust is demonstrated when we apply what we believe is true.)*

Advance the Conversation

- How does knowing that Jesus is God allow us to trust him? *(Discuss your child's answer, then read Romans 8:31–37. Nothing can stand against his plan or separate us from an eternity with him.)*
- There are many things Jesus promised in the Bible. Why do you think Christians should trust those promises? *(The Bible is God's Word, and God doesn't lie. Read the promises and verses from this chapter.)*
- Read Romans 8:28. Do you think Christians can always see how God is working things out for the good of those who love him? Why or why not? *(No, because we don't have a view of eternity. But because of who God is, we can trust him.)*
- *(Recount the brief story line from the book on bullying I described.)* Do you think this story teaches a good lesson about what it means to trust in Jesus? Why or why not? *(Read Matthew 5:10–11; John 16:33; 2 Timothy 3:12. Explain that the Bible teaches us to expect suffering—Jesus will not always protect us from harm.)*
- The Bible tells us to take all our concerns to Jesus in prayer (Phil. 4:6–7). Do you think that when we pray for physical healing, we should trust that Jesus will always heal us? Why or why not? *(The Bible never promises that everyone will be healed. We don't have the eternal perspective of Jesus to understand why some are healed in this life and others aren't.)*
- What if you prayed over and over for a certain classmate to become your friend and they never did? Would that mean you shouldn't trust Jesus with your prayers? Why or why not? *(We must trust that Jesus will always answer in the best way*

in view of eternity. That's not always the same as the outcome we prayed for.)

Apply the Conversation

- How would you respond to the woman quoted at the beginning of this chapter?

30. Why Do Christians Want to Share Their Faith with Others?

For my son's end-of-season baseball party, the team went to one of those family entertainment centers with miniature golf, a few rides (which look like they'll fall apart at any moment), and an arcade. While the coach was giving out awards, my husband gave our girls some change to go play games. They came back later carrying two stuffed animals. Apparently, they got lucky playing a game where you spin a wheel to win tickets that you can redeem for various toys. The spinner landed on the jackpot, and they won a thousand tickets.

After redeeming some of the tickets for stuffed animals, they brought several hundred back to share with their brother. Much to their annoyance, however, he didn't care about the tickets at all. He was busy hanging out with his friends, and at some point before we left, he threw the tickets away. When the girls eventually found out, they were furious. They asked, "Why did you throw them away? Why didn't you give them back to us so *we* could buy something else?"

My son replied, "What do you mean? You could *buy* something with the tickets? I thought they were just tickets to show how many points you earned! I didn't know I could *get* anything with them!" Tears welled up in his eyes as he realized he had thrown away something of significant value.

When it comes to sharing our faith with others in a secular world, we often don't realize how far people are from appreciating the value of what we're talking about. They dismiss conversations about Jesus as quickly as my son tossed those tickets in the trash, assuming there's no worth to what we have to say. If our kids are going to follow Jesus's command to make disciples of others (see chapter 25), they're going to need help understanding what that looks like in today's world.

Understanding the Great Commission

Recall from chapter 25 that just before Jesus ascended to heaven, he told the disciples, "Go and make disciples of all nations, baptizing them in the name of the Father and of the Son and of the Holy Spirit, and teaching them to obey everything I have commanded you" (Matt. 28:19–20). This is what Christians today call the Great Commission. We see how the apostles began to fulfill Jesus's command in the book of Acts. The gospel was first preached in Jerusalem (Acts 1–7), then it spread to Judea and Samaria (Acts 8–12), then to the lands beyond (Acts 13–28). Christians today are to continue sharing the gospel to "the ends of the earth" (Acts 1:8). That, of course, looks different for all people because we have varied life circumstances—different personality types, strengths, weaknesses, jobs, geographic locations, cultural environments, physical abilities, mental abilities, family situations, and much more. Some people may end up sharing the gospel in a remote part of the world, while others may never leave their hometown.

That said, why is it so important to Jesus that we tell others about him? If you're a longtime Christian, the answer might be obvious to you. But it's not always obvious to kids. You might recall from chapter 10 that although 96 percent of millennials agree that part of their faith "means being a witness about Jesus," almost half also agree that "it is wrong to share one's personal beliefs with someone of a different faith in hopes that they will one day share the same faith." It seems there's a disconnect between knowing that sharing about Jesus is important and understanding why; when we understand the why, we can't possibly believe it's wrong.

Understanding this starts with acknowledging the fact that God "wants all people to be saved and to come to a knowledge of the truth" (1 Tim. 2:4). And why does he want that? Because he knows the grim reality of the human situation we discussed in chapter 28: we're condemned because of our sins. As we learned, he made provision for our forgiveness on the cross and offers salvation to those who put their trust in what Jesus has done. Those who respond will have eternal life, but those who do not will bear the punishment for their sins themselves (Matt. 25:46; see chapter 8).

If we know and believe what the Bible says about these things, how can we think it's wrong to share this with others in the hope that they, too, will have salvation? Christians are motivated by a desire to be obedient to Jesus's command *and* by a genuine love for others—which includes caring for their souls (see chapter 10).

The Difference Jesus Makes

There are two beliefs people commonly have in today's culture that can make sharing the gospel particularly difficult for Christians: (1) Christianity isn't true, and (2) *all* religions are true. Those who hold these beliefs devalue what Christians have to say, but for very different reasons.

When People Believe Christianity Isn't True

Almost everyone in our society has at least some knowledge of Christianity. That means a good number of people we want to share the gospel with have not only heard about Jesus but also consciously rejected him. They may be:

- rejecting Jesus based on an inaccurate or incomplete understanding of Christianity
- reacting emotionally to past hurt from Christians or a church
- convicted that another religion is true
- convicted that no religion is true (because there's no God)

These are just a few examples of the possibilities. Whatever their rationale for rejecting Jesus, however, they typically come to the conversation with strong feelings, believing they've already given Christianity as much of a fair shake as is needed. Because of this, it's important to begin faith conversations by asking questions to understand where a person is coming from rather than sharing your faith as if they've never heard anything about Christianity before. In particular, it's helpful to learn (1) what a person currently believes about God, Jesus, and the Bible; (2) how they came to those conclusions; (3) what their understanding of the core message of Christianity is; (4) how they describe their current beliefs; and (5) why they understand their current beliefs to be true. With this insight, we're in a better position to speak about Jesus in a more personally relevant way.

When People Believe All Religions Are True

Though this may sound surprising, it can be even more difficult to have faith conversations with those who assume that *all* religions are true. People with this belief often don't understand why you would try to share why Christianity is true in the first place—they already accept that it's one of *many* truths! The reality, however, is that religions make contradictory claims about the nature of reality—things such as where we came from, why we're here, where we're going, who God is, and what he asks from us. Ironically, Jesus said that no one comes to the Father except through him (John 14:6), so if all religions are true, then Christianity must be false. (Think about that for a minute . . .)

Don't assume that people who believe all religions are true have thought through these implications. It's helpful to ask questions to learn (1) *in what sense* they believe all religions are true and (2) *why* they believe all religions are true. As conversation progresses, share the exclusive truth claim of Jesus (that he's the only way to God) and explain why that means Christianity can't be true if other religions are true. If a person gets to the point of acknowledging that all religions can't be true at the same time, it's a great opportunity to then talk about the evidence for the truth of Christianity specifically.

Finally, just because we're *called* to share the gospel and *want* to share the gospel doesn't mean people will *listen* to the gospel. We aren't called to tackle people to the ground to make them listen! Ultimately, a person must be willing to have a conversation. Building genuine relationships with people is often the only thing that opens that door.

Two excellent books to help Christians share their faith are *Tactics: A Game Plan for Discussing Your Christian Convictions* by Greg Koukl and *Relational Apologetics: Defending the Christian Faith with Holiness, Respect, and Truth* by Michael Sherrard.[1]

KEY POINTS

- Jesus commanded us to make disciples of all nations. This is called the Great Commission.

- God wants all people to be saved and to come to a knowledge of the truth.
- If we know and believe what the Bible says about salvation and eternity, we will want to share the gospel out of love for Jesus and love for others.
- There are two beliefs people commonly have in today's culture that can make sharing the gospel particularly difficult for Christians: (1) Christianity isn't true, and (2) *all* religions are true. Our approach in each case should be to first ask questions, though the nature of those questions will differ.

CONVERSATION GUIDE

Open the Conversation

- When have you shared your Christian faith in some way with someone? *(If your child can't think of a time, go on to the next question.)*
- Do you think it's easy or hard to share about Jesus with others? Why?

Advance the Conversation

- One of the final things Jesus told his disciples before he ascended to heaven was that they should make *more* disciples around the world. Why do you think Jesus wanted the disciples—and wants us today—to tell others about him? *(He knows people need salvation and the abundant life he offers.)*
- A study has shown that about half of young Christians believe it's *wrong* to share one's personal beliefs with someone of a different faith in the hope that they will one day share the same faith. Given that this is the opposite of what the

Bible teaches, why do you think so many Christians think this way today? *(Culture places a higher value on not upsetting people.)*

- If you tried to share about Jesus with a friend but they told you they already know about Christianity and don't believe it's true, what are some questions you could ask to better understand where they're coming from? *(Walk through the questions listed in this chapter.)*

- Some people today believe that *all* religions are true. Do you think that belief makes it easier or harder to share about Jesus with a person? *(It can make sharing about Jesus more difficult because they see no reason to be convinced of why Christianity is true—but Jesus claims he's the only way to God. Talk about the two questions we should ask someone with this belief.)*

Apply the Conversation

- A person in an online forum asked, "Why do Christians seek to convert everyone, especially people who have no interest in being converted? It always comes off like a drug dealer saying, 'Try it, you'll like it—trust me. Would I lie to you?' If the point is to make the world a better place, wouldn't a less aggressive approach be more effective?"[2] How would you respond?

Notes

Introduction

1. "5 Things People with Tidy Homes Don't Do," Nesting Place, March 20, 2016, https://thenester.com/2016/03/5-things-people-with-tidy-homes-dont-do .html.

2. Natasha Crain, *Keeping Your Kids on God's Side: 40 Conversations to Help Them Build a Lasting Faith* (Eugene, OR: Harvest House, 2016).

3. Natasha Crain, *Talking with Your Kids about God: 30 Conversations Every Christian Parent Must Have* (Grand Rapids: Baker Books, 2017).

4. I discuss this in detail at Natasha Crain, "How Sunday Schools Are Raising the Next Generation of Secular Humanists," *Christian Mom Thoughts*, January 7, 2019, https://christianmomthoughts.com/how-sunday-schools-are-raising-the -next-generation-of-secular-humanists/. For an excellent summary of studies, see J. Warner Wallace, "Are Young People Really Leaving Christianity?," Cold-Case Christianity, January 12, 2019, https://coldcasechristianity.com/writings/are-young -people-really-leaving-christianity/.

5. See *Christian Mom Thoughts* (blog), https://www.christianmomthoughts .com/low-grade-tidying/.

Part 1 The Identity of Jesus Overview

1. "The Jesus Seminar," The Westar Institute, accessed June 10, 2019, https:// www.westarinstitute.org/projects/the-jesus-seminar/.

Chapter 1 Is Jesus a Myth?

1. Raphael Lataster, "Did Historical Jesus Really Exist? The Evidence Just Doesn't Add Up," *Washington Post*, December 18, 2014, https://www.washing tonpost.com/posteverything/wp/2014/12/18/did-historical-jesus-exist-the-tradi tional-evidence-doesnt-hold-up/.

2. "What Do Americans Believe About Jesus? 5 Popular Beliefs," Barna, April 1, 2015, https://www.barna.com/research/what-do-americans-believe-about -jesus-5-popular-beliefs/.

3. "Jesus 'Not a Real Person' Many Believe," BBC, October 31, 2015, https:// www.bbc.com/news/uk-34686993.

4. For the mention of James, the brother of Jesus, see Josephus, *Antiquities of the Jews* 20.9.1; for the longer passage about startling deeds, etc., see *Ant.* 18.3.3.

5. For a more detailed discussion of sources, as well as objections to the sources discussed here, see Josh McDowell and Sean McDowell, *Evidence That Demands a Verdict* (Nashville: Thomas Nelson, 2017), chap. 6.

6. McDowell and McDowell, *Evidence That Demands a Verdict*, 150.

7. Historian and atheist activist Richard Carrier debated Christian apologist Jonathan McLatchie about this theory on the radio show *Unbelievable*: "Unbelievable: Mythicism Debate: Did St. Paul Believe in a Real or 'Celestial' Jesus? Richard Carrier vs. Jonathan McLatchie," Premier Christian Radio, March 3, 2018, https://www.premierchristianradio.com/Shows/Saturday/Unbelievable/Epi sodes/Unbelievable-Mythicism-debate-Did-St.-Paul-believe-in-a-real-or-celestial -Jesus-Richard-Carrier-vs-Jonathan-McLatchie.

8. Bart Ehrman, *Did Jesus Exist? The Historical Argument for Jesus of Nazareth* (New York: HarperOne, 2012), 133.

9. An excellent resource on the subject is Craig Blomberg, *The Historical Reliability of the Gospels* (Downers Grove, IL: IVP Academic, 2007).

10. Ehrman, *Did Jesus Exist?*, 92.

11. Valerie Tarico, "5 Reasons to Suspect That Jesus Never Existed," *Salon*, September 1, 2014, https://www.salon.com/2014/09/01/5_reasons_to_suspect _that_jesus_never_existed/.

Chapter 2 Is Jesus the Jewish Messiah?

1. For in-depth background on this, see Michael F. Bird, *Are You the One Who Is to Come?* (Grand Rapids: Baker Academic, 2009).

2. For those interested in the historical evidence for these events, I highly recommend Darrell L. Bock, *Who Is Jesus? Linking the Historical Jesus with the Christ of Faith* (New York: Howard Books, 2012).

3. Bock, *Who Is Jesus?*, 110–11.

4. For further (still introductory-level) discussion of fulfilled prophecy, see Lee Strobel's interview with Dr. Michael Brown in *The Case for the Real Jesus* (Grand Rapids: Zondervan, 2007), chap. 5.

5. David Wilkinson, "Why Do Some People Believe Jesus Is the Messiah?," Quora, July 3, 2014, https://www.quora.com/Why-do-Christians-believe-that -Jesus-was-Christ?

Chapter 3 Is Jesus God?

1. Robert M. Bowman Jr. and J. Ed Komoszewski, *Putting Jesus in His Place* (Grand Rapids: Kregel, 2007).

2. For more on this subject, see Richard Bauckham, *Jesus and the God of Israel: God Crucified and Other Studies on the New Testament's Christology of Divine Identity* (Grand Rapids: Eerdmans, 2009).

3. Bowman and Komoszewski, *Putting Jesus in His Place*, 82.

4. Bowman and Komoszewski, *Putting Jesus in His Place*, 236.

5. "Christians That Believe Jesus Is Not God (Me)," Christian Forums, October 7, 2003, https://www.christianforums.com/threads/christians-that-belive-jesus-is-not-god-me.61090/.

Chapter 4 Did Jesus Really Perform Miracles?

1. *Merriam-Webster*, s.v. "miracle," accessed June 10, 2019, https://www.merriam-webster.com/dictionary/miracle.

2. Craig S. Keener, *Miracles: The Credibility of the New Testament Accounts* (Grand Rapids: Baker Academic, 2011), 24.

3. Keener, *Miracles*, 23–24.

4. Craig S. Keener, "Will the Real Historical Jesus Please Stand Up? The Gospels as Sources for Historical Information about Jesus," February 2010, https://www.bibleinterp.com/articles/keener357924.shtml.

Chapter 5 Did Ancient People Believe in Miracles Because They Were More Gullible?

1. If you'd like to read academic research on Matshishkapeu and the Innu people, a study is available online at Peter Armitage, "Religious Ideology among the Innu of Eastern Quebec and Labrador," accessed June 10, 2019, https://www.religiologiques.uqam.ca/no6/armit.pdf.

2. Richard Carrier, "Kooks and Quacks of the Roman Empire: A Look into the World of the Gospels (1997)," The Secular Web, accessed June 10, 2019, https://infidels.org/library/modern/richard_carrier/kooks.html.

3. John N. Oswalt, *The Bible among the Myths* (Grand Rapids: Zondervan, 2009), 142.

4. See Keener, *Miracles*, for an extensive discussion on ancient miracle claims.

5. Keener, *Miracles*, 93.

6. Keener, *Miracles*, chaps. 2 and 3.

7. N. T. Wright, *The Resurrection of the Son of God* (Minneapolis: Fortress, 2003), 82–83.

Chapter 6 How Can Jesus Be Both God and Human?

1. For the full Chalcedonian Definition and a more detailed discussion, see Wayne Grudem, *Systematic Theology* (Grand Rapids: Zondervan, 1994), chap. 26.

2. Bassam Zawadi, "Mark 13:32: The Verse That Christians Have No Answer Around," accessed June 10, 2019, http://www.answering-christianity.com/bassam_zawadi/mark13_32.htm.

Part 2 The Teachings of Jesus Overview

1. Rachel Hollis, *Girl, Wash Your Face* (Nashville: Thomas Nelson, 2018), 40.

Chapter 7 Did Jesus Teach That He's the Only Way to God?

1. Leonardo Blair, "Saying You're Going to Hell If You Don't Believe in Jesus Is 'Insanity' Megachurch Pastor Michael A. Walrond Jr. Says," *Christian Post*, March 12, 2018, https://www.christianpost.com/news/belief-jesus-is-only-way-to-heaven-is-insanity-megachurch-pastor-michael-a-walrond-jr-says-221123/.

2. Robert Herguth, "Prominent Presbyterian Pastor: 'God's Not a Christian . . . We Are,'" *Chicago Sun-Times*, March 7, 2018, https://chicago.suntimes.com/2018/3/7/18318384/prominent-presbyterian-pastor-god-s-not-a-christian-we-are.

3. "Many Americans Say Other Faiths Can Lead to Eternal Life," Pew Research Center, December 18, 2008, https://www.pewforum.org/2008/12/18/many-americans-say-other-faiths-can-lead-to-eternal-life/.

4. Neela Banerjee, "Survey Shows U.S. Religious Tolerance," *New York Times*, June 24, 2008, http://www.nytimes.com/2008/06/24/us/24religion.html.

Chapter 8 What Did Jesus Teach about Hell?

1. This chapter does not discuss the more philosophical question of how a loving God can send people to hell. That's the subject of chapter 4 in *Keeping Your Kids on God's Side*. Please refer to that chapter for help discussing questions such as "Why does God need to punish *anyone*?," "Who should be punished?," and "What should the nature of that punishment be?"

2. Roger Wolsey, "To Hell with Hell," *The Holy Kiss*, March 7, 2015, https://www.patheos.com/blogs/rogerwolsey/2015/03/to-hell-with-hell/.

3. For an extended discussion on the word translated "punishment" and how it's clear this is what Jesus had in view rather than some idea of correction, see Francis Chan and Preston Sprinkle, *Erasing Hell* (Colorado Springs: David C. Cook, 2011), 80–85.

4. Chan and Sprinkle, *Erasing Hell*.

5. Caryle Murphy, "Most Americans Believe in Heaven . . . and Hell," Pew Research Center, November 10, 2015, https://www.pewresearch.org/fact-tank/2015/11/10/most-americans-believe-in-heaven-and-hell/.

Chapter 9 What Did Jesus Teach about Religion?

1. Jefferson Bethke, "Why I Hate Religion, But Love Jesus: Spoken Word," YouTube video, January 10, 2012, https://www.youtube.com/watch?v=1IAhDGYlpqY. Bethke has nuanced his views in subsequent writings. I'm not evaluating those clarifications but rather addressing the message of the original video that was attractive to so many.

2. Jefferson Bethke, *Jesus > Religion: Why He Is So Much Better Than Trying Harder, Doing More, and Being Good Enough* (Nashville: Thomas Nelson, 2013).

3. The blog post from which this is taken has been removed from the internet. As of July 8, 2018, it was at Mike Gantt, *Blog for the Lord Jesus*, https://www.blog forthelordjesus.com/2011/06/22/jesus-organized-religion-biblical-christianity/.

4. *Merriam-Webster*, s.v. "religion," https://www.merriam-webster.com/dic tionary/religion.

5. Mick Mooney, "Why I Choose to Live My Faith Outside of Organized Religion," *HuffPost*, February 16, 2015, https://www.huffingtonpost.com/mick -mooney/why-i-choose-to-live-my-f_b_6339134.html.

Chapter 10 What Did Jesus Teach about Loving Others?

1. "The Arrogance of Evangelism," Atheist Revolution, June 5, 2013, https:// www.atheistrev.com/2013/06/the-arrogance-of-evangelism.html.

2. "Almost Half of Practicing Christian Millennials Say Evangelism Is Wrong," Barna, February 5, 2019, https://www.barna.com/research/millennials-oppose -evangelism/.

3. Harm Reduction Coalition, https://harmreduction.org/.

4. See the Homeless Youth Alliance as one example: https://www.homeless youthalliance.org/.

5. Josh McDowell and Sean McDowell, *The Beauty of Intolerance: Setting a Generation Free to Know Truth and Love* (Uhrichsville, OH: Shiloh Run Press, 2016), 24.

6. It's not clear if this originated with Del Rey, but it's commonly attributed to her. See Lana Del Ray (@LDelRayQuote), Twitter, February 24, 2019, 3:16 p.m., https://twitter.com/LDelReyQuote/status/1099810264436887552.

Chapter 11 What Did Jesus Teach about Judging Others?

1. Natasha Crain, "10 Signs the Christian Authors You're Following Are (Sub-tly) Teaching Unbiblical Ideas," *Christian Mom Thoughts*, September 25, 2018, https://christianmomthoughts.com/10-signs-the-christian-authors-youre-follow ing-are-subtly-teaching-unbiblical-ideas/.

2. "A New Generation Expresses Its Skepticism and Frustration with Chris-tianity," Barna, September 21, 2007, https://www.barna.com/research/a-new-gen eration-expresses-its-skepticism-and-frustration-with-christianity/.

3. Hannah K. Brinnier, "Hey Christians, Can We Please Stop Being So Judg-mental?," Odyssey, July 3, 2017, https://www.theodysseyonline.com/christians -please-stop-being-judgmental.

Chapter 12 How Can We Know What Jesus Would Have Taught on Sub-jects He Didn't Address?

1. Tony Campolo, *Red Letter Christians: A Citizen's Guide to Faith and Politics* (Ventura, CA: Regal, 2008), 23.

2. For more on slavery, see Crain, *Keeping Your Kids on God's Side*, chap. 30.

3. Scott Klusendorf, *The Case for Life: Equipping Christians to Engage the Culture* (Wheaton: Crossway, 2009).

4. "I May Regret This Thread . . . Cherry Picking the Bible?," Wedding Bee, September 2013, https://boards.weddingbee.com/topic/i-may-regret-this-thread -cherry-picking-the-bible/.

Part 3 The Death of Jesus Overview

1. Ex Preacher, *Obsessed with Blood: The Crazy Things Christians Believe— Book 1* (CreateSpace Independent Publishing Platform, 2013), from the back cover.

2. For more on progressive Christianity, I highly recommend the blog posts and podcasts of Alisa Childers: https://www.AlisaChilders.com.

3. Anna Skates, "The Trouble with Easter: How to (and Not to) Talk to Kids about Easter," Unfundamentalist Parenting, April 12, 2017, https://www.patheos .com/blogs/unfundamentalistparenting/2017/04/trouble-easter-not-talk-kids -easter/.

4. I am not implying that the specific people quoted in this overview are per- ishing. Only God knows their status before him.

Chapter 13 Did Jesus Predict His Violent Death and Resurrection?

1. Michael Licona, "Did Jesus Predict His Death and Vindication/Resurrec- tion?," *Journal for the Study of the Historical Jesus* 8 (2010): 47–66.

2. Licona, "Did Jesus Predict His Death and Vindication/Resurrection?," 53.

3. "Review of 'The Case for the Resurrection of Jesus' by Habermas and Licona, Chapter 1: Why Jesus Probably Did NOT Predict His Resurrection," Escaping Christian Fundamentalism, March 2, 2017, https://lutherwasnotborn againcom.wordpress.com/2017/03/02/review-of-the-case-for-the-resurrection -of-jesus-by-habermas-and-licona-chapter-1/.

Chapter 14 What's the Relationship between Old Testament Animal Sacrifices and Jesus's Death?

1. Peter Barney, "Why Many Religions Require a Sacrifice (an Animal, a Lamb, a Cow ecc) in God's Name? Is He Happy That We Kill Another Creature That He Created?," Quora, March 29, 2016, https://www.quora.com/Why-many-re ligions-require-a-sacrifice-an-animal-a-lamb-a-cow-ecc-in-Gods-name-Is-he -happy-that-we-kill-another-creature-that-he-created.

Chapter 15 Did Jesus Die Willingly?

1. William Paul Young, *Lies We Believe about God* (New York: Atria Books, 2017), 149.

2. For more on these and other passages related to the subject of human sacrifice, see Crain, *Keeping Your Kids on God's Side*, chap. 32.

Chapter 16 What Did Jesus's Death Accomplish?

1. "A Progressive Christian Wades into the Waters of Baptism," Pastordawn, January 7, 2015, https://pastordawn.com/2015/01/07/a-progressive-christian -wades-into-the-waters-of-baptism-2/.

Chapter 17 If Jesus Is God, How Could He Die?

1. Quoted from "The Muslim World," in J. Dudley Woodberry, ed., *Muslims and Christians on the Emmaus Road* (Monrovia, CA: MARC, 1989), 164.
2. "What If Jesus Died for His Own Sins?," Atheist Forums, August 18, 2016, https://atheistforums.org/post-1367781.html.

Chapter 18 Where Was Jesus between His Death and Resurrection?

1. Joel Osteen, Easter service message at Lakewood Church, sermon #CS_002— 4-23-00, accessed June 10, 2019, https://web.archive.org/web/20040408215244 /http://www.lakewood.cc/sermons/cs_002.htm.
2. Grudem, *Systematic Theology*, 586.
3. Grudem, *Systematic Theology*, 582–94.

Part 4 The Resurrection of Jesus Overview

1. See Operation Christmas Child, Samaritan's Purse, https://www.samari tanspurse.org/what-we-do/operation-christmas-child/.
2. For more on how the Bible defines faith, see Tim Barnett, "Getting Faith Right," Stand to Reason, October 15, 2015, https://www.str.org/articles/getting -faith-right#.XDZvDVxKhPY.
3. Michael Shermer, "What Would It Take to Prove the Resurrection?," *Scientific American*, April 1, 2017, https://www.scientificamerican.com/article/what-would -it-take-to-prove-the-resurrection/. I wrote a critique of this piece at "Your Kids Need to Think Critically about the Resurrection Because the Secular Media Does Not," *Christian Mom Thoughts*, April 6, 2017, https://christianmomthoughts .com/your-kids-need-to-think-critically-about-the-resurrection-because-secular -media-does-not/.
4. See this church's statement of faith as one example: "Progressive Christianity," Church of the Foothills, Santa Ana, California, accessed June 10, 2019, https://www.churchofthefoothills.org/about-us/progressive-christianity/.
5. "Richard Dawkins: You Ask the Questions Special," Independent, December 4, 2006, https://www.independent.co.uk/news/people/profiles/richard-dawkins -you-ask-the-questions-special-427003.html.

Chapter 19 Why Does It Matter If Jesus Was Resurrected?

1. Kimberly Winston, "Can You Question the Resurrection and Still Be a Christian?," *National Catholic Reporter*, April 17, 2014, https://www.ncronline .org/news/theology/can-you-question-resurrection-and-still-be-christian.

2. Quoted in McDowell and McDowell, *Evidence That Demands a Verdict*, 234.

3. "Do I Have to Believe That Christ Literally, Physically Rose from the Dead in Order to Be a Christian?," Explorefaith.org, accessed June 10, 2019, https://www.explorefaith.org/christ.html.

Chapter 20 What Historical Evidence Is There for Jesus's Resurrection?

1. For the number geeks out there (like me), I understand there is a difference between quantitative interpolation and historical analysis. This is meant only to illustrate a general concept.

2. Gary Habermas and Michael Licona, *The Case for the Resurrection of Jesus* (Grand Rapids: Kregel, 2004), Kindle, introduction to part 2.

3. Habermas and Licona, *The Case for the Resurrection of Jesus*, chap. 3.

4. Sean McDowell, *The Fate of the Apostles: Examining the Martyrdom Accounts of the Closest Followers of Jesus* (Surrey, UK: Ashgate, 2015). The term *apostles* refers to the inner circle of Jesus's twelve disciples (minus Judas) plus others who met certain qualifications of having been with Jesus during his earthly ministry, having personally witnessed his resurrection, and having been empowered by the Holy Spirit to perform signs (Acts 1:21–22; 10:41; 2 Cor. 12:12). Paul was an exception as an apostle in that he wasn't with Jesus during his earthly ministry, but Jesus appeared to him specially (Acts 26).

5. McDowell, *The Fate of the Apostles*, chap. 4.

6. Sean McDowell, "Could the Apostles Have Been Executed against Their Wills?," October 27, 2015, https://seanmcdowell.org/blog/could-the-apostles-have-been-executed-against-their-wills.

7. Habermas and Licona, *The Case for the Resurrection of Jesus*, loc. 616.

8. "What Is the CENTRAL Truth of Christianity?," Catholic Answers Forums, accessed June 10, 2019, https://forums.catholic.com/t/what-is-the-central-truth-of-christianity/140999/127.

Chapter 21 Was Jesus's Tomb Really Empty?

1. Bart Ehrman, *How Jesus Became God: The Exaltation of a Jewish Preacher from Galilee* (New York: HarperOne, 2015), Kindle.

2. Ehrman, *How Jesus Became God*, loc. 2450.

3. Craig Evans, *How God Became Jesus: The Real Origins of Belief in Jesus' Divine Nature—A Response to Bart D. Ehrman* (Grand Rapids: Zondervan Academic, 2014).

4. Evans, *How God Became Jesus*, 76.

5. Evans, *How God Became Jesus*, 88.

6. Piet Bakx, "Is Jesus' Empty Tomb Evidence for His Resurrection? If Not, Why?," Quora, February 16, 2018, https://www.quora.com/Is-Jesus-empty-tomb-evidence-for-his-resurrection-If-not-why.

Chapter 22 Did Jesus's Disciples Lie about the Resurrection?

1. Richard Carrier, "Did the Apostles Die for a Lie?," Richard Carrier Blogs, April 7, 2016, https://www.richardcarrier.info/archives/9978.

2. Craig A. Evans, *Matthew*, New Cambridge Bible Commentary (Cambridge: Cambridge University Press, 2012), 473.

3. J. Warner Wallace, *Cold-Case Christianity: A Homicide Detective Investigates the Claims of the Gospels* (Colorado Springs: David C. Cook, 2013), 112.

4. Wallace, *Cold-Case Christianity*, chap. 7.

5. Wallace, *Cold-Case Christianity*, 113.

6. Wallace, *Cold-Case Christianity*, 114.

7. "Romulus and Remus vs. Jesus," Lion of the Blogosphere, accessed October 1, 2019, https://lionoftheblogosphere.wordpress.com/2015/12/13/romulus-and-remus-vs-jesus/.

Chapter 23 Were Jesus's Disciples Mistaken about the Resurrection?

1. Gerd Lüdemann, *The Resurrection of Christ: A Historical Inquiry* (Amherst, NY: Prometheus, 2004), 175–76.

2. Joseph Bergeron and Gary R. Habermas, "The Resurrection of Jesus: A Clinical Review of Psychiatric Hypotheses for the Biblical Story of Easter," Scholars Crossing, 2015, https://digitalcommons.liberty.edu/lts_fac_pubs/402. Bergeron summarizes his work for a popular audience in *The Crucifixion of Jesus: A Medical Doctor Examines the Death and Resurrection of Christ* (Suwanee, GA: St. Polycarp Publishing House, 2018).

3. Bergeron and Habermas, "The Resurrection of Jesus."

4. Jake O'Connell, "Jesus' Resurrection and Collective Hallucinations," *Tyndale Bulletin* 60 (2009): 69–105. Available online at legacy.tyndalehouse.com/Bulletin/60=2009/5%20O'Connell.pdf. Though O'Connell refers to these experiences as collective "hallucinations," I refer to them here as visions, following Bergeron's use of this language, to distinguish them from medically defined hallucinations. Per Bergeron, no current scientific data substantiate the occurrence of identical, simultaneous, collective group hallucinations.

5. William Lane Craig, "Visions of Jesus: A Critical Assessment of Gerd Lüdemann's Hallucination Hypothesis," Reasonable Faith, accessed June 10, 2019, https://www.reasonablefaith.org/writings/scholarly-writings/historical-jesus/visions-of-jesus-a-critical-assessment-of-gerd-ludemanns-hallucination-hypo/.

6. Bergeron, *The Crucifixion of Jesus*, 194.

7. For instructions, see Wayne Kawamota, "Magic Tricks for Kids: The Rubber Pencil," The Spruce Crafts, April 17, 2019, https://www.thesprucecrafts.com/rubber-pencil-kids-magic-tricks-2267012.

8. Petter Häggholm, "If You Think Christianity Started by Visions of a Risen Jesus, Then What Caused the Disciples to Hallucinate?," Quora, September 11, 2016, https://www.quora.com/If-you-think-Christianity-started-by-visions-of-a-risen-Jesus-then-what-caused-the-disciples-to-hallucinate.

Chapter 24 Did People Invent the Resurrection Many Years Later?

1. Bob Seidensticker, "Jesus a Legend: A Dozen Reasons," Cross Examined, November 29, 2012, https://www.patheos.com/blogs/crossexamined/2012/11/jesus-a-legend-a-dozen-reasons/.

2. An excellent book-length introduction to this topic is Peter J. Williams, *Can We Trust the Gospels?* (Wheaton: Crossway, 2018).

3. If you're interested in how this is determined, see this article for a detailed explanation: Ryan Turner, "An Analysis of the Pre-Pauline Creed of 1 Corinthians 15:1–11," Christian Apologetics and Research Ministry, accessed June 10, 2019, https://carm.org/analysis-pre-pauline-creed-1-corinthians-151-11.

4. Gerd Lüdemann, *The Resurrection of Jesus: History, Experience, Theology*, trans. John Bowden (Minneapolis: Fortress, 1994), 38.

5. Michael Goulder, "The Baseless Fabric of a Vision," in *Resurrection Reconsidered*, ed. Gavin D'Costa (Oxford: Oneworld, 1996), 48.

6. Robert W. Funk and The Jesus Seminar, *The Acts of Jesus: What Did Jesus Really Do?* (San Francisco: HarperOne, 1998), 466.

7. Michael R. Licona explains this idea further in *The Resurrection of Jesus: A New Historiographical Approach* (Downers Grove, IL: InterVarsity, 2010), 163.

8. "'No Resurrection,' Say One in Four Christians," The Day, April 13, 2017, https://theday.co.uk/stories/no-resurrection-say-one-in-four-christians.

Part 5 The Difference Jesus Makes Overview

1. C. S. Lewis, *The Weight of Glory* (New York: HarperOne, 2001), 141.

Chapter 25 What Is a Christian?

1. Natasha Crain, "Committed Christians Are Now a Minority and Kids Need to Know It," *Christian Mom Thoughts*, September 12, 2018, https://christianmomthoughts.com/committed-christians-are-now-a-minority-and-kids-need-to-know-it/.

2. "Religious Landscape Study," Pew Research Center, https://www.pewforum.org/religious-landscape-study/.

3. Ed Stetzer, "Barna: How Many Have a Biblical Worldview?," The Exchange, March 9, 2009, https://www.christianitytoday.com/edstetzer/2009/march/barna-how-many-have-biblical-worldview.html.

4. We don't have the space to evaluate the validity of books that claim to augment, clarify, or change the teachings of the Bible (for example, the Book of Mormon or the Quran). Suffice it to say that if a person is following "the teachings and ways of Jesus" as defined by another book, that will mean something very different. The question, of course, is whether there is good reason to believe these other revelations are true. For those interested, I recommend Corey Miller and Lynn K. Wilder, eds., *Leaving Mormonism: Why Four Scholars Changed Their Minds* (Grand Rapids: Kregel, 2017); and Nabeel Qureshi, *No God but One: Allah or Jesus? A Former Muslim Investigates the Evidence for Islam and Christianity* (Grand Rapids: Zondervan, 2016).

5. As one example, listen to this interview on the radio show *Unbelievable*: "Unbelievable? Religious Fictionalism: Can You Believe a Believer Who Doesn't Believe? Kristi Mair and Philip Goff," Premier Christian Radio, May 4, 2019, https://www.premierchristianradio.com/Shows/Saturday/Unbelievable/Episodes /Unbelievable-Religious-Fictionalism-Can-you-be-a-believer-who-doesn-t-be lieve-Kristi-Mair-and-Philip-Goff.

6. "Can I Be a Christian but Not Believe in God?," Quora, August 24, 2016, https://www.quora.com/Can-I-be-a-Christian-but-not-believe-in-God.

Chapter 26 How Is a Person's View of the Bible Different as a Christian?

1. See https://americanheritagegirls.org for more information.

2. These categories are highlighted in Gregg R. Allison, *50 Core Truths of the Christian Faith: A Guide to Understanding and Teaching Theology* (Grand Rapids: Baker Books, 2018), 11. This book is an excellent reference for succinct explanations of Christian doctrine, including the inspiration of Scripture.

3. Systematic theologies are great resources for exploring these issues in more depth.

4. A great overview of the differences between Christian denominations is Ron Rhodes, *The Complete Guide to Christian Denominations: Understanding the History, Beliefs, and Differences* (Eugene, OR: Harvest House, 2015).

5. Whisper, "I'm a Christian, but I Don't Believe in the Bible," accessed June 10, 2019, wis.pr/whisper/0518ad9d6fda11315345eb487bde84e787c1f9/Im-a-Chris tian-but-I-dont-believe-in-the-bible-I-believe-that-there.

Chapter 27 How Is a Person's View of God Different as a Christian?

1. See Crain, *Talking with Your Kids about God*, parts 1 and 2, for help with these conversations.

2. See Crain, *Talking with Your Kids about God*, part 3.

Chapter 28 What Does It Mean to Be Saved?

1. See chapter 8 for a discussion of hell.

2. Thomas Murphy, "What Does It Mean to Be Saved?," Quora, November 7, 2018, https://www.quora.com/What-does-it-mean-to-be-saved-1.

Chapter 29 What Does It Mean to Trust in Jesus?

1. We don't have space to discuss the general "problem of evil" in this chapter. I recommend D. A. Carson, *How Long, O Lord? Reflections on Suffering and Evil* (Grand Rapids: Baker Academic, 2006); and Clay Jones, *Why Does God Allow Evil? Compelling Answers for Life's Toughest Questions* (Eugene, OR: Harvest House, 2017) on this subject.

2. Lindsey T, "Health Anxiety—Root Is Not Trusting God to Heal," Christian Forums, May 15, 2018, https://www.christianforums.com/threads/health-anxiety -root-is-not-trusting-god-to-heal.8064282/.

3. For more on this subject, I recommend this article (and other resources) from Mama Bear Apologetics: Hillary Morgan Ferrer, "MBA 29: Does God Heal Every Time If We Ask in the 'Right Way'?," Mama Bear Apologetics, March 13, 2018, https://mamabearapologetics.com/mba029-god-heal-ask-right/.

Chapter 30 Why Do Christians Want to Share Their Faith with Others?

1. Greg Koukl, *Tactics: A Game Plan for Discussing Your Christian Convictions*, updated and expanded (Grand Rapids: Zondervan, 2019); and Michael Sherrard, *Relational Apologetics: Defending the Christian Faith with Holiness, Respect, and Truth* (Grand Rapids: Kregel, 2015).

2. "Why Do Christians Seek to Convert Everyone?," Christianity Stack Exchange, March 2013, https://christianity.stackexchange.com/questions/14179/why-do-christians-seek-to-convert-everyone.

Natasha Crain is a national speaker, author, and blogger who is passionate about equipping Christian parents to raise their kids with an understanding of how to make a case for and defend their faith in an increasingly secular world. In addition to *Talking with Your Kids about Jesus*, she has authored two other apologetics books for parents: *Keeping Your Kids on God's Side* and *Talking with Your Kids about God*. Natasha's articles have been featured in the *Focus on the Family* magazine and the *Christian Research Journal*, and she's been interviewed on radio shows across the country. She has an MBA from UCLA and a certificate in Christian apologetics from Biola University. A former marketing executive and adjunct professor, Natasha lives in Southern California with her husband and three children. She writes at www.natashacrain.com.

Connect with Natasha!

To read Natasha's blog and learn about additional resources for Christian parents, visit ChristianMomThoughts.com.

f @ChristianMomThoughts 🐦 @Natasha_Crain

LIKE THIS
BOOK?
Consider sharing it with others!

- Share or mention the book on social media. Use the hashtag **#TalkingWithYourKidsAboutJesus**.

  - Share this message on **FACEBOOK**: "I loved #TalkingWithYourKidsAboutJesus by @ChristianMomThoughts"

  - Share this message on **TWITTER**: "I loved #TalkingWithYourKidsAboutJesus by @Natasha_Crain"

- Write a book review on your blog or on a retailer site.

- Pick up a copy for friends, family, or strangers— anyone who you think would value and be challenged by its message!

- Use this book as curriculum for your small group, church class, youth group, or Christian school.

- Follow Baker Books on social media and tell us what you like.

  f Facebook.com/ReadBakerBooks

  y @ReadBakerBooks